John Brown

The courts of Sweden and Denmark from 1766 to 1818

John Brown

The courts of Sweden and Denmark from 1766 to 1818

ISBN/EAN: 9783337724344

Printed in Europe, USA, Canada, Australia, Japan

Cover: Foto ©ninafisch / pixelio.de

More available books at **www.hansebooks.com**

SECRET MEMOIRS

OF THE

COURTS OF EUROPE

FROM THE

16TH TO THE 19TH CENTURY

VOLUME VII

THIS EDITION, PRINTED ON JAPANESE VELLUM PAPER

IS LIMITED TO

ONE THOUSAND NUMBERED COPIES

NO. 115

Secret Memoirs

MEMOIRS OF THE
COURTS OF SWEDEN AND DENMARK

VOLUME I

CAROLINA-MATILDA
WIFE OF CHRISTIAN VII

After an engraving by Maria Anne Bourlier, from the painting by Francis Cotes

MEMOIRS

COURTS OF SWEDEN AND DENMARK

CAROLINA MATILDA
WIFE OF CHRISTIAN VII

After an engraving by Marie Anne Bourlier, from the painting by Francis Cotes

PHILADELPHIA
GEORGE BARRIE & SON   PUBLISHERS

Courts of Europe

MEMOIRS

OF THE

COURTS OF SWEDEN AND DENMARK

FROM 1766 TO 1818

BY

JOHN BROWN

VOL. I

Illustrated

PHILADELPHIA
GEORGE BARRIE & SON   PUBLISHERS

PREFACE

The present work was originally intended by the Author to have been a miscellany; and the sketches of the reigns of the different Sovereigns were to have been given as an Appendix, made up of selections. It was, however, discovered that one volume would not contain the matter that was indispensably necessary, which was then divided into two volumes; but such was its redundancy that the lives of the late and present Kings of Sweden, and the late and present Kings of Denmark, as well as some intended comments on the political opinions respecting Russia by Mr. Leckie and Lieut.-General Sir Robert Wilson, were necessarily omitted; they must otherwise have been reduced to the limits of an index.

In December last a pause occurred in the execution of the work, during which the Author endeavoured to procure, from various sources, those authentic and original facts which were essential to complete his work, and calculated to distinguish it from a mere compilation.

The Swedes are eminent for hospitality and every social virtue, and their character has been wilfully assailed, or casually misunderstood, by British tourists. In the hour of persecution Mr. Brown found a secure and most agreeable asylum there. It was an act of duty to those whose friendship he had enjoyed to publish the criticisms on the works of travellers in Sweden which appear in the second volume, not with a view to decry the general merits of the authors alluded to, but to display their local errors and correct their too frequent acerbity.

The sources whence he borrowed matter for his work are so generally given with the quotations that he is not conscious of a single omission of importance.

CONTENTS TO VOL. I

CHAPTER I

PAGE

Reflections on the Danish Revolution of 1660 1

CHAPTER II

Frederick V.—His character—The cause of his intemperance—Character and anecdotes of Juliana Maria—Anecdotes of Christian VII., when Crown Prince 10

CHAPTER III

The character and person of Christian VII.—Demoralised by his cruel step-mother—Portrait of Caroline Matilda at fifteen years of age—Reflections on, and instances of, the unhappiness of Royal females—Secret memoirs of Gustavus III. and his Queen—The Princess Albertina—Unhappy love—An extraordinary expedient, its detection—The secret history of the birth of Gustavus IV., Adolphus, now Count Gottorp 22

CHAPTER IV

Matilda's reception in Denmark—The machinations of Juliana Maria—Weakness and depravity of Christian VII.—His motive for setting out on his travels—His adventures in Amsterdam and London. 43

CHAPTER V

Queen Matilda—The Counts Struensee and Rantzau—Court intrigues—Peter III., Count Rantzau the cause of his death—Madame Göhler—First confidential interview between Queen Matilda and Struensee—Its result—Reflections on their comparative criminality 66

CHAPTER VI

Melancholy state of the King—A Royal tour to the Duchies of Holstein and Sleiswick—Count Rantzau's hospitality—History of Gourmand, the King's favourite dog—Anecdotes of the Court—A Circassian Princess—Altered manners of Queen Matilda: wears leathern small-clothes, and sits her horse like a man—Prosperity more difficult to endure than adversity—Struensee and Brandt admonished by Count Rantzau—The last interview—The arrest of Matilda, Struensee and Brandt 85

CHAPTER VII

Critical situation of Juliana Maria, Count Rantzau and the other conspirators—The courage of Queen Matilda—Cowardice of Struensee—A singular riot: its source developed—The execution of Brandt and Struensee . . 124

CHAPTER VIII

Character and conduct of Count Rantzau—His disgrace—Benevolence of Matilda—Gratitude—*Lex talionis*—Sensibility and gratitude—A fascinating mistress—Visit to Zell—A fair penitent—Reconciliation of Matilda and Rantzau—Their deaths 148

CHAPTER IX

The Danish Court after the fall of Struensee—Wise and dignified conduct of George III.—Memoir of Count Andreas Petrus Bernstorff—A celebrated tourist quoted, and censured—

PAGE

Violation of the Danish flag—Source of that abuse—Its consequence—The armed neutrality of the Northern Powers—Count Bernstorff retires—The Crown Prince Frederick seizes the reins of government—Count Bernstorff restored 211

CHAPTER X

THE SWEDISH OLIGARCHY 247

CHAPTER XI

GUSTAVUS III.

Sophia Magdalena, consort to Gustavus III.—Auspicious commencement of his reign—His secrecy and self-command—Profound dissimulation—The Diet of 1771—Further proofs of deep hypocrisy—Outwits the Senate—Overthrows the oligarchy in 1772—His gross impiety on that occasion—Anecdote of Count Ugglus—Gustavus lives apart from his Queen—The Duchess of Sodermanland—A Royal expedient—Increased splendour of the Court—Gustavus encourages trade and manufactures—Becomes a monopolist of brandy distilleries—General discontent—Insurrections—Failure of his commercial speculations 274

CHAPTER XII.

Vast projects of Peter the Great—Their progressive realisation—Gustavus attempts to counteract Russia—Catherine II. and Gustavus—Their opposite views and preparations—Great national undertakings begun or completed by Gustavus at Carlscrona and Sveaborg—Visits his provinces—Reforms local abuses, and punishes several unjust judges—His great and varied talents and acquirements—Effeminacy of his Court—Honours paid by Gustavus to the memory of Sir Charles Linné—Suffers his invaluable collection to be sold—Embellishes Stockholm—Practises the utmost profusion—Recommends frugality to his subjects—Sumptuary laws—Corrupts the national manners—Lavishes his treasures on idle pageantry 292

SECRET HISTORY

OF THE

COURTS OF SWEDEN AND DENMARK

CHAPTER I

Reflections on the Danish Revolution of 1660.[1]

OUR historians inform us that in the seventeenth century the tyranny, insolence, and rapacity of the Nobles had attained such a height that, to deliver themselves from the humiliating and oppressive yoke, the Clergy, burghers and peasantry surrendered to the Crown all their rights and privileges; making the Monarch absolute, and themselves and posterity slaves! But why do I say *posterity?* Can the rights of the unborn to freedom be done away with by the folly or baseness of their ancestors? Certainly not; and we have

---

[1] This interesting portion of the "Secret History of the Courts of Sweden and Denmark" was copied and translated from a Danish MS. found on board the United States merchantman, the *Clyde*, Alcorn, master, laden with French and Dutch colonial produce, and bound from New York to Amsterdam; detained off the Start by the *Dapper* gun-brig, Lieutenant Gardner, commander, and sent into Plymouth, February, 1807.

now a greater right to restore the freedom of Denmark than our weak and infatuated forefathers had to lay it at the feet of Frederick III. Of all the stains on our annals, this is the most disgraceful. It is also one of the most extraordinary events recorded in modern history. There is no doubt but some creatures of the Crown, playing upon the exasperated feelings of the burghers, persuaded them that the only effectual mode of avenging *their* wrongs consisted in making the Monarchy absolute! Yet, it still seems incomprehensible how a race of men illuminated by the light of the Reformation, who were far from illiterate, well versed in their political rights, and who had recently covered themselves with glory in defending the metropolis, could be so completely infatuated as to act in this base and wicked manner. Their infamy is the more apparent as they were inured to war, were flushed by victory, had their weapons still in their hands, and their vile oppressors were cooped up within the walls of their city! By the same effort of mind, and at a less personal risk than it required to reduce themselves and posterity to the condition of slaves, they might have humbled the accursed oligarchy that devoured and degraded Denmark, have stripped them of their territorial spoils, their feudal *rights*—as their tyrannies were improperly called—and every other usurpation; and, with all facility, have elevated themselves to the rank of freemen. While borrowing from England that representative system which our ancestors, the Goths, carried thither in their first expeditions, they might have laid the deep and broad foundations of a free commonwealth, with a constitutional king at its head; by which means Denmark would at this day have equalled England in wealth, power and fame! The Crown was at that moment elective, and the oligarchs lorded it with equal insolence over the King and the people. If, therefore, this base conspiracy on the part of the commonalty had been discovered by the aristocracy in time enough to have prevented its execution, the fierce, haughty, vindictive oligarchs would have washed out the crime meditated by the silly commoners with their blood! Not so if they had aimed at establishing a government altogether republican, because, under that system, the Nobles would not have been subjected to the King, who was before subjected to them; and it was the sole object of the burghers to reduce the Nobles to a state of slavery and degradation! The heroism displayed by Frederick III. in defending his capital against the Swedes had rendered him deservedly popular, whilst the Nobles were detested on account of the disaffection, if not the cowardice, that many of them had displayed in the unfortunate wars with Sweden. The King, to secure his Crown from the power of the Nobles, would, no doubt, have readily entered into the views of the people, and have ratified their freedom in return for their rendering the Crown hereditary and independent of the oligarchy. Instead of acting thus nobly and wisely, with a frantic hand they tore the laurels from their brows and surrendered unconditionally and without any equivalent—for what is there equivalent to such a sacrifice?—their lives, liberty, property and honour, to the King: investing him and his heirs male for ever with the uncontrolled power to wage war, negotiate peace, to cede provinces, levy taxes, expend treasures, spill the blood of his people by unnecessary wars, by the axe of the executioner; and plunge them into solitary dungeons, there to rot in darkness, without the King or his ministers being accountable to any human being! Stupendous folly and wickedness! I blush as I write at the degeneracy of my ancestors. This vile, polluting and degrading Revolution was brought about by a few of the leading burghers in Copenhagen, backed by the blind confidence and heated passions of the lowest classes, and aided by the secret influence, the gold and the power of the Crown. The blow was struck; the liberties of the Danes, existent or to be born, were clandestinely surrendered, and the Crown elevated on the ruins of liberty ere the great mass of the people knew that the dire expedient was in agitation! In a delirium of joy the burghers of Copenhagen sung "Io Pæans," that the tyranny of the Nobles was no more. Silly wretches! A short time taught them that the Crown, to prevent the enraged oligarchs from calling in the Swedes, made a compromise, and left that obnoxious class of privileged men all their territorial domains, however acquired; all their feudal claims and exactions. They could no longer dictate to the King, but each could play the petty tyrant on his own estates, and spread desolation and misery among their unhappy dependents, who were still left subjected to their insolence and power. A short time opened the eyes of the infatuated burghers, but the mischief was done; and a standing army protected the throne which the stupid burghers had made absolute, and rendered their regrets and remorse alike unavailing.

Our historians in vain endeavour to palliate this act of political suicide. Amongst innumerable attempts to extenuate its infamy, they pretend that so transcendently great were the merits of Frederick III. that the nation had no other means of affording him an adequate proof of its gratitude and devotion! Silly casuistry. Contemptible sophists. What individual had so much to lose as the King? Certainly no one; and, consequently, no one had a stimulant equally strong to propel him to great exertions. His wisdom, fortitude, valour, were admitted and admired by friend and foe; by the Swede and by the Dane. He preserved his throne and his metropolis. The glory of the achievement, and the love and praise of his people and of posterity, offered the only recompense to which he ought to have aspired.

The same historians,[1] as an excuse for this sad monument of popular frenzy and delinquency, tell us that the Nobles were corrupt, tyrannical and oppressive; that, in their legislative capacity, they levied enormous burdens on the labouring hind and the industrious citizens, from which those drones not merely remained exempted, but contrived, in their capacity as generals, governors, or ministers, to intercept a large proportion of those taxes wrung from the hard hand of the toil-worn, sinewy labourer and his half-famished family. Our time-serving historians assert that this foul oligarchy (to get rid of which moral pestilence our liberties were all destroyed),

---

[1] Holberg, &c.

with one hand oppressed and controlled the Crown, obtruding their creatures and partisans into all places of high trust and great emolument; whilst, with the other hand they scourged, debased, plundered and enslaved the people. This venal class of privileged men met with mockery and contempt the remonstrance and petitions of the commonalty, insolently denying the truth of self-evident grievances; and not merely denying them redress and adding insult to to their wrongs, but visiting them with still heavier burdens, and laying them under more humiliating restraints! Hence, our *courtly historians* infer that there remained no other way of getting rid of those accursed devourers than by making the Crown of Denmark arbitrary and hereditary. The people, from one extremity of the Danish dominions to the other, should have destroyed the power of those despicable and cruel oligarchs, levelled their moated and turreted castles with the earth, and set the bondsman free; thus should they have got rid of that oligarchy which, like a huge and loathsome wen on the human body, impaired its strength and disfigured its beauty. Instead of which, surely in a moment of general madness, to gratify an absurd spirit of vengeance, the citizens of Copenhagen established *despotism by law!* That their posterity have not suffered by the folly and delinquency of their ancestors in an equal degree with those unhappy nations whose harder destiny bowed their necks to a Bourbon yoke, has arisen from the superior quality of our princes, who, since this scandalous Revolution, have ruled Denmark and its dependencies. Possessing unlimited sovereignty in the fullest and most ample meaning of the term, it redounds to the glory of our autocrats—for such are our kings, as well as the czars of Russia —that they have permitted us to be governed by law instead of by ukase; that they have allowed us the liberty of discoursing or writing with freedom on political subjects, instead of shedding our blood on scaffolds, or, *à la Bourbon*, throwing us into lonesome cells and there leaving us to perish. But this clemency, so honourable to our illustrious kings, has the dangerous tendency of rendering despotism less odious, less frightful, less disgusting than it appears when hung round by chains and implements of torture, by *lettres-de-cachet* and Bastilles, which decorated the splendid despotisms of the Bourbons ere their merited fall and eternal banishment from France. It is to the mercy of our kings, and not to the prudence of our ancestors, that we are indebted for an exemption from most of the evils attendant on despotism. The example of justice and moderation afforded by our mild monarchs, each of whom, had he been a Nero in heart, might, like Nero, have wallowed in the blood of the most illustrious citizens, goes a considerable length towards establishing the justice of Pope's dubious aphorism:

> "On forms of government let fools contest,
> Whatever's best administered is best."

One of the greatest calamities that can befall any nation; one of the most certain omens of its speedy fall, is the declining state of the labouring classes, on whose labour the wealth of every superior class is grounded. That degrading Revolution, which calls a blush into my cheeks as I treat of its baseness, reduced the political, but not the *seigneurial*, power of our Nobles, and was fatal to our poor hinds; for the monarchs, assuming a degree of pomp unknown to their electoral predecessors, fearful of offending the wealthy burghers, increased the burdens of the agriculturists, and the weight of this cumbrous pomp fell principally on the labouring peasant. The nobleman, driven from the Court and the Treasury, forced into an involuntary rustication, sought, by increasing his exactions in every possible way, to gain in wealth what he had lost in power; whilst our poor peasantry fared even worse than the beast of the field belonging to his lord; for, having a property in the beast, the lord had an interest in providing it with provender and shelter from the severity of our northern winters. Not so with the poor hind; he was left to struggle with famine and taxation. His sole inheritance was ignorance and bondage. From his birth, in some squalid hovel, he has been, till lately, exposed to privations of every kind, to humiliations of the most debasing description. If Nature blessed his wife or daughter with beauty, the lust of his lord demanded its possession. In his cheerless hut reigned want and wretchedness. Filthy in his habits, base in his propensities, he exhibited the bitter fruits of aristocratical despotism in its most appalling form; and his whole life, from his cradle to his grave, was but one continual scene of wretched and hopeless servitude.

The two greatest errors of our monarchs have been these: the too great splendour of their Courts, and the too great extent of their standing armies—that dreadful pressure and incessant drain on the feeble resources of their country. The splendour of our Court in the last reigns, and the early part of this,[1] illustrated the truth of that bold assertion made by a celebrated American writer, that in despotic States and voluptuous regal Courts, the mere trappings and embellishments of a Monarchy cost more money than, under a frugal system of Republican government, would suffice for all the expenses of the State! Yet how few of our kings have really exercised the sovereignty conferred on them in 1660! During all the latter part of the reign of Frederick V. he was a mere automaton; governed by Count, *alias* King, Molckte, or by his ambitious consort, Juliana Maria. As to the present King (Christian VII.), it was only during a very short interval that he really reigned. A Holcke, a Struensee, a Juliana Maria, by turns possessed and abused the sovereignty. In short, he that wears a despotic crown is seldom the person who exercises the sovereign power; and after all, I am decidedly of opinion that the President of the United States enjoys, under the sanction of the law, more real political power than any despotic prince in either of the four quarters of the globe.

Copenhagen, 1804.   V. D.

---

[1] Christian VII.

CHAPTER II

Frederick V.—His character—The cause of his intemperance—Character and anecdotes of Juliana Maria—Anecdotes of Christian VII., when Crown Prince.

FREDERICK V., the father of our present Monarch (Christian VII.), was a wise, magnificent, liberal prince; the patron of men of genius, science and learning, and the idol of a grateful people. Suddenly, a marked change took place in his habits and his manners; he lost all relish for those exalted pursuits to which he had been attached, and gave himself up to excessive and continual inebriety, whereby he impaired his faculties, physical and mental, and shortened his days. Whilst the memory of this solitary vice that sullied his character is generally known, the secret and powerful cause that led to this melancholy alteration (except to a few, who, during the lifetime of his second Queen, dared not give it utterance, and most of whom have since descended to the grave), has remained buried in oblivion. This accomplished Monarch had two consorts; the first, and deservedly the best-beloved, was the English princess, Louisa, daughter of George II., by whom he had the wretched and imbecile Prince who yet bears the title of King of Denmark, and Sophia Magdalena, married to Gustavus III., of Sweden, who fell by the hand of Ankarstrom. For his second wife, our favourite Monarch, in an evil hour, took Juliana Maria, daughter of Ferdinand Albert, Duke of Brunswick Wolfenbuttle; an unhappy choice that was the source of many and heavy domestic calamities.

Bad passions will obtrude into palaces as well as cottages, and when they chance to obtain full possession of a queen they are likely to hurry her to acts more atrocious than a female of humble rank, because her power to commit wickedness is so much greater. The events of common life too often exhibit the most lamentable scenes, arising from the jealousy and hatred of callous and unfeeling step-mothers who oppress the children of their predecessor. Such was the character of Juliana Maria. She hated the presence of the children of the deceased Queen; and, if she had dared, would have quickly sent them to follow their mother to the grave, for the propensities of her nature were mostly of a selfish and ambitious kind. At an early age, in her father's petty Court, she was a great dabbler in political intrigues; in her temper sullen, cruel and vindictive; extremely penurious; forgetful of benefits, but seldom failing to avenge an injury tenfold; above all, a most profound dissembler, and able to wear a smile on her face, and show all manner of civilities to the person most mortally hated, and whose destruction, at that very moment, she might be planning.

Such was the step-mother whom Frederick V. placed over the children of Queen Louisa! The King possessed great sensibility, and, in spite of all the pretended fondness of his new consort, he soon ascertained that she did not love them. Frederick often indulged his feelings so far as to have the children brought to him, whom he caressed with every mark of strong affection. On these occasions the crafty stepmother would participate in his affectionate regard of the innocent babes, whilst her black heart cherished the most deadly rancour. Finding herself pregnant, she flattered her ambition with the hope of presenting her lord with a new object of affection that should not fail to wean his regards from the fair and white-haired boy of Louisa, who was the King's darling. Instead, however, of a child calculated to prove a successful rival to the beautiful Christian, the cruel and envious Queen brought forth a weakly, deformed infant, whose appearance was calculated to excite commiseration mingled with disgust, rather than love. This deformed child—contrary to expectation—lived; and, as its strength and size increased, it showed a disposition the exact reverse of Christian's, and—owing, perhaps, to organic defects—was cross, sullen and unmanageable. This was a source of sorrow to the good and humane King, and of unutterable misery to the Queen, whose aversion towards Christian increased as she saw the healthy, playful, volatile boy becoming more and more the pride and hope of his fond father, who, nevertheless, did not neglect the deformed Frederick, nor fail to bestow upon him proofs of a regard truly paternal. At length, to such a pitch did that wicked woman suffer malice and envy to carry her, that, to secure the Crown for her deformed son, she resolved to cut off the blooming young Christian by poison. Having determined to commit murder, she soon found what she believed to be a favourable opportunity. The young Prince happened to be indisposed. The cruel step-mother, under the specious pretext of fondness, was frequent in her visits ere an opportunity of attempting the horrid deed presented itself. At length, she found the Prince's favourite nurse preparing some gruel for her young charge over a silver lamp, and there was no other attendant in the chamber. She ordered the nurse to go to her closet to fetch her something, and, as soon as the door closed, she approached the lamp and instantly infused a mineral poison into the gruel—a small part of which, if it had been swallowed by her unconscious victim, would have occasioned his death. The nurse in question was by birth a Norwegian, and had been for years a confidential servant of the Royal Family. She attended Queen Louisa at the birth of Prince Christian; she strove to soothe the last moments of her existence, and she really felt towards her children all the affection of a mother. Having long entertained suspicions of the Queen's intentions, she was ever suspicious and watchful of Juliana Maria's proceedings that in any way affected the young Prince. At the moment the Queen entered the apartment, her heart fraught with murder and the poison in her hand, there might, in spite of all her circumspection and self-command, have been some peculiar expression imprinted on her countenance, her eye, or tone of voice that alarmed the worst fears of the faithful and vigilant matron, who, instead of going to the Queen's apartments that were in the grand front, went only a few steps and returned softly to the door, and distinctly perceived the Queen infusing something from a paper into the gruel, which she appeared to stir in the silver saucepan that contained it; which done, she then replaced it on the lamp-flame in the same position as the nurse had left it. Horror curdled the blood in the veins of the nurse as she beheld this scene. Had the Queen offered the gruel to the Prince she would have rushed in and torn it from her; but Juliana paced the room with a quick and hurried step—her hands clenched together and a strong expression of suppressed misery playing on her stern features. Just then the nurse saw a domestic named Wolff cross the gallery;[1] him she beckoned to come near, and in a whisper told him to go to Count Molckte, and give him a ring that she handed to him, and request his Excellency to make haste to the apartment of the Crown Prince. She knew that when the Count saw that token it would not fail to fix his attention and produce immediate acquiescence. This done, she re-entered the room, her looks and manner betraying the painful emotions that filled her heart. The Queen, without noticing her coming in sooner than she could, if she had gone to the front of the palace, told her to take the gruel to the Prince, as it was sufficiently boiled, and would no doubt *do him good!* Every limb shook with horror as the nurse took up the saucepan. "Why do not you go with it to the Prince?" said Juliana. "Pardon me, gracious Queen," said the honest-hearted woman, "it is my duty

---

[1] In the Mezzanine, or low wings that connected the principal fronts of this vast edifice.

to disobey you." Darting a withering look at the nurse, she exclaimed: "How dare you disobey my commands?" The nurse replied not, but, as the tears streamed from her eyes, she looked significantly at the gruel, and mournfully shook her head. Thrown off her guard by passion, the Queen ordered the nurse out of the room; who stood immovable as a statue, holding the saucepan in her hand. Equally torn by rage and fear, on seeing her wicked plot thus frustrated, and infamy and ruin suspended over her head, like the sword of Damocles, by a single hair, the Queen, ever fertile in resources, took the desperate resolution to accuse the nurse of having attempted to commit the crime she herself came to perpetrate! Sudden as lightning she acted on this diabolical impulse; and turning towards a bell, rang it furiously; a gentleman of the Prince's suite entered, and beheld, in silent amazement, the scene before him. "Go," said Juliana, "to M. Guldberg, and tell him to come instantly to me." The gentleman bowed and withdrew. "Now, wretch," said the furious Queen, her eyes flashing fire, "thou shalt feel the full weight of my vengeance; thy limbs shall be broken on the wheel for having attempted to poison the Crown Prince; the proofs of thy guilt are now in thine own hands!"

"May God forgive you, Queen," said the astonished woman, "as I can pardon you for my death, if I am the humble means of saving the son of my beloved mistress." Just then, Count Molckte entered the room. "Behold in that wicked woman," said the pale and passion-torn Queen, "a wretch whom I have detected in the very act of administering poison to the Crown Prince! Call in the guards! when the King returns he will order her to be put to the severest torture, to force her to confess by whom she has been suborned to the commission of this horrible crime." The Count heard the Queen in respectful silence. In a grave and severe tone, he said, "I wish to speak with Your Majesty alone; shall I attend Your Majesty in your own apartment, or order the nurse to withdraw?" Little suspecting that this minister had long kept a watchful eye over her conduct, and was in possession of other evidence of a criminating tendency—besides that of the nurse, who stood calm and undaunted amidst this storm of guilty passion—Juliana exclaimed, "What! are you too, Count, an enemy to the Crown Prince, and the accomplice of this trembling culprit?" "How can Your Majesty harbour such a thought?" he coolly replied; "*my son* would not succeed to the throne if the Crown Prince were no more!" Count Molckte was a man of keen penetration, and perfectly a courtier. His looks implied more than his words. The abashed and guilty Queen, awed and confounded, said, "If your Excellency pleases, let the woman retire." The Count then took the saucepan from her hand, and the nurse went into the Prince's bedroom. What passed between Count Molckte and Juliana can only be surmised; but in less than an hour he went to the Prince's room, and, after paying his compliments, told him that his favourite nurse must go immediately to Norway. He was so affected at the news that, clinging round her neck, the fond boy said,

"Then I will go to Norway too; you shall not take away my mother." It was in vain the Count strove to pacify him. "I will apply to my father," said he in an angry tone; "I am sure he will not suffer *this mother* to be taken away from me." The Count appeared embarrassed and retired; he soon came back again, when, calling the nurse into an ante-room, he artfully strove to convince her that she had been deceived, and that the Queen had merely stirred the gruel to keep it from burning. The nurse shook her head, saying: "Will your Excellency allow me to carry the gruel to the Prince's apothecary?" "Yes," said the subtle minister, "you may." She ran for the saucepan, but found it empty and perfectly clean! More alarmed than ever, and fearful that the Count had entered into the Queen's hostile views against the Crown Prince, she secretly determined to address the King on the danger which awaited his darling boy. The insidious minister, reading in her ingenuous countenance what was passing in her mind, whilst he applauded her courage and fidelity, told her he meant to have sent her home to Norway merely to secure her from the Queen's power, but he now wished her to remain, assuring her if she pledged herself by a solemn oath to secrecy, she should be safe from the effects of the Queen's dislike, and remain in attendance on the Crown Prince, at the same time pledging himself in the most solemn manner for the perfect safety of the Prince. To these terms, for the sake of continuing her attendance, the faithful nurse assented. The wicked Queen, humbled and defeated, abstained from visiting the Prince's apartments. The same day she was reported to be indisposed, and the next day went to Hirschholm Palace. But the affair did not end here. The King (Frederick V.) was then absent at a small hunting lodge called Jagersprest, situated near the Palace of Charlottenborg. Thither the gentleman repaired whom the Queen had commanded to call M. Guldberg. He obtained an audience, and told the astonished King not only what he had seen and heard in the ante-chamber of the Prince, but many important circumstances besides. It is not in language to express the agonising feelings excited by this intelligence, for his own life was less dear to Frederick than that of his darling son. He applauded the conduct of his informer, and such was his haste to return to Christiansborg Palace, that he fell down stairs and broke his leg. The agitation of his mind produced a fever that nearly proved fatal. As soon as his fractured limb was set, he caused the Norwegian nurse and Count Molckte to be summoned before him, taking precautions to prevent any previous intercourse. The result was that he had no cause to doubt the guilt of Juliana, or that the life of the Crown Prince had been preserved by the courage and fidelity of his nurse, whom he liberally rewarded. From this moment he never cohabited with his guilty Queen; but the thoughts of her wickedness, and the danger of his son and heir, preyed continually on his feeling mind. As a resource—a sad resouce it proved—this excellent King gave himself up to drinking; and Count Molckte being at once master of the Queen and the favourite minister of the King, was, *de facto*, Autocrat of Denmark, exercising the sovereign authority in the name of his master, who rapidly became but the shadow of what he had formerly been. Juliana secretly intended to make M. Guldberg minister, who was a man of great talent and cool judgment; but this detection foiled her plans,[1] and forced her to bow to the man whom she hated and feared. It was by this means Count Molckte acquired that unlimited power which, during the latter part of the reign of Frederick V., he exercised in a way so despotic as to procure him the ironical appellation of "Koning Molckte." This is generally the case with autocracies: Some favourite governs the autocrat, who thereby governs the State—frequently reducing the autocrat himself to a mere cipher. Few, indeed, have been the number of absolute monarchs who were not themselves as far from being free as the meanest of their slaves. But to quit this digression; though the mind of the mild and benevolent Monarch, Frederick V.,

---

[1] The machinations of this envious Queen against the life of Christian VII. did not cease with this attempt. She strove, by gold and promises of preferment, to seduce the attendants of the child. It happened, according to Latrobe's translation, as the King and Royal Family were taking the recreation of sailing in a Royal yacht on the coast of Zealand, near the palace of Fredensborg (about five Danish miles north of Copenhagen), that the young Prince Christian being rather unruly, one of the attendants, named Brocdorph, seized the boy, held him over the stern of the yacht, and threatened to throw him into the water. From the boy's struggles to get free, or from treachery, down he fell into the sea, whence he was rescued; but, as long as reason held its seat, the Prince imputed this act to the agency of his fell step-mother, with a view to procure the Crown for her beloved son Frederick. So far, the anonymous author; and what, in some respect, corroborated this opinion, Brocdorph, being forbidden to appear in the Prince's presence, was immediately engaged in the service of the Queen, and placed as an officer in her palace.—EDITOR.

was thus clouded, he was never happy except the Crown Prince was in his presence. As he grew in years, Christian became more and more the favourite of the King and people. In the wildest sallies of his father, the Prince had more command over him than any other person; and he often had influence enough to prevent him, when tipsy, from lavishing away his treasures on the companions of his cups, and even of inducing him to retract those improvident gifts when sober.

In one of these fits, the King made Count Molckte a present of the magnificent Palace of Hirschholm[1] and all its costly furniture! The Crown Prince, hearing of this lavish act, went to his study, and taking in his hand a plan of the palace, carried it to Count Molckte, saying, "Content yourself with this, I beseech your Excellency; and believe me, unless you possess the Crown, the Palace of Hirschholm shall never be yours."

On another occasion, the King desired Prince Christian to fill the glasses for himself and the Count. The Prince coloured and hesitated. The King repeated his commands, telling him to fill for himself also. Upon which the spirited youth first filled to the brim the glass that stood before the Count, the King's glass only half full, and in his own he scarcely poured any wine. "Hey day! What do you mean by this, Christian?" said the King. "I mean, Sire," said he, "to denote hereby our relative consequence in the State. Count Molckte being *King* and minister, I

---

[1] The Isle of Stags.

filled the glass commensurate with his authority. You, my father, being the *next* person in the State to the Count, I half-filled your glass; as for myself, being of no consequence whatever, I took *no* wine." Weakened and obscured as was the intellect of the King, he pressed his son to his bosom, and a tear glistened in his eye at the reproof thus conveyed. It was, however, only a momentary impression. He still continued his career, till Nature, vanquished by his excesses, and not worn out by time, could endure no more. He died in the year 1766, in the forty-sixth year of his age and the twenty-third of his reign. The Crown Prince Christian, whom Juliana Maria hated and would fain have murdered, was then proclaimed King by the name of Christian VII. Seldom was the dawn of any reign more auspicious than his. He was young, handsome, affable and generous, and the idol of the people. This event knocked the stage from under *King* Molckte, and the sovereign power was, for a short time, really exercised by him who wore the Crown.

CHAPTER III

The character and person of Christian VII.—Demoralised by his cruel step-mother—Portrait of Caroline Matilda at fifteen years of age—Reflections on, and instances of, the unhappiness of Royal females—Secret memoirs of Gustavus III. and his Queen—The Princess Albertina—Unhappy love —An extraordinary expedient, its detection—The secret history of the birth of Gustavus IV., Adolphus, **now Count Gottorp.**

THE person of the young King, though considerably under the middle height, was finely proportioned, light and compact, but yet possessing a considerable degree of agility and strength. His complexion, remarkably fair; his features, if not handsome, were regular; his eyes blue, lively and expressive; his hair very light; he had a good forehead and aquiline nose; a handsome mouth and a fine set of teeth. He was elegant rather than magnificent in his dress; courteous in his manners; of a very amorous constitution; warm and irritable in his temper; but his anger, if soon excited, was easily appeased; and he was generous to profusion. Such was the person and disposition of Christian VII. when he ascended the throne of Denmark.

The reigning Queen, Juliana, failing in her attempts to take the life of the heir-apparent, adopted a method scarcely less cruel to effect the destruction of this young and thoughtless Prince. It was her influence that, during his father's lifetime, opened the doors of the palace and connived at his nocturnal sallies to the haunts of lewd women. It was Juliana, through the agency of M. Guldberg, who surrounded him with a crowd of voluptuous and gay young courtiers, in whose society his morals were corrupted and his constitution undermined. In some of his wild sallies he beat waiters, broke glasses and furniture, attacked watchmen, and more than once was actually taken into custody. These traits resemble the youthful follies of that favourite hero, Henry V., and like him, Christian might have been a hero and a conqueror if he had had similar means and opportunities, and had not been betrayed into all manner of precocious excesses by those whose duty it was to have watched, admonished and protected him.

Being so completely a libertine as to women, he would not, if left to himself, have thought of marrying so soon, if at all. A consciousness of the evil designs of the Queen-Dowager, and a desire to counteract them, rather than any sense of public duty, induced the young and giddy Monarch to listen to those who advised him to strengthen his throne by an alliance with his fair young cousin Matilda, sister to the King of England. He consented; negotiations were opened, and the Princess Matilda became Queen of Denmark.

Caroline Matilda was the youngest child of Frederick, Prince of Wales, and, as well as her husband, a grandchild of George II. She was very tall, of a majestic rather than elegant make, and a very pleasing rather than a beautiful countenance. Her complexion was uncommonly fine—she might, without flattery, have been termed the fairest of the fair. Her hair was very light flaxen, almost as white as silver and of luxuriant growth; her eyes, light blue, clear, large and expressive; her lips, particularly the under lip, full and pouting; her teeth, white and regular. Even at this early age, Matilda was much inclined to what the French call *embonpoint*. Her education had been carefully attended to; her temper was generally mild and gentle, though sometimes rather quick; her demeanour towards the lower and middle classes full of condescension. Towards the supercilious Queen-Dowager, Matilda soon displayed traits of that impetuous and haughty turn that is said to be characteristic of the Guelphs. She was neither profuse nor generous, but her extreme youth, her freshness and apparent good-humour, endeared her to every liberal mind. I saw this ill-fated Princess when she first set her foot on the soil of Denmark. I did not join in the shouts of the multitude, but I was charmed with her appearance. Everything she saw was grandeur and festivity: she was received like a divinity, and almost worshipped, at least by those of the masculine gender. Her animated, beautiful features, her fine blue eyes, beamed with delight on all around her. How kind it was of fate to shut from her view the dreadful reverse that soon snatched the diadem from her brows, her infants from her bosom, and sent her forth from Denmark repudiated into perpetual exile.

That youth must have been a stoic whose heart, if

not devoted to some prior object, would not have been enslaved by this fair foreigner, who was but little more than fifteen years of age at this period. She had not done growing, and though a woman in stature, was a mere child in point of judgment. As to the Prince destined to be her husband, though a youth under his twentieth year, he was older in constitution than many a hale man of threescore; and almost before he had arrived at the age of manhood he had well-nigh ceased to be a man—a circumstance that should be duly considered by all who would form a just opinion of the virtues or frailties of this unfortunate lady.

Entitled to our pity, rather than our envy, is the fate that too often awaits the daughters of Royalty. Dearly do they pay, by the misery they are too often doomed to suffer, for the empty pomp that awaits them. Seldom, if ever, they enjoy the natural affection of their parents, for the loss of which no pageantry can atone. Their mothers are not allowed, even when inclined, to nourish with their own breast their tender offspring, to press their infants with ardour to their bosom, or to perform those endearing offices dictated by Nature and claimed by their helpless young. How much more happy is the wife or the child of a peasant, when health, peace and plenty fall to their lot. The children of kings, from the hour of their birth, are consigned to mercenary hands: they are suckled by mercenary breasts, by mothers who, for the sake of gain, rob their own children of their natural inheritance to sell it to a wealthy stranger. On such hirelings those infantine marks of affection are bestowed, that are never returned with the warmth which marks the caresses of a fond mother. As soon as their intellects admit, the Royal babes are consigned to the tuition of numerous individuals, most of whom they fear, hate or despise, and by whom their manners and habits are formed. Thus the children of kings, the daughters in particular, become a sort of artificial beings, who, having no equal, must form no tender attachment, but hold their subdued affections in a state of abeyance, debarred their natural right of reserving the heart and hand for the man they love. They may fairly be considered as the most elevated class of *Royal slaves*, a sort of kingly merchandise, of which ambassadors are the salesmen; sometimes they are offered to a conqueror to appease his ire; some are bartered away to procure political influence in a foreign Court; or coveted by some cold, calculating prince as the medium whereby he hopes to gain possession of the territories to which she is heiress. Such was the case with the lovely and unfortunate ancestor of our Matilda, the Princess of Zell. Though she was lovely in her person, gentle and amiable in her manners and temper, highly accomplished, and in the flower of her youth, she was yet regarded as a mere appurtenance to the Duchy, and soon treated by her brutal lord with cruelty and contempt. The cowardly assassination of Count Konigsmark and the incarceration of this injured Princess, are subjects too well known to need repetition.[1]

---

[1] The Electoral Prince had, for some time, not only deserted

To a female of real delicacy, what can be conceived more revolting to modesty than to form a union with a man whom, till that moment, her eyes never beheld? How tremendous is the risk she runs that her peace of mind shall cease with her celibacy. Obedient to the call of the oligarchs of Sweden, Gustavus, III., then Crown Prince, married in 1766 the Princess Royal of Denmark, Sophia Magdalena. She, too, was a fine young woman, such as the epicurean debauchee would make almost any sacrifice to obtain. What a singular destiny was hers! Betrothed to one of the most ele-

---

her entirely, but corresponded with his mistress* openly, of which Her Royal Highness not only complained to the Elector and Electress, though without effect, but enlarged upon the affront offered to her, in pretty severe terms, to the Prince himself; who, instead of using the least address to mollify her, gave way to such a transport of rage that, utterly forgetful both of her sex and her quality, he fiercely seized the Princess by the throat, then pregnant and near her time! The whole palace immediately took the alarm, and everybody who dared rushed in to prevent further mischief; notwithstanding which, the Prince was so lost in passion as publicly to avow that henceforward she was to consider him as her mortal enemy; but his threats were not heard by her to whom they were addressed, grief and terror had oppressed her so strongly that she fainted in the arms of those who had come to her relief, and in that condition she was removed to her apartment.

* This celebrated woman afterwards figured in England as Duchess of Kendal. The "Memoirs and Secret Negotiations of John Ker, of Kersland, Esq." (2 vols., London, 1726), treats largely of this mercenary adventuress. Mr. Ker, of Kersland, had been highly instrumental in promoting the Hanoverian Succession; he was a Scotchman, and to gain the favour of the House of Hanover, even during Queen Anne's reign, he betrayed the interests of his own country. He was promised a place, but because he would not give a large *douceur* to the German agent of this German-Anglo Duchess he was disappointed, and thereby totally ruined. Mr. Ker exposed the venality of this wholesale trafficker in politics, &c., and she caused him to be prosecuted *ex officio*. The once-favoured instrument, now no longer needful, was suffered to pine in the King's Bench, borne down by her baleful influence, where he died poor, deserted, and broken-hearted, in July, 1726.

gant and accomplished princes of Europe, then in the bloom of youth, she was received by him with confusion and restraint; during many years this restraint continued, and neglect and insult followed. I have often seen her at the Swedish Court when she lived in compulsory retirement as Crown Princess, and afterwards when she was Queen of Sweden. In spite of all her efforts to dress her face in smiles whilst her heart was a prey to misery, I saw that she was unhappy; and, falling into the prejudice of the day, I imputed her sorrows to the moroseness of the Queen-Mother. I became acquainted with her confidante, Madame ———. I was then young and chivalrous, and beloved by this lady. Master of her entire affections, it will not be deemed surprising if I also became master of many particulars respecting her Royal mistress that, in strict honour, ought not to have been revealed, the strange nature of which excited in my bosom sorrow, pity, disgust and indignation! Neglected and despised by the creature called her husband—borne down by the austerity of that great and inflexible woman, Louisa Ulrica, the sister of Frederick the Great, and consort to the mild and benevolent Monarch, Adolf Frederick, our Princess found herself, in the flower of her youth, a wife without a husband, without peace and without hope! Being a Dane, though of humble rank, my steps were watched with jealous caution; the unguarded conversations of Count Ulric Scheffer enabled me to see my danger. I was romantic enough to endeavour to persuade Madame ——— to prevail on my fair, neglected countrywoman to imitate the conduct of the Queen-

Dowager, Maria Eleonora,[1] widow of Gustavus Adolphus, and mother of that heroic Queen, Christina. I scarcely need say that my counsel was not followed. Madame —— said to me reproachfully, "What! would you take our Princess from the open enmity of a great and magnanimous woman like Louisa Ulrica to place her at the mercy of that fiend, Juliana Maria?" I was

---

[1] This Princess was the daughter of John Sigismund, Elector of Brandenburg, born the 11th of November, 1599, married to Gustavus Adolphus, King of Sweden, the 25th of November, 1620, and crowned the 28th of the same month. Their only child, Christina, succeeded her illustrious father on the throne of Sweden, who was killed at the Battle of Lutzen, or treacherously murdered, as others suppose, on the 16th of November, 1632. Thus was Maria Eleonora born, married, crowned, and widowed in the month of November; she survived her daughter's abdication only nine months, dying the 18th of March, 1655, and was buried near her husband in the Gustavian sepulchre in Ridderholm Church, Stockholm. The following narration of her extraordinary flight is translated from Carl Frederick Ljungman's description of Gripsholm Castle, printed in Stockholm 1790, p. 16, &c., from which compilation it appears that this curious record was originally written in German in Apelblad's description of Saxony, page 47.

"The Queen-Dowager, Maria Eleonora, on the 23rd of July, went secretly away from Gripsholm Castle, and on the 25th embarked on shipboard near Trosa, a small bay ten leagues from Sodertelje. The Government being informed on the 29th of what had happened, despatched messengers after the Queen in five different directions, but in vain. On Thursday, the Burgomaster of Calmar arrived (at Upsala), who informed the Government that, in an unfrequented bay, he had seen a vessel lying at anchor, and a man walking on the deck who had a pistol on each side of him. As soon as the Regency had this intelligence communicated to them, they immediately despatched a messenger to Trosa to enquire into matters. Upon his arrival he found affairs as they had been represented, and he returned with tidings of her conduct in effecting her escape. It seems that, two years pre-

silenced. Not to proceed too far in this digression from the fate of Matilda, I shall merely state that Gustavus totally neglected his Danish bride and indulged in propensities that my pen shall not be polluted by naming.[1] Suffice it to say, that she was made the scoff of those debased wretches, her husband's favourite associates. The Queen, however, kept her

---

ceding this elopement, the Queen-Dowager had attempted to effect her escape from Gottenburg; but, not being able to execute her project there, upon her arrival at Gripsholm Castle, she gave out that, during three days in each month, she should remain with her waiting-woman in her chamber to celebrate religious duties, during which time no one was to be admitted to her; nor would she see anyone. What she required to eat and drink was ordered to be placed in her apartment to serve the whole time. Her chaplain said prayers outside her door, and this custom the Queen continued till July 21st, 1640, when she said to her spiritual guide, 'My vow will shortly expire; I will double my number of days of fasting and prayer and close therewith.' She had sent the Marshal of the Palace to Stromsholm, near Westeros, to make everything ready for her reception there within ten days. As soon as he was got rid of, the Queen-Dowager introduced six pieces of coarse wrappering into her apartment, in which she secretly packed up her valuables.

"When the 23rd of July arrived, she said, 'To-morrow I commence my fast and thanksgiving; therefore prepare everything for six days that I shall have occasion for, as during that time I shall not suffer any one to see me.' She had already procured from Nykoping two side-saddles covered with velvet for herself and her young waiting-woman, which were concealed in the chamber of George Pagreln the page; and fourteen days prior to this period the prudent Queen had caused two palfreys to be turned into the park, under pretext that those nags ought to have grass, by which stratagem she avoided the risk and trouble of procuring horses from the Royal stables; and with a view to promote the great object of all these preparations, she caused a covered way to be made from her chambers to the gardens, of such an extent that she could go a considerable way, and which she contrived so that no one could

[1] See Lewis Goldsmith's "Crimes of Cabinets," p. 16.

shame and sorrow to herself, and strove when in public to dress her face in smiles. And so complete an adept in the practice of the most profound dissimulation was Gustavus, that when they met in public, which was as seldom as possible, he acted the part of a fond, nay, even an uxorious husband. Detestable hypocrite! —I have seen the arch-dissembler practising those

---

observe her when she walked under it; this was finished only four days previous to her last *long fast!*

" The 23rd July being come, provisions and necessaries to serve for six days were carried into the Queen's apartment; into which she went with a young lady named Bulowein, who, the preceding year had arrived from Denmark to take service with Maria Eleanora. But at night, the covered passages concealing their movements, and the nags prepared, the one for herself and Miss Bulowein, and the other for the page George Pagreln, and a Danish painter, the party got off undiscovered, and passing by Trosa, went to a farm about two leagues distance, called Dargenge, where it was pretended that the Queen-Dowager was the daughter of a citizen of Nykoping, and the Danish painter her lover, whose parents would not permit her to marry him, and he had prevailed on her to quit her country to go with him over the sea; their horses, saddles, pistols and riding coats they left at this farm; those were sent forward by a messenger, and on Friday the party went into a boat and proceeded six leagues, where they found a galliot, on which they went on board, and after sailing two leagues in this vessel they reached two Danish ships of war that were waiting for them, on board of which the Queen and her party went; and on Saturday, which was St. Jacob's day, the 25th of July, the ships of war sailed away.

" The country-people stated that all the men who were in the boat or upon the galliot, as well as the men-of-war, spoke pure Danish, and that the Queen shed tears in profusion when she left the farmhouse at Dargenge. The Danish painter said to her in Swedish, 'Do not weep, my love, tranquillise your mind: rest assured everything will terminate happily.' The whole of her party when she embarked amounted to thirty persons. The young lady Bulowein left her knife and a silver sheath behind her, upon which her name was engraved at length.

LOUISA
WIFE OF FREDERICK V

After an engraving by François-Germain Aliamet.
Artist Unknown

secret vices of her sons, particularly Gustavus, and Duke Charles of Sodermanland (now Charles XIII.), thought herself comparatively happy in the affectionate regards of an only daughter, the Princess Sophia Albertina. She was indeed a charming woman, and worthy of a different fate! It was the lot of this lovely and amiable Princess to possess a heart full of sensibility, which even the formalities of Royalty could not extinguish. Many princely suitors, some of them Sovereigns, sought her hand, but not feeling any affection for either, she nobly declared she would rather forego her rank and title and descend from the palace to a cottage than marry a man she could not love. Such was the propriety of her demeanour, that the tongue of calumny, which so much delights in endeavouring to sully the fame of high-born and beautiful ladies, had not even breathed upon her virgin fame. At length the day arrived that she surrendered her heart to an accomplished and virtuous foreigner who appeared at her brother's Court. They were privately married, and everything was ready for their flight; but cruel was the blow that awaited the anxious pair: her husband *suddenly expired*—expired the very day preceding that appointed for their flight; and the priest who had married them, and an old domestic who had witnessed the ceremony, were nowhere to be found. In an instant, the unhappy Princess was bereft not only of her youthful and adored husband, but the means of proving that she was a wife. The shock nearly deprived her of life and reason; but she survived, and, to complete her misery, found herself pregnant. To cut the story short—after mature deliberation, the widowed bride made a confidante of the young and amiable Duchess of Sodermanland, who advised her to conceal her pregnancy; offering to take on herself the appearance, and adopt as her own the child with which Albertina was teeming. The plan was acceded to; the pregnancy of the young Duchess was officially announced, and public thanksgivings ordered in the churches of Sweden.[1] The cannon are said to have been loaded that were intended to celebrate her happy delivery, when an event took place that spoiled the well-conducted project of the two exalted females, and, according to the author of the work just alluded to, "Put the King as well as the Duke out of humour,"—an expression that strongly corroborates the conjecture that, whoever was the father of the expected infant, the King and the Duke were both privy to the intended adoption of Albertina's child. The immediate cause of its failure was, that the Queen-Dowager (and thereto hangs a tale full of the marvellous) suspected the reality of the assumed pregnancy. Knowing that the Duke could not have been its cause, and believing the Duchess to be a virtuous woman, she guessed at the fraud and its object that was already so far advanced. Louisa Ulrica was bold, firm, open and decisive in her conduct and resolves. Without regard to private feelings, she was bent on defeating this project, which she threatened to expose. Despotic as he was, Gustavus could not avert the blow.

---

[1] *Vide* "Characters and Anecdotes of the Court of Sweden," vol. i., p. 7.

The Friherre Benzelstjerna, one of the Secretaries of State, was the bearer of the Queen-Dowager's stern message to the young and playful Duchess, which could not be parried. "Well," said she, "if it is not at present, it may occur hereafter"; and the same day it was announced that the Duchess had, from inexperience, mistaken her situation and been deceived by a "false conception!"

Meantime, the Princess Albertina was secretly delivered of a fine female child, which—reared as the posthumous daughter of a burgher of Stockholm, under the protection of its accomplished and amiable mother—is known in the Court of the Princess as Mademoiselle F——. Whilst these stratagems were formed and frustrated, year after year rolled away and still Sophia Magdalena remained a "mourning bride." Though commanded by the King to hold levées and receive the Nobility, though gratified with splendid dresses, and attended with the utmost pomp whenever she went out from her palaces, there was still a void in the heart that neither power nor pageantry could supply. She had been eleven years the wife of a man who had never yet consummated his marriage! But this strange story runs away with me. I am losing sight of the lovely Matilda and the reflections into which her melancholy destiny hurried me, and describing events too minutely for a sketch like this. Suffice it, therefore, to say that the false and perjured King, finding that an heir was necessary to give stability to the government he had formed, adopted the extraordinary expedient of proposing to his wife that she should admit his bosom friend, Major Muncke, to her bed! Such is the odious complexion of this assertion, that those happy people who have been reared where the decencies of life are more prized than its luxuries, will spurn this as a base and foul aspersion on the memory of Gustavus III. But this is not the case; and I have as much belief in its truth as in the truth of the assassination of that splendid and depraved Monarch.

When the graceful Abelard wooed the lovely and yielding Elosia, the suit of that eloquent lover could not have been urged with more ardour than this strange mortal sued for his own dishonour. With tears suborned, and sighs that seemed to rise from a heart oppressed with grief and shame, he confessed that physical inability alone had kept him from her bed; and to bring her the readier over to his vile ends, he insinuated that his own mother was the wilful source of his misfortune. Although it is hard to believe he was not privy to the expedient that was frustrated by the masculine firmness of his mother, the insidious King imputed it to the ambition of the Duke and Duchess of Sodermanland, and strove hard to impress her with the belief that the stability of his throne depended on her consent. He offered her a "letter of licence" and to be sworn to eternal secrecy. The Queen, however, knew the dissembler too well to trust her honour in his keeping. Covered with blushes, trembling from the force of conflicting passions, almost unable to speak, and not daring to trust herself to look at the recreant King, she made signs for him to retire and afford her time to recall her agitated spirits. When next they met, the Queen mustered courage to tell him that having duly considered his extraordinary proposal, she thought he ought first to divorce her, and then marry her to Major Muncke, adding, if his Majesty pleased so to do, she was willing to meet his wishes; if not, the religious and moral principles in which she had been reared, and of which she had never lost sight, would for ever prevent her acceding upon any other terms. The King, unable to move her from these terms, yielded with a good grace. To give a colour to the reconciliation of this singular pair, it was given out that whilst the King was in Finland, by means of a young minion named Rosenstein, he discovered that his Queen, whom he had accused of being deficient in love and tenderness, was the reverse of all this, and distractedly fond of her beloved Gustavus. My fair countrywoman, Madame ———, who was paid sufficiently well to console her for the execrations of a people she never liked, or intended to see again, was accused, and pleaded guilty to the charge, of having falsely transcribed the Queen's letters, of omitting all the tender sentences they contained, and foisting upon the generous and deceived Monarch her own base language. In short, the lawyers and parsons made quick work of the divorce; and on that day, when the good people of Stockholm were invited to meet the King and Queen in Riddarlolm Church, to return to God their solemn thanks for this happy reconciliation, on that day, and in that church, in the Royal pew, the ex-Queen who had been legally divorced was solemnly married to Major Muncke. The most brilliant festivities followed; and, from this pseudo marriage that extraordinary being, Gustavus IV., Adolphus, owes his existence.[1]

---

[1] This circumstance is well known to the principal statesmen of Europe, and was the *real cause* of his abdication in 1809.

As a lasting monument of his friendship and affection for Major Muncke, the King gave the name of "Muncken's Backen" (Muncke's Hill), to a huge mass of naked granite, that was left in its pristine state when the costly garden at Drottningholm was constructed. The space of ground was covered with huge rocks, on a barren, unwholesome morass. The rocks of granite were blown up, the morass—at an enormous expense—was underdrained, and the surface, made smooth and level, was covered with a fine vegetable soil. To denote its native wildness, one hideous mass lifted its naked head in this wilderness of sweet flowers and shrubs. It was a good idea, and had a fine effect. Soon after the birth of this pseudo Crown Prince (now Count Gottorp, late Gustavus IV.), this rock was wholly covered with earth, and made into a regular circular eminence, covered with greensward and planted on basket beds with shrubs and flowers. Upon its crest, on a fine pedestal of Swedish granite, stands a group in Carrara marble, large as life, representing Gustavus III. and his friend Muncke in the characters of Castor and Pollux. This piece of statuary (which is not to be compared with Sergel's or Canova's works,) was executed in Italy, having been ordered by the King, in 1783, when on his travels in that country. The figure to the right was intended for the King; that to the left for Muncke. The savage rock, once naked and unproductive, now decorated by flowers and shrubs and shaded by beautiful trees, were, perhaps, intended as symbols, first of the Queen's sterility, and next of her fruitfulness when committed to the hands of Count Muncke.

A third source of strong corroborative evidence exists in the mysterious "Iron Chest," mentioned by Sir John Carr and other northern travellers, which is preserved in a room belonging to the library of the University of Upsala, whether *inviolately*, after the Revolution of 1809, may be questioned. The contents of this chest are known to few who are now living (except it has been opened as before observed). Sir John Carr, with his usual sagacity, says: "Conjecture and expectation frequently hover over this chest, which

Such has been the fate of the sister of Christian, our imbecile King. She is yet acknowledged as Queen of Sweden. What has become of Muncke I know not. It is reasonable to suppose that he stood bound by the strongest obligations never to claim the privilege of a husband after the purpose was answered for which he was appointed; and that he was not, in any way, to divulge to the children whom the Queen might have by him, that Gustavus III. was not their sire; nor, in the event of the King's death, ever to claim his supposed widow. All these very hard conditions he probably fulfilled. I believe that Muncke is a Finlander by birth; and I have heard that he is now residing there on an estate bestowed upon him by Gustavus III. Other accounts say that he has been assassinated;—which of these accounts be the truth, or if either account be correct, I am unable to determine.

---

will one day unfold to Sweden much interesting memoir and literary treasure." It would be presumption to speak too decidedly on so doubtful a point, but my opinion is grounded on that of the patriots of Sweden who effected the Revolution of 1809, which drove a weak and imbecile tyrant from his throne: that is, that *this chest contains the secret history of the birth of that Prince.* The chest was ordered to be kept unopened till half-a-century had expired; and there is no proof that even then it was directed that its secret should be made public. The chest is large; has three locks and keys, and was sealed by the present King when he was appointed Regent; by the University great seal; and by the Ryks Drotts, or Lord Chancellor, of Sweden. The keys were deposited, one with the Sovereign for the time being; one with the Ryks Drotts, or Lord Chancellor; and the third with the University of Upsala. So many formalities and precautions would scarcely have been taken to preserve the Royal manuscripts if they were merely of a literary nature.—EDITOR.

As to the personal character of this pseudo son of Gustavus, he is said to possess no great nor splendid quality; but, on the contrary, to be stubborn, penurious and mean in his disposition, irritable in his temper, and a complete bigot in matters of religion.[1]

But to return to our Danish Queen Matilda. That atrocious woman, Juliana Maria, failing in her hellish projects against the life of her Royal step-son, the crafty, cruel and unrelenting woman insidiously and but too successfully endeavoured to enfeeble both his mind and body; thereby to render him not only unfit to rule a nation, but physically unable to leave an heir of his own begetting to the Crown of Denmark. A mode of destruction more cruel than any of her former attempts to destroy the unfortunate Prince in his days

---

[1] It is recorded that this young King put the greatest public affront on Catherine II. that she ever sustained, in rejecting her fair and youthful grand-daughter when the Court was assembled in grand gala, and the bride was waiting him at the altar; and this upon a point of religion that was not of vital importance to either party, and was capable of arrangement. He was right in resisting the encroaching power of Catherine, but surely he might have done it in a way less offensive to her innocent grand-daughter.* This affront, however, has since been too fully avenged by the triumph of Russian power in wresting Finland from the feeble hand of Gustavus; and the present Emperor Alexander may be said to have rejected Frederica Dorothea, the beautiful, virtuous and *divorced* Queen of this eccentric Prince, who, at an early period of her life, was, with her sister, actually sent from Baden to St. Petersburg for examination and selection. What base subserviency in the Grand Duke of Baden! It is not singular that our Danish commentator on the unhappiness of Royal females, seized on this disgusting picture of Regal meanness.—EDITOR.

* Full particulars of this occurrence are to be found in another of our series of Court Memoirs, viz., "The Secret History of the Court of St. Petersburg," 1 vol. —PUBLISHERS' NOTE.

of childhood and adolescence. I have read in the interesting letters of the Countess d'Aunoy that the mother of Charles II. of Spain wilfully and wickedly destroyed the intellectual and physical powers of that Prince to prolong her own reign as Queen Regent. "The whole life of that wretched being (Charles) from his cradle to his grave," says the Countess d'Aunoy, "might be termed one continual malady. The formation of his mind was, of the two, more infirm than that of his body; and he was kept by the Queen-Mother in such profound ignorance, that he knew neither the names, situation, nor the extent of the provinces and cities that composed the kingdom of Spain. When he was about fifteen years of age he happened to exhibit some faint sparks of intellectual energy; when, alarmed at the prognostication, the wicked wretch is accused of having caused some pernicious drugs to be mixed with his chocolate, the effect of which was to stupefy and debilitate the understanding." In one point, this infamous mother went beyond Juliana Maria in crime, because it was her own child whom she thus cruelly devoted to destruction; and in the case of the Queen-Dowager, she was only a step-mother to the being whose destruction she sought with unwearied perseverance and unrelenting hatred.[1] After this long and tortuous digression I

---

[1] Transactions black as these are by no means rare occurrences in Regal courts, although from the shackled state of the Press in despotic monarchies, and the rank and power of the delinquents, they are not, as they ought to be, held up to universal obloquy and execration. The Electress Dorothea, step-mother to Frederick I. of

shall once more return to the eventful and tragical history of Queen Matilda, from her arrival on our shores to her melancholy exile to Zell, where she died.

Prussia, was accused of having attempted to poison that Prince; failing in which design, she strove to deprive him of his inheritance in favour of her own son, by unjustly exciting the resentment of his father against him. The scandalous conduct of the Queen of Charles VI. with Godoy, the *ci-devant* life-guardsman of Madrid, might be quoted as additional proof that the possession of a Regal Crown is no preventive against the worst of propensities.

CHAPTER IV

Matilda's reception in Denmark—The machinations of Juliana Maria—Weakness and depravity of Christian VII.—His motive for setting out on his travels—His adventures in Amsterdam and London.

IT was neither the powerful connections, the high lineage, nor the ample dowry which this young and interesting Princess brought to my country that commanded universal admiration and esteem; but her youth, her innocence, her beauty, and her modest, retiring, graceful demeanour that fascinated all who saw her. The venerable mother of Frederick V.[1] could not suppress emotions tainted by envy on beholding the lovely girl; but the enmity of Sophia Magdalena was harmless compared to the intense malice that glowed in the bosom of Juliana, whose heart was torn by hatred, jealousy, and disappointed ambition at the moment when, with well-dissembled smiles and flattering blandishments, she hailed Matilda as the Consort of Christian VII. This task, however painful, she performed in her best style, and if her malice had not been as much a matter of notoriety as her ambition,

---

[1] Sophia Magdalena, Consort to Christian VI., was then sixty-six years of age. Juliana Maria was in her thirty-eighth year.

Matilda might have believed she should find an affectionate friend, a second mother, in Juliana Maria, to whose odious machinations the vices of the young Monarch were principally owing. This cruel stepmother artfully masked all her own ambitious desires of reigning, under the plausible pretext of regard for the welfare of her son. But Juliana's known qualities forbid the belief that it was for his sake she meditated and committed so many black crimes. The intellectual faculties of Christian VII., until eclipsed by excessive debauchery, were strong and brilliant; her son's, on the contrary, were dull and feeble; hence, this artful woman knew that if she could procure the Crown for her son, the sovereignty would be all her own.

It is difficult to say with precision if Matilda ever felt real affection towards her husband. It is, however, but too certain that he had little regard for her, for he continued secretly to visit the same impure haunts of loose women to which he resorted before marriage. And here again the malice of his implacable enemy was too successfully played off, for those licentious courtiers whom she purposely placed in his way used all their efforts to detach him from his young bride, finding fault with her complexion, her manners, and omitting no opportunity of exciting indifference in hopes of its soon becoming confirmed disgust.

The conduct of Matilda, on her arrival at Denmark, was such as left no room but for approbation—possessing much of that hauteur by which her family are distinguished, she certainly did not forget the dignity of her station. Whilst the King, descending from his rank, made companions of his gay young courtiers, Matilda exacted all the homage from the ladies of her Court to which her exalted station entitled her. She seemed more fond of the show and pageantry of Royalty than desirous of political influence. Notwithstanding the vices of her husband, as he had a large fund of good nature and generosity she might have avoided the calamity that too soon overtook her, had it not been for the intrigues of conflicting Nobles emulous for power; and the ceaseless intrigues of Juliana Maria. The acclamations that resounded wherever Matilda appeared in public smote the envious heart of Juliana as the death-knell of her ambitious hopes of securing the Crown of Denmark for Prince Frederick, who was then in his thirteenth year. Still, she did not relinquish her darling project. Her malice ever fertile, her hopes ever buoyant, impelled her to pursue her destined victims. Even amidst the enthusiastic popularity of Matilda's first reception in the colossal Palace of Christiansborg, the wicked step-mother was secretly preparing means whereby she hoped to effect the destruction of the hated pair, on whose youth, levity and inexperience her impious hopes of their ruin were founded. She was overwhelmed by secret grief when the marriage between young Christian and Matilda was consummated; but then, one great source of hope remained in the ravages which an excessive indulgence in illicit pleasures had made on his constitution, and inexpressible was the mental torture she underwent when the pregnancy of the young bride was officially announced. Her hopes were blasted by the tidings that filled all Denmark with exultation, for nothing was more dreaded by the cultivated and liberal part of the community than seeing her own son ascend the throne. For upwards of two months she buried herself, as it were, in her palace at Fredensborg—but which edifice might, with more propriety, have been termed " Pandemonium," from the iniquitous designs of its owner and her agents. To complete her dismay, on the 28th of January, 1768, the thunder of a thousand pieces of ordnance, from the forts and fleets of Zealand, proclaimed the safe delivery of the young Queen and the birth of a male child.

Juliana Maria was never popular; and when her notorious partiality in favour of her son, and her secret attempts to set aside the heir-apparent to her husband's throne, were known in Denmark, she became an object of general dislike. Everyone foresaw that if Christian VII. died without male issue, this ambitious woman would exercise the sovereign power in Denmark in the name of her son Frederick. These considerations operated with powerful and genial influence in favour of Matilda. Juliana would, perhaps, have expired of chagrin, amidst the blaze of illuminated palaces and the shouts of applauding multitudes, had it not been communicated to her that Christian was weary of his bride, and that his constitution had been so deeply impaired by his debaucheries as left but little room for her to fear he would ever beget another child. As to the infant just born, it was of a slight frame, and rather feeble and sickly than robust, and therefore the more liable to fall a prey to some of the many serious maladies to which infants are subject. On such contingencies she supported an existence that was scarcely tolerable; with such fuel she strove to feed the expiring embers of her hopes of ruling Denmark in the name of her son.

The imbecility of the worn-out boy, his corrupted morals and aversion to his wife, were the real sources of that expensive tour which, a few months after the birth of his son, Christian VII. made through Holland, Great Britain, France and Germany. The motive assigned was to acquire wisdom, to perfect himself in the art of governing, and gather, from a personal review of foreign institutions, materials for the improvement of those established in Denmark, or suggestions for new ones. He visited William V., then recently married to a haughty and tyrannical princess of Prussia, whose pride and insolence, in a few years time, involved her weak, good-natured husband in a contest with the burghers of Amsterdam and other cities that led to the invasion of Holland by the Prussian army in 1787, and, ultimately, to the expulsion of the Princes of the House of Orange. It has ever been my opinion that this little Republic contained more useful institutions than all the Monarchies of Europe put together. On those our young King had but little time for observation and reflection; and the want of superior intellect in his cousin, William V., rendered it impossible to derive useful instruction in the art of governing from that source, who was himself governed by his wife and the Cabinets of Berlin and St. James's. The time he passed there was consumed by a succession of splendid feasts and delightful excursions by land and water. Whilst he was in Amsterdam, he gave Count Bernstorff and all his suite the slip; and, disguised as an English sailor, went with Count Holcke to the Rondeel, a temple consecrated to Cyprian traffic, where he supported his assumed character with great spirit in every point save one. Not content with this frolic, they bent their steps to the Pyl (arrow), a noted brothel in the Pyl Steeg, where a bevy of mercenary beauties crowded round the strangers, one of whom, deceived by the fair complexion of our King and his effeminate appearance, accused him of being a lady come in disguise to witness their mysteries, and she was proceeding to disrobe her temporary lover, when she perceived a rich silken vest, and a star and blue riband beneath his sailor's jacket, and at the same moment his flaxen locks fell about his shoulders. In a moment he was recognised as Count de Travendahl. The youthful King of Denmark, perceiving he was detected past retrieval, flung a handful of ducats on the floor, and whilst the girls were scrambling for the golden prize, the King and Count Holcke ran down stairs, leaped over the hatch door and, making good use of their heels, avoided all pursuers.

From Holland, the gay and giddy youth proceeded by Antwerp and Brussels to Calais, where a Royal yacht, the *Mary*, Captain Cambell, awaited his arrival to convey this brother-in-law of George III. to Dover. One of his chamberlains proceeded as an *avant* courier to St. James's[1] to announce the arrival of the Royal

---

[1] Christian VII. was lodged in those apartments in the Stable-

Dane, and see that the accommodations were suited to his master's taste. A train of Royal carriages and domestics were sent down to Dover to convey the King and his numerous suite to London; but such was his impatience to see the famed metropolis of Great Britain, that he declined those sumptuous vehicles and travelled by post-chaise. Having heard that the Clergy and Corporation of Canterbury and Rochester intended to receive him with all possible pomp, he was

---

yard that are now occupied by the Duke of Clarence, and where the King of Prussia was lodged when he visited this metropolis in the summer of 1814. When Count Holcke, a gay, extravagant, dissipated young nobleman, first saw the exterior of the place, he exclaimed, "By God, this will never do! this is not fit to lodge a Christian in!" When he saw the interior, the Count was more dissatisfied—an impression not to be wondered at; the extreme splendour of Christiansborg Palace being fresh in his memory, compared with which St. James's appeared mean and insignificant. The Danish Monarch hired his horses of a man named Baker, who died about the year 1797—a master hackney-coachman in Bond Street. This person drove the King's carriage in his peregrinations about the metropolis. He used to take a pride in showing himself to those females who seemed most desirous to see his Royal person. From some of these, who supposed he could not understand them, he occasionally met with coarse compliments—such as: "What a little Jack-a-dandy!" "What a squinny thing it is!" &c.,—all of which he took in perfect good humour. One day, as his coach drove to the door of his residence, a fine-looking girl burst through the double line of attendants, caught the King of Denmark in her arms as he leaped from his carriage, and, kissing him heartily, said: "Now kill me, if you please; I can die contented since I have kissed the prettiest fellow in the world!" The King, far from being offended, gently disengaged himself from her embrace, and ran laughing and skipping upstairs. He used to carry gold coins in one pocket and silver in another, which he gave away, often by handfuls, to those who attracted his notice.
—EDITOR.

thrown almost in a passion, not being at all partial to formalities of any kind; and as to the Clergy as a body, he held them in contempt and spoke of them with derision. He said to Count Bernstorff: " The last King of Denmark who entered Canterbury laid the city in ashes and massacred the inhabitants. Would to God they had recollected this, and would let me pass quietly through their venerable town where our ancestors have committed so many crimes. Is it conformable to etiquette that I should appear by proxy? If so, pray let me proceed to announce *your* approach, and be you my proxy. Really, the unwieldy pomp and pedantic speeches of the priests and the burghers fill me with dreadful apprehensions. If this is inadmissible, and I must, sooner or later, undergo this visitation, may it not be deferred till I return to this port for embarkation? Believe me, the thing would be infinitely more agreeable and quite as useful, and one ceremony would do for all." The Count told him, with a smile, that the good citizens of Canterbury would find less difficulty in forgetting all the outrages suffered by their ancestors, than in being deprived of the honour of making him a speech and kissing his Royal hand. Finding there was no escape, he entreated the Count to intimate beforehand that the King had a mortal antipathy to long speeches.

In disposition, person, manners and habits, Christian VII. was the reverse of his cousin and brother-in-law, George III., whose regularity and dignified demeanour were objects of ridicule to our wild and giddy King and his dissolute associates; and, instead of this example reclaiming Christian from his vicious habits, he laughed at him as a domestic quiz—alike void of elegance or spirit.

As the periodical publications of the day present a faithful detail of the festivities and illuminations, balls, concerts and masquerades, military and nautical spectacles, and tours by land and excursions by water that occurred in England in honour of our young King, and marked the popularity he enjoyed, it would be superfluous to go into those events. He was pleased with the Dutch, but the English quite amazed and fascinated the wild and giddy boy. The dazzling whirl of dissipation in which his hours were passed was enough to turn the brain of a wiser head than his. Such a rapid succession of splendid spectacles was calculated to pall the senses, enervate the frame, and exhaust the animal spirits of him who was the idol of the day, the object of all those joyous scenes of dissipation. Out of every twenty-four hours, eighteen at least were thus employed! Where, then, was the leisure for the voluptuous youth to learn lessons of wisdom and store his mind with knowledge? Unlike Telemachus, this Royal wanderer had no mentor but his own unbridled passions—no pilots but servile courtiers, who, to gratify their Sovereign, flattered every folly, and sought with lamentable avidity, even in the paths of infamy and vice, the means of making themselves useful or agreeable.[1] His errors and vices are, however, entitled to more than ordinary

---

[1] In the "Walpoliana," vol. ii., p. 94, is the following article, headed, "Court Promises": "I have sent the Strawberry Hill Books to the Prince of Denmark as I was requested, except the 'Anec-

indulgence, so much pains having been taken to eradicate the seeds of virtue from his mind, and render him an adept in the exercise of libertinism and profligacy.

Whilst Christian was in London, he acted as he used to do in Copenhagen, namely, visited in disguise the haunts of courtesans of every class, from the purlieus of St. James's to the lanes in Wapping and the cellars of St. Giles's. His youthful bride, his child, his rank, his health, all were forgotten. These nocturnal rambles in search of adventures were generally commenced after midnight, and after the King had been exhausted by twelve or fourteen hours spent in paying or receiving visits of ceremony, in promenades, drives, or dances. He opened the ball given at Sion House by the Duke of Northumberland, with his sister-in-law, the Queen of Great Britain; he danced with the Princesses of Saxe Gotha and the Duchess of Ancaster, and within an hour after quitting those scenes of Regal grandeur, he would throw off his gorgeous habiliments, disguise his rank by the dress of a sailor, and, making the best of his way to St. Giles's, join in the rude dances of labourers and their lasses with as much glee as if he had never moved in a higher sphere: for which performance, indeed, his former rambles amongst the sailors of Copenhagen had qualified him. Count Holcke, in the same disguise as the King, and passing for his brother, accompanied Christian to these vulgar haunts, and, on emergencies, protected him—though,

---

dotes of Painting,' which I was forced to buy at a high price to present to the King of Poland. I have no answer from Denmark, which I much wonder at."

to give the young King his due, he was by no means deficient in personal courage. On such occasions the *incognito* sometimes met with adventures that put his courage and forbearance to a severe test. It happened in St. Giles's, as he was going through a dance with a fine healthy looking girl, who had been crying cherries all day behind a barrow in the streets, a gigantic Irishman, her lover, gave him a slight blow for presuming too far, calling him a foreign puppy and bidding him keep his hands from the bosom of a girl that had an Irishman for her protector! In a moment the King returned the compliment; when Holcke, stepping between the combatants, told the assailant he must turn his rage on him, as his brother was no match for a man of his strength. "By J——," exclaimed the Irishman, "your brother is a hero; and I am sorry I gave him the pat. Here's my hand and my heart; I am ashamed of having hit you, and if you will but forgive me, you shall *bate* me afterwards till you are tired!" Instinctively the King and his magnanimous enemy shook hands; gin was called for; Christian drank his glass to the girl whose modesty he had offended, and whom he was, by the lover, invited to kiss as the pledge of peace. The blow he had received called the blood into his fair and delicate cheeks; the girl was a fine healthy-looking brunette, though a good deal tanned; the wild youth kissed her cherry lips, and sliding his purse full of gold into her half-exposed bosom, made good his retreat, followed by his associate, Count Holcke, laughing heartily at the adventure—the blow giving the King less pain than the heroism of the gigantic Irishman had excited admiration. Such was the manner in which Christian VII. passed his time in London, by which it may be supposed that his health was more deeply impaired; as to his morals, they were in so bad a state before he left Denmark, that it was scarcely possible they could be further contaminated. If Christian VII. had adopted a disguise for the purpose of enabling him the better to observe the manners and morals of the middle and lower orders of British society, he might have reaped abundance of amusement and much useful knowledge of the world, of which Princes in general are lamentably ignorant. But his motives had their source in those lascivious images which continually floated in his mind and excited his passions, whilst every day he became less capable of enjoying the frail beauties whose society he sought, promiscuously, in Cleveland Row or St. Catherine's. Like Tantalus, though from a different cause, he was continually tormented, and his desire after women increased in proportion as his strength decayed. Stimulants and restoratives were in constant requisition; and the too-celebrated Struensee, who attended Christian during this Regal tour, saw, with unaffected sorrow, the certain misery he was drawing upon himself by practices alike ruinous to body and soul. All his efforts were in vain, for the King, without restraint, abandoned himself to those destructive habits, whose rapid progress within a couple of years left him nothing but a shattered and debilitated hulk, afflicted in the morning of life with all the imbecility of body and mind incidental to extreme old age. The condition of the King soon became known. His mother-in-law, the Princess-Dowager of Wales, was amusing herself, one day, with a lady of her Court (to whom, it was conjectured for certain gratifications, Christian had presented a superb set of jewels), by telling fortunes with cards. Christian said to her: "My dear mother, how do you designate my Majesty in your paper Court?" "Lady ——," said the Princess, with an arch smile, "calls you the King of Diamonds!" "And what do you call Holcke?" rejoined the conscious youth, colouring as he spoke. "Oh! by a title far more flattering; that rake, who is so formidable to careful fathers and jealous husbands, is called the King of Hearts." "Then, pray, my dear mamma," said Christian, piqued by her ironical allusions, "under which of the suits do you designate Lord Bute?" This repartee, as severe as it was unexpected, crimsoned the face of the Princess, who soon afterwards retired, evidently offended with her incorrigible son-in-law.

One day, Holcke and Christian VII. went to a well-known public-house, not far from the Bank, which was much frequented by Danish and Swedish ship-masters. Here they listened to the conversation of the company, which, as might be expected, was full of wonder and admiration at the splendid festivities daily given in honour of Christian VII. Count Holcke, who spoke German in its purity, asked an old skipper what he thought of his King, and if he were not proud of the honours paid to him by the English. "I think," said he, drily, "that, with such counsellors as Count Holcke, if he escapes destruction it will be a miracle." "Do you know Count Holcke, my friend," said the *incognito*, as you speak of him thus familiarly?" "Only by report," said the Dane; "but everybody in Copenhagen pities the young Queen, attributing the coolness which the King showed towards her, ere he set out on this voyage, to the malice of Count Holcke!" The confusion of this minion may be easier conceived than described; whilst the King, giving the skipper a handful of ducats, bade him "Speak the truth and shame the devil." The moment the King spoke in Danish the skipper knew him, and, looking at him with love and reverence, said in a low, subdued tone: "Forgive me, Sire, but I cannot forbear my tears to see you exposed to the temptations of this vast and wicked metropolis, under the pilotage of the most dissolute nobleman of Denmark." Saying this he retired, bowing profoundly to the King and casting at Count Holcke a look full of defiance and reproach. Holcke was a good deal confused and not a little hurt, seeing that the King in a manner countenanced the rudeness of the skipper.

When the King returned to St. James's he told Struensee what the blunt skipper had said respecting Count Holcke. Struensee's reply was so ambiguous that it might be be construed or explained in more ways than one; yet so obviously reflecting on the Count as a person dangerous to the King, that the latter said: "I thank you very sincerely, M. Physician, for these hints; I think I must transfer your talents from the path you are now in, and make you a *Conferentie Raad*"[1]—at the same time extend-

---

[1] Counsellor of State.

ing his hand to Struensee, who, bending his knee to the ground, gracefully touched it with his lips, saying: "Ah, my King! seeing as I do every day the treachery of courtiers, and the slippery ground on which favourites stand, wisdom warns me to shun the allurements of ambition." This was the first step towards the fall of Holcke and the advancement of Doctor Struensee which followed, but not immediately. Struensee saw with secret rapture the brilliant path opening to his view, that rapidly led him to the highest pitch of fortune and suddenly precipitated him to the lowest depths of debasement and misery.

To give all the anecdotes that I have heard connected with the conduct of Christian VII. whilst he stayed in England would fill a moderate volume. Some of the most interesting are already before the world, and many more are of a nature unfit for publication. The following is, I believe, original. For the better supply of his wants, the King had caused an unlimited credit to be opened with a very rich but penurious merchant in the city, under the assumed name of M. Frederickson. Dressed as private gentlemen, the King and Count Holcke went to the merchant's counting-house and took up five thousand pounds. The merchant was very desirous of knowing more of M. Frederickson—he even employed a lad to watch them; but in spite of his dexterity, the strangers got off unperceived. It happened as the same clerk who had attempted to watch the King and Count Holcke in the city was passing St. James's Palace, he saw the same gentlemen enter, by a private door, the building in which the King resided; and, asking a sentinel on duty if he knew who they were, he was told they must belong to the Danish King, as no persons but his attendants were allowed to pass or repass by that door! Well pleased with this discovery, the lad, as soon as he got home, communicated it to his master, by whom it was told to his spouse—taken from the kitchen—and whose pride and arrogance was only surpassed by her ignorance. The wife urged her husband, when next those strangers called, to invite them to tea, she being much inclined to ask them to show her the King and his apartments; and the husband the more readily agreed, as he conjectured that this M. Frederickson might take up the money to lend to the King on very advantageous terms. Thus, though from very different causes, the merchant and his wife were alike desirous of cultivating the acquaintance of the mysterious stranger.

The next time M. Frederickson called, he again demanded a very large sum, for which the merchant gave him a cheque on his banker. The man of business had barely time to ask them to take a cup of tea with his wife some afternoon before the King and Holcke hastened away, telling him they would talk of that next time they came. The lad who had before tried to watch them home, saw them go into the banker's, and thence to the bank, where a carriage was standing, the door of which was opened the moment the gentlemen appeared, and which drove off with such rapidity that the boy was obliged to give up a fruitless chase.

It was not long before the strangers called again, when M. Frederickson drew a further and considerable sum of money. The merchant had by this time made up his mind that the cash was for the use of the King, and that M. Frederickson made an enormous profit by these advances. To obtain a share of this gain was the object of his study; but the ambition of his spouse was of a more exalted kind, aspiring to no less an honour than that of being presented to the King of Denmark!

Leaving the Count engaged in conversation with his wife, the merchant took the King by the lappel of his coat and led him a little distance from his companion; and, after a long and tedious detail of the courses of exchange being much against him and the great risk of going too deep on one speculation, asked the Count in direct terms if the money was not taken up for the use of Christian VII. The King thought at first he was detected, but finding that not to be the case, and that the merchant only wanted to get a share of a good thing, resolved to allow him to proceed, in hopes of deriving amusement by the adventure; thence, he answered in the affirmative. The merchant's eyes sparkled with joy at this confession. "I am told," said he, "that Christian VII. is one of the most extravagant and thoughtless young dogs living, and cares no more about money than if it could be raked out of the kennels. Of course, you make him pay handsomely? Eh! you understand me?" It was with difficulty the King could restrain from laughter; but he contrived to avoid this rudeness, and, as gravely as he could, told the man of traffic that he had drawn a correct picture of the King's character. "And pray, sir," said he, significantly, "what is the nature of your employment?" "My chief employment," said Christian, "consists in dressing the King and looking out for amusements." "Just the thing!" said the merchant; "then you are the more likely to have influence. Perhaps you pick him up a tit-bit now and then, eh?" "No man has more influence with him than I have; of that be assured." "Then, of course, you make a handsome thing out of these advances?" "Upon my word of honour, I never made a profit by any pecuniary transaction in my life." The merchant's face lengthened considerably, as he turned his small eyes obliquely towards the King's. After a pause, he began on another tack, and said he supposed he knew nothing of money-dealings, nor how to make the best of his capital? "Nothing whatever!" "How does the King dispose of these sums?" "Gives them away; sometimes in coin or banknotes—oftener in presents of jewellery or other precious articles." "Harkee, sir," said the merchant, delighted by these confessions; "would you not wish to make the best of your influence with the King?" "Certainly I would." "Then, if you will suffer me to instruct you, I will teach you how to make fifty per cent. on the capital. Let me buy the jewels and presents." Just at that instant one of the King's pages arrived, and desired the clerk to call his master, who was never less disposed to be interrupted. "Pray, sir," said the messenger, "is not the King of Denmark in your house?" "The King of Denmark? No, sir; there is no King of Denmark; only a M. Frederickson." "That is the King! the son of Frederick V.; the gentleman with him is Count Holcke, Master of His Majesty's Wardrobe; I am sent by the Princess-Dowager of Wales, and am ordered to deliver this letter into His Majesty's own hands." It would be in vain to attempt to describe the stiffening horror that seized on the humbled and mortified son of traffic; the big drops of sweat poured down his face, and every limb shook. The page, alarmed at his agitation, pressed for an explanation, which, in the best manner he could, was given. The page laughed heartily, and told him not to fear that any bad result would follow his proposal to the King to help to cheat himself. It was, however, impossible to induce the man of business to reappear. As soon as the page, with all the reverence usual on such occasions, presented the letter to the King, the merchant's wife, who had been urging the Count to introduce her, was taken in a way somewhat similar to her husband. But the Count, in the most gentle and soothing manner, bade her be comforted; and, taking her by the hand, introduced her to the King, saying to her, "I have thus, madam, unexpectedly the happiness of fulfilling your flattering wish." This speech was lost upon the woman, whose stupid stare showed the complete confusion of her mind, and who might have changed colour if the paint that covered her cheeks had not prevented it. The King, pitying her confusion, drew from his own finger a valuable ring, which he would, if her fingers had not been too large, have put on one of hers. And desiring her to tell her husband that the King would never feel offended at what he had said confidentially to M. Frederickson, skipped down stairs, laughing heartily at the adventure, and regretting that it had so suddenly terminated.

Such was the profusion of this Prince, that although his brother-in-law supported a table for himself and his suite that cost nearly five hundred dollars per diem, he got rid, in various ways, of five times that sum; drawing on Hamburg for more than one hundred thousand dollars per month. This enormous drain of specie was sensibly felt on the Exchange of Copenhagen; and the more so, as the absence of the King and his principal minister threw a gloom over the metropolis and injured trade and commerce. From the sketches already given, it will be conceived that Christian VII. rather scattered his treasures than bestowed them; that, acting on the impulse of the moment, he gave without discrimination; and it is too probable, from the audacity of impostors and the modesty of suffering merit, that the former class of applicants swallowed by far the greater part of his largesses. But, wherever real misery met his eye, his hand went, as it were, spontaneously to his pocket; and if that chanced to be empty, his ring, watch, or any other valuable about him was bestowed instead of money. He saw a poor tradesman put into a hackney-coach by two bailiffs, followed by his weeping wife and family, from whom he was about to be torn and thrown into prison. To avoid observation he ordered Molckte to follow the coach to the Marshalsea; he paid the debt and costs, and setting the poor man free from every other demand, gave him five hundred dollars to enable him to begin the world anew. He distributed considerable sums generally amongst the poor debtors confined in the different gaols of the metropolis. To men of science he paid but little attention; nor was he a warm patron of literature or the fine arts. All the faculties of his mind were concentrated on voluptuous pursuits. He was struck by the marked superiority of the British stage, and David Garrick had the honour of an audience. The King paid homage to his genius, repeating a line of Shakespeare as he presented him with a very valuable snuff-box set with brilliants. M. Martin of Stockholm, a Swede, and an eminent landscape painter, was then in London. Having recently seen the Queen Magdalena Sophia, the sister of Christian VII., and being much admired as an artist, he was admitted to an audience, and received a valuable present as a token of affection towards his Royal sister, the Queen of Sweden, and of respect to the artist, who offended the King by telling him, in reply to a question, "Whether the Queen, his sister, was happy?" that, "She was as happy as a young woman could be expected who had been married nearly three years and yet remained a virgin." The King coloured at the insinuation contained in this imprudent reply, which, finding its way to Stockholm, injured M. Martin very materially.

After distributing many magnificent presents, and taking leave of the King, Queen and Royal Family, the

King of Denmark, on the 13th of October, 1768, set off for Dover, where he embarked for Calais, and proceeded to Paris. There he was received with all the *éclat* and magnificence in the power of that voluptuous Court to bestow on a Prince who had travelled so far to visit the most polished Court in Europe. Here the treasures of France and Denmark were poured forth in a mingled stream, and the King plunged anew into dissipation. The Duke of Orleans initiated him in Parisian voluptuousness. It was, perhaps, mere caprice that induced Christian to travel in Holland, *incognito*, as Prince of Travendahl, in England as a King, and in France as Count of Oldenburgh. After dining at Versailles with the French King, Queen and Court, a large curtain was withdrawn, and disclosed a fine view of his great Palace of Christiansborg, at Copenhagen. The Prince of Condé gave him a grand hunt by torchlight in an illuminated forest. Such splendid spectacles, even in France, were scarcely ever before witnessed. No wonder that the youthful King was completely entranced and lost, as it were, in a flood of pleasure. Whilst he was in this capital, in defiance of Struensee's remonstrances, he abandoned himself with more fury than ever to unrestrained habits of debauchery, whilst his health more than ever suffered, not only by former taints, but still more severely by a recent infection, which rendered his case almost hopeless. At the Court of Versailles our King left a very mean character behind him as to his prowess in feats of love; and there, as in London, Christian was "King of Diamonds," and Holcke, "King of Hearts."

On the 8th of December, the King and his suite quitted Paris, on his return to the capital of Denmark, *viâ* Strasburg and Altona, which he reached by the beginning of January, 1769, after an absence of rather more than six months, and the expenditure of nearly £200,000 sterling.

CHAPTER V

Queen Matilda—The Counts Struensee and Rantzau—Court intrigues—Peter III., Count Rantzau the cause of his death—Madame Göhler—First confidential interview between Queen Matilda and Struensee—Its result—Reflections on their comparative criminality.

DURING the absence of her giddy lord, Matilda resided principally at the Palace of Fredericksborg, in the vicinity of Copenhagen, and her conduct was free from reproach. Though courted and menaced by conflicting factions, she joined with none, nor showed the least ambition for political power. She appeared to feel a truly maternal affection for her child, and in spite of remonstrances, had the infant and nurse to sleep in her own apartment. She sometimes visited, and was visited by, the Queen-Dowager and Prince Frederick, but lived very retired. She was grown in stature, and appeared much more womanly than when she arrived in Denmark. The glow of robust health was on her cheek; she often nursed her child, and a more interesting object could scarcely be conceived than this healthy and lively young Queen playing with her babe. During this state of retirement, Matilda visited the houses of the farmers and peasants who resided near the palace; and though she could not converse fluently with these poor, grateful people, she gained their warm hearts by her condescension in visiting their cottages, smiling graciously on their wives and daughters, and distributing useful presents. Thus innocently, Queen Matilda passed her time during the travels of her wild and dissipated husband.

During all this time, the different factions were struggling for ascendency. The chiefs of those domestic curses sent home to Denmark such accounts of the conduct of the King and the overweening influence of Count Holcke, as awakened the most serious apprehensions in the minds of those who really felt for their country. Matilda ranked Count Holcke as her most formidable enemy; and she strove in vain to prevent his accompanying the King. Count Charles Schak Rantzau, Governor of Gluckstadt, a general in the army, a Knight of the Order of the Elephant, the head of one of the most powerful families under the Danish Crown, being ambitious of power, found means to induce Count Holcke and Enevold Brandts to favour the appointment of Doctor John Frederick Struensee as Physician in Ordinary to the King, and to accompany his Majesty in the grand tour that he meditated through Holland, England, France and Germany.[1] There is scarcely a doubt, though the

---

[1] The following account of the unfortunate Count Struensee, and his father and brothers, is extracted from the "Conversion of Struensee," pp. 55—57.

"Adam Struensee, his father, was born at New Rippon, educated at Brandenburg, and studied at Halle and Jena. In 1730, he was made chaplain to Count Witgenstein; he married the

5—2

immediate consequence of this step was beneficial to Struensee alone, that General Count Rantzau had his own interest in view; and that he hoped, by the talents and influence of Struensee, to ascertain and counteract the machinations of Count Holcke, and once more obtain a post of consequence in the Court of Christian VII.

Struensee was a libertine and a freethinker. He possessed considerable talents, and became a favourite with this nobleman, whose morals were of the same loose stamp. Count Rantzau married his first cousin, the daughter of his father's brother, Count Oppendorff, of Kiel. It was rather a union of the two estates of Rantzau Oppendorff and Rantzau Aschberg. The Count and Countess had not been long married before she retired from the Count's residence. Her husband ever used to speak of her as a good creature, a little

---

daughter of the Count's physician. Frederick V. advanced him to the high post of General Superintendent to the Two Duchies, a clerical rank nearly equal to that of a bishop.

"John Frederick, afterwards Count Struensee, was born at Halle, on the 5th of August, 1737; studied medicine; was appointed Physician to the districts of Rantzau and Pinneberg; resided at Altena. In April, 1768, was appointed Physician to the King; in May, 1769, *Lecteur Royale*; on the 19th of May, 1770, Counsellor of Conference and *Maitre du Requestes*; in July, 1771, First Minister of the Crown, created a Count, and invested by the Queen with the Order of Matilda; was arrested on the 17th of January, 1772, and beheaded, &c., on the 28th of April following. Charles Struensee, now a Minister of the Crown (1817) in Prussia, with the rank of Baron, was born in 1735, and was Professor of Mathematics at Liegnitz, in Silesia. He was called to Denmark by Struensee; made Minister of Justice, and arrested with him; as was also the case with a younger brother, to whom he had given a commission in the horse-guards."

beside herself. It was too probably his libertine pursuits that destroyed her health, her peace, and affected her intellect. He frequently visited the Countess when he was near her residence, and showed her respect when she was no longer capable of being gratified by his attentions.

When young, the Count was a very fine man. He was of a profuse disposition, caring so little about money that, when he was colonel of a regiment and wanted to light his pipe, if no other paper were within reach, he would make use of Danish banknotes of ten, twenty or thirty dollars each. His purse and his table were always open to his friends. He was munificent to the poor, a liberal landlord, a brave officer, an accomplished courtier, and a universal lover. He possessed that cool kind of courage which denotes the firmest nerves. He had been engaged in several duels, some of a political, but more of a female origin (if the expression may be allowed), and more than once he laid an opponent dead at his feet. In one case, where he had debauched the daughter of a gentleman whom he could not avoid fighting, and who rushed on the sword of his child's betrayer, the Count was for a time inconsolable; he threw himself at the feet of the widow with every mark of penitence, imploring her forgiveness; he married, with the *left hand*,[1] the unfortunate lady he had seduced, and settled an ample provision on the mother

---

[1] An intermediate state, between that of wife and mistress, in use in Germany, and called "left-hand marriages"; mostly used where a great inequality exists as to birth and rank. It is said that George I. married the person, afterwards Duchess of Kendal, in that way.

and her other children. Time and new amours soon effaced the melancholy inspired by this domestic tragedy, and the Count became as gay and dissolute as ever.

His estates were very considerable, and lay principally at Aschberg, about four English miles from Ploën and twenty from Lubeck. His residence in Copenhagen was the Princens Palace, to the west of Christiansborg. At at early age this distinguished nobleman served the Emperor of Austria. He was at St. Petersburg when Peter III. avowed his determination to make war on Denmark for the recovery of the territories ceded in 1737 in Holstein and Sleiswick.

At that eventful crisis Count Charles Schak Rantzau was not an idle spectator of his country's danger. He gained the confidence of Prince Orloff and the Empress by communicating the secret designs of the unfortunate Emperor, who, true or false, was accused by Count Rantzau of intending to put the Empress to death. The result is too well known to require repetition. Peter was dethroned and murdered; his wife ascended the throne.[1] Holstein was saved from invasion, and the unoffending Hamburgers were forced to pay Frederick V. a million of dollars, because the Autocrat of All the Russias had menaced Denmark with invasion. Thus, in Russia too, he helped to depose a legitimate Sovereign and elevate a —— and a —— to an Imperial throne.

---

[1] To prove that Peter came to his death by natural means, his disconsolate widow had his corpse exposed naked to the view of all the world, although a company of grenadiers, with fixed bayonets, surrounded it on every side, threatening instant death to anyone who should dare approach to examine it.

Ten years afterwards he seized a young and interesting Queen, the wife of his own Sovereign, in the dead hour of sleep, and hurled her from a throne to a prison. Strange events these to have fallen to one man's share. It is neither my object to vilify the memory of this extraordinary nobleman, nor conceal his failings. He was a marked character, signalised from the ordinary herd of courtiers by splendid qualities. I have never yet seen anything like a correct biographical sketch of his eventful life; all I can do is to supply a few leading traits that may, perhaps, remove the mystery that envelops his motive and conduct on the fatal night that consigned a young and beautiful Queen to shame, ruin and exile.

It is already mentioned that, in the spring of 1768, Count Rantzau was the cause of Struensee being placed near the person of Christian VII. It is probable that the real intention of Rantzau was to gain early and correct intelligence of the conduct of Counts Holcke, Bernstorff, Molckte, &c.—particularly the former—with the view of counteracting Holcke and ingratiating himself with the Queen. Whether Struensee had secret instructions or not, it is certain he omitted no opportunity of undermining Holcke in the esteem of the King; for he was admirably calculated to perform a secondary part, though wholly incapable of striding the whirlwind and directing the storm.

During the King's stay in Paris, Count Holcke fell under serious displeasure; and just then arrived the celebrated Count—then Chamberlain—von Brandt, a sort of dependent and partisan of Rantzau's, the bosom friend of Struensee, a man of polished manners, undaunted courage, a deist as to religion, and a libertine as to love. From the period of Brandt's arrival in Paris, the influence of the giddy and voluptuous Count Holcke was shaken and diminished; but the time of his dismissal, and of Brandt's elevation to his high post, had not then arrived.

Those politicians, the Counts Bernstorff and Molckte, saw without alarm the King's fondness of the gay and dissipated Count Holcke, because, absorbed in voluptuous pursuits, those statesmen thought him perfectly indifferent to State affairs; he might dissipate the King's treasures, contaminate his morals, and destroy his constitution without censure, as long as he did not presume to interfere with the government of the kingdom.

Count Rantzau took the best means in his power to convince Queen Matilda of these facts, and that the great object of each faction was to keep Her Majesty from meddling with affairs of State. The partisans of Juliana have accused Struensee of transmitting anonymous letters to the Queen, containing the most exaggerated pictures of the King's debaucheries; and they have even asserted that Struensee himself was the instigator of the King's most criminal excesses, on purpose that, on his return to Denmark, he might infect his Queen!—aspersions which I notice only to illustrate the rancorous malice of the enemies of Struensee.

As to Count Rantzau, he felt all the esteem of an affectionate brother towards Frederick V. He was not ignorant of the base designs of Juliana Maria. He promised her dying husband on his oath and his honour that he would never desert his favourite boy, Christian. He now saw that son surrounded by dissolute minions, who were urging him to destruction. It is, therefore, allowable to presume that Count Rantzau had no dishonourable views in the part he acted, as it were, behind the scenes; and that, in seeking to obtain power, he intended to use it for the public good.

The King's irregularities led to more frequent personal interviews between him and Struensee, who knew so well how to use them that, insensibly, he acquired not merely an influence, but such kind of authority over the King as a man might be supposed to possess who is the keeper of another's honour, a witness of his secret vices, and a mild and eloquent declaimer against them. And though the giddy Prince took no pains to improve his mind by the intercourse with distinguished foreigners which his recent tour had afforded, Struensee was not so remiss, for, whilst he revelled in voluptuous pleasures, he dedicated a considerable part of his time to the acquirement of knowledge. During this tour, his manners, always insinuating and pleasing, had acquired a polish and dignity before unknown. Even the giddy and dissolute Count Holcke perceived it; Struensee was a deist when a mere boy at Halle; and, of course, his intercourse at Paris with philosophers and wits had not increased his reverence for revealed religion. In short, Struensee returned to Denmark a corrupted atheist and as refined a sensualist as ever Paris produced.

It was a gross mistake of the true state of things that led Latrobe and so many writers to believe that Matilda once felt aversion towards Struensee.[1] It was a master-stroke of policy, intended to blind and deceive Counts Molckte and Bernstorff; for if the Queen had shown any tokens of preference or solicitude before Struensee had intrenched himself, as it were, in the good graces of his imbecile Sovereign, the suspicions of Holcke would have been awakened, and means found to remove the intruder before he had taken too deep a root.

Such was the situation of affairs on the return to Denmark of Christian VII. and his suite, at the beginning of 1769.

In proportion as the King declined and degenerated in his physical and intellectual powers, Matilda had made more than proportionate advances. Her person was much increased in height and breadth; her air and appearance more dignified and imposing; her mind seemed to have acquired firmness, and, on their first interview, her conscious husband absolutely started at the improved appearance of his Queen; reflecting on his own imbecility, he seemed half reluctant, half ashamed to meet her.

Unfortunate victim of the crimes of an unprincipled step-mother! At that moment his whole system was tainted; and he should not have approached Matilda,

---

[1] "Authentic Elucidation of the History of Counts Struensee and Brandt," p. 40.

to tantalize her imagination and pollute her wholesome blood. Like the snail that crawls over the blushing nectarine, he defiled his youthful bride; the poison, spreading through her veins, soon displayed its destructive influence. To whomsoever she had applied, of all the medical men in Denmark, Struensee was the man whom she should have most avoided.

Amongst the ladies with whom Matilda associated, her favourite was Madame Göhler,[1] the beautiful, accomplished, fascinating and wanton wife of the general of that name. Philosoff, the Russian Minister, and Struensee were favoured rivals in this lady's good graces, who made her charms subservient to her political views. She aimed at supplanting Count Holcke, to promote the influence of the Queen, and through her favour to advance herself to the rank of chief female favourite. Her Russian lover declared against the Queen's interest, and on this account Madame Göhler excluded him from her boudoir, and Struensee was preferred, much less from personal advantages than the political power she hoped to obtain by making him her instrument. The Courts of Russia and France were each supporting their favourite agents. Those were Bernstorff, Molckte, Schimmelman, Thott, and Lauerig. The Russian Minister, imputing his declin-

---

[1] Lady Göhler was at this time about twenty-seven years of age; her figure good; her complexion remarkably clear and fine; features small and regular, yet expressive; her eyes dark and piercing; she was rather too much inclined to *embonpoint*; her style of dress was greatly admired. General Göhler was a good-looking man; rather short and stout; he commanded the artillery, and resided in the Storm Gadan.

ing influence with Madame Göhler to the superior accomplishments of Struensee, and knowing that his rank as an ambassador forbade the physician lifting an arm against him, he, like a cowardly ruffian, fell unawares upon his rival and gave him a very severe castigation with a cane—a mode of discipline to which he had himself often submitted at St. Petersburg from the hand of Peter III., in whose murder he was afterwards instrumental. His associate, Salder, was born in Holstein, and dismissed, on a charge of embezzlement, from his post as bailiff over the Royal domain called Trittau; an appoinment that marked the contempt felt by Catherine and her ministers towards the Danish Court.

Madame Göhler made love subservient to ambition; she dismissed the Russian boyard the moment her interest required it; and, instead of monopolizing the attentions of Struensee, she did all she could to advance his interest with the Queen, to whom she spoke of Struensee as a man worthy of the esteem and confidence of any woman, and earnestly advised Matilda to allow her to state Her Majesty's case to the general, that he might make it known to Struensee.

The interview that decided the fate of Matilda and Struensee took place, under the mediation of Lady Göhler, in the King's hunting lodge at Travendahl. On this occasion Struensee adorned his person with more than common care, and he certainly formed a striking contrast to the King his master. Struensee was fully five feet ten inches high and very robust, his complexion fair, his eyes blue, his luxuriant hair was flaxen—rather inclined to yellow—a high forehead, prominent nose, well-formed mouth, and a good set of teeth.[1] His personal defects consisted in his appearance being too heavy to be graceful—his neck was short, and he was a little in-kneed. From these particulars it will readily be conceived that he made a better figure on horseback than on foot. Struensee took particular pride in dressing with elegance. He fenced and danced well, and whilst he was in England he took lessons from Mr. Astley, and greatly improved his horsemanship. He wore his hair dressed like the Queen, namely, four curls on each side, a high *toupee*, the hair behind plaited and made fast with a comb; he wore a black silk waistcoat, small clothes and stockings, and a coat of blue cloth with gilt buttons. The suit which he then wore having been made by the first tailor in London. Struensee was then just in the flower of his days; the glow of robust health tinged his florid cheeks and sparkled in his fine blue eyes; and if he were not an Adonis, he was a noble-looking fellow, whose physiognomy and manners were calculated to make too deep an impression on an amorous, neglected, insulted and injured woman.

It cannot be believed that Matilda attended this assignation without experiencing emotions painful and humiliating; and she inherited her full share of the hauteur that marks her family. Struensee was, of course,

---

[1] In the "Conversion of Struensee," the portrait is rather a caricature than a likeness. In Mr. Jens Wolff's "Northern Tour," p. 80, there is a more natural representation, but the attitude is bad.—EDITOR.

all deference. He said but little, for Lady Göhler had beforehand apprised the Queen of all the vices of her degenerate husband—polluting her ear by the description of habits, the very knowledge of which was heretofore hidden from her, and which cannot be told by a woman of real modesty. But the fair Matilda did not possess that extreme delicacy that would lead some females to perish by inches rather than reveal their sexual infirmities to a stranger. On the contrary, she discoursed relative to her health with great composure. But her bosom swelled with scorn and indignation, and tears of anger, rather than sorrow, fell in profusion from her fine eyes as Madame Göhler recited those disgusting articles of impeachment against Christian VII., that are too indelicate to be inserted. This fatal interview, brought about by Lady Göhler to promote her own personal views, was the first important error committed by a young and inexperienced Queen. Matilda's first impulse was to write home to her mother and brother and demand a separation, with liberty to retire to England. "I have experienced little else," said the Queen, "than mortifications; the King's family are all secretly my enemies; the Ministers of the Crown are my enemies, and my husband is the worst foe of all! I will take my child and quit these hated shores." Whilst grief and indignation thus shook her frame, Madame Göhler appeared affected by the sorrows of Matilda almost as powerfully as the fair sufferer herself. Struensee stood in an attitude as if he were bowed down by grief: his left hand pressed his bosom; with his right he covered his face, as though to conceal the tears that, whether they were real or suborned, trickled down his manly cheeks. The first burst of passion over, Matilda was pleased by the silent, insidious homage paid by the accomplished Struensee. "You pity me, sir," said she; " Madame Göhler has convinced me how truly you are my friend; be, then, my counsellor as well as my physician, and try if you cannot restore my peace of mind, as well as my health!" Struensee could scarcely conceal his transports; Madame Göhler was in secret raptures at the complete success that appeared to attend her scheme. Bowing low, in an attitude of classical propriety, the exulting flatterer said: "It would ill become me, revered Queen, to offer any other than professional advice; and were I to presume thus far, and offer my humble opinion, I could not improve upon your own noble and just intention of appealing to the protection of your august family; but there is one point that probably Your Majesty may not have considered: your infant, madam, is the Heir-Apparent to the Crown of Denmark, and, should you resolve to quit these shores, your child must be left behind—left, perhaps, to perish under the cruelty of those who were the first great cause of all his Royal father's misfortunes." Struensee never looked better, or spoke more gracefully or impressively. Matilda was overcome; she almost screamed when, by a master-touch, Struensee alluded to her separation from her husband and return to England as necessarily occasioning a separation from her beloved child! All the fears of the tenderest mother rushed in a flood to her agitated bosom; she almost screamed as, with a convulsed voice, she exclaimed, "Never! never will I abandon my child!" Madame Göhler wept in silence. Struensee, when Matilda appeared more calm, bade her assume her proper station, banish Count Holcke, and gradually take the reins of government into her own hands, "Which," said he, "your unhappy lord will never more be in a position to exercise"—telling the afflicted Queen that although the King might live many years, yet he thought his intellectual faculties could never be restored.

Madame Göhler then, with earnest humility, entreated the Queen not to quit a Court of which she was the pride and ornament, and leave her child and friends to the mercy of Juliana. This name, as by magic, roused all her pride and resentment. "No!" said Matilda, with energy; "I will not flee; I will face my foes, and conquer them or perish!" This was the very point to which Madame Göhler and Struensee wished to work her feelings. "Thanks be to God! for this resolve," exclaimed the beauteous Dane, as she dropped on her knee to promise, in the name of her Creator, eternal fidelity to her Royal mistress and her child. Struensee, whose heart was really touched, sobbed audibly. Secretly soothed by this proof of attachment and sensibility, Matilda extended her hand, saying, "Henceforth, be you my knight!" Struensee, dropping on his knee opposite to Madame Göhler, bedewed her hand with tears as he breathed a solemn oath to be a true knight to his Queen. This interview decided the destiny of Matilda and Struensee; though

t-..., she almost screamed as, with a convulsed ..., she exclaimed, "Never! never will I abandon my child!" Madame Göhler wept in silence. Struensee, when Matilda appeared more calm, bade her resume her proper station, banish Count Holcke, and gradually take the reins of government into her own hands. "Which," said he, "your unhappy lord will never more be in a position to exercise"—telling the afflicted Queen that although the King might live many years, yet he thought his intellectual faculties could never be restored.

Madame Göhler ... with earnest humility, entreated the Queen ... a Court of which she was the pride and ornament, and leave her child and friends to ... "No!" said Matilda ... "I will not flee; I will face ... rather than ... or ... !" This was ... Madame Göhler and Struensee ... her feelings. "Thanks be to God!" ... the beauteous Dane, as she ... bade ... to promise, in the name of her ... fidelity to her Royal mistress and her ... whose heart was really touched, ... Secretly soothed by this proof of ... and sensibility, Matilda extended her hand, ... "Henceforth, be you my knight!" Struensee, ... on his knee opposite to Madame Göhler, ... her hand with tears as he breathed a solemn ... a true knight to his Queen. This interview ... the destiny of Matilda and Struensee; though

JEAN - FREDERIC
Comte de Struensée
Premier Ministre d'État de sa Majesté Danoise
Décapité en 1772

JEAN FREDERIC, COUNT STRUENSEE

After an old engraving. Artist Unknown

probably at this moment not one of the interesting group harboured a thought of the consequences that ensued. From this moment the intercourse between Matilda and Struensee grew more frequent; her health was soon restored, and he that was her physician gained her heart. The Queen was young, her passions at their flood, her feelings violent, her judgment weak, as must ever be the case where our passions are strong enough to subdue our reason. And if ever a woman merited pardon for a frailty it was Matilda. Let anyone look at such a female and such a husband! Let them consider her tainted by a loathsome disease, unbosoming herself to a man of high endowments, in the flower of manhood. The temptation was too powerful for human nature, under such circumstances, to resist: she yielded, and they fell; but that Deity who filled their too susceptible hearts with those warm passions that precipitated them from their high estate, will wipe from his tablets the record of their crime, which is amply expiated by their sufferings. If Matilda had been of more mature years, if her passions had been less ardent, a proper sense of her duty would have curbed resentful feelings; for it cannot be doubted that the vast distance between their stations, and the solemn nature of his duties as physician to the King her husband, must have restrained Struensee, and kept him in awe, however ardent were his passion, or daring his ambition. Real, inborn modesty is one of the sweetest graces, as well as the strongest guards, of female chastity. Perhaps the palaces of kings and princes are not the places where this virtue thrives; thence Matilda, even were she deficient in that quality, is rather an object of compassion than censure. Madame Göhler was an able auxiliary, and if Struensee brought his deistical principles into play—if he were able, as I have been assured was the case, to eradicate from her mind all belief in revealed religion and a state of future punishment or reward—then, indeed, the fortress was dismantled, and, when betrayed by the traitor passions within, incapable of resistance. It is really hard to decide where lay the preponderating weight of blame. The first impulse of Matilda's feelings, in the eventful interview at Travendahl, took a proper direction; which Madame Göhler and Struensee's insidious counsel turned aside. Even at this period, the disposition of Matilda had lost much of that gentleness and good nature which distinguished her on her first arrival. Her carriage had become more bold and confident; her temper more quick, severe, and imperious. It is not likely she ever felt a very strong affection towards a worn-out debauchee, who grew tired of her before the honeymoon expired; and it is consistent with the decided character of Matilda to imagine, when she found her blood tainted with a loathsome disease by an imbecile and depraved husband, that every vestige of respect vanished, and hatred, scorn, and the fiercest thirst for vengeance took its place in her bosom. The enemies of Struensee accused him of having, through Count Charles Schak Rantzau, communicated to the Queen all the follies and vices that disgraced her husband during his travels the preceding year. These accusations, like a multitude more with which the memory of the guilty favourite has been loaded, had probably no other foundation than the black and horrible malice of his enemies, who literally carried their enmity beyond the grave.

Matilda must have made unequivocal advances to Struensee; but let not her memory be stigmatised by this remark, for, if she resolved to transfer to him the heart that her husband had relinquished, it was then her business to save the man, to whose affections she aspired, the guilt and peril of seducing her. These facts, however, offer no apology for her lover. What insult, wrong, or provocation had he to plead? With all his faults, the King had been to him a kind master. He ought to have warned the young and irritated Queen of the fearful precipice she was ascending. Struensee was guilty of the most heinous breach of faith that can be conceived, and he had neither the levity of youth, nor the want of a thorough knowledge of the world to plead as an excuse for his delinquency. Struensee was as great a sensualist as his Royal master; but he had more self-command, and husbanded his stock of health and manhood with more skill. This superior judgment blackens the turpitude of Struensee's conduct. It was impossible for him to stifle the voice of honour in his conscience even if he were ever so firmly resolved to disregard its dictates; nor could he blind himself to the dangers that beset him on every side—dangers that were so formidable and so palpable that, when his principles proved too much relaxed to restrain his licentious passions, common sense, supplying the place of honesty in many cases, warned him in vain to desist.

Struensee, in his defence, affirmed, and probably

with justice, that, during his attendance on the King in his travels, he strove by every means in his power to wean him from his vicious propensities; warning him of that swift and sure destruction in which their continuation would involve both body and mind. Happy had it been for himself and for Matilda if he could have subdued his own master passion, and taught the young indignant Queen to curb her vindictive feelings and avoid dishonour. If he had pursued this direct, straight and honourable course; if, with all the pathos and eloquence of which he was master, he had told the Queen that his life she might command, but his honour he must preserve, and that, although as a humble friend he might serve her, as a lover he should entail eternal ruin and disgrace on both their heads, it is highly probable that pride would have averted the calamity and disgrace that followed; and Struensee, faithful to his Sovereign and respected by the woman whom he had saved from dishonour, might still have gratified the utmost scope of laudable ambition. Instead of which, with his eyes open, he rushed upon infamy and destruction, dragging his unfortunate Queen with him to perdition.

CHAPTER VI

Melancholy state of the King—A Royal tour to the Duchies of Holstein and Sleiswick—Count Rantzau's hospitality—History of Gourmand, the King's favourite dog—Anecdotes of the Court—A Circassian Princess—Altered manners of Queen Matilda: wears leathern small-clothes, and sits her horse like a man—Prosperity more difficult to endure than adversity—Struensee and Brandt admonished by Count Rantzau—The last interview—The arrest of Matilda, Struensee and Brandt.

IT is exceedingly difficult to comprehend the real state of the King's intellect at this period of his life.[1] His senses were so far unimpaired that he knew everybody with whom he was acquainted, and conversed rationally enough on common-place subjects. He had the most fixed abhorrence of public business, and signed his name, without investigation, to everything proposed by his ministers. During his recent tour through the

---

[1] Count Reventlau had a daughter who was a confirmed idiot. She was inoculated for the small-pox, and had a very fine sort. This being communicated to Frederick V., he had matter taken from her arm for the inoculation of his son Christian. Strong prejudices prevailed at that time against the practice, on the score of its impiety; and the subsequent decay of intellect that befell this Prince was imputed to the person being an idiot from whom the infection was received.

principal parts of Europe his excesses of every kind were multiplied, and those secret vices to which in early youth he was initiated, through the wickedness of Juliana, grew so strong upon him that even the presence of his attendants was no restraint upon their filthy indulgence; and as though Nature intended a two-fold punishment for those who so scandalously violated her laws, the effect of these vices smite the understanding, and paralyze the intellectual as well as the physical faculties. During the seven months that Christian VII. spent in his travels his mind was kept in a state of intense exertion by the fascinating objects that every hour assailed his senses. He seemed unusually depressed and abashed when he first saw the Queen and his child after his return from France. The excessive draughts upon his spirits accelerated the catastrophe, and he declined rapidly from that period; which change was, by the enemies of Matilda and Struensee, imputed to drugs administered by their orders, and to the brutal coercion to which he was subjected. He was reduced to a state of incapacity to govern before Matilda and Struensee seized the helm; but he was not in a condition that required the vigilance of a keeper. From being quick and sensitive he grew dull, lethargic, sullen, and dreadfully furious if greatly irritated.

Whilst Struensee was lord of the ascendant, the King was held in a state of liberal confinement, debarred from the intercourse and society of everyone, save those who were placed about his person by the Queen and Struensee; yet during all that period he dined in public with the Queen, accompanied her in the field sports to which she was addicted, appeared at the French and Italian operas, danced at their balls, and took part in their card parties; but little if any attention was paid to what he said, except as far as his wants were concerned; and all the subaltern attendants and domestic servants had orders never to speak to the King. One Sunday, coming from the Royal Chapel, the King turned the wrong way, and lost his way in the vast passages of his enormous palace. Seeing Struensee's valet, he asked him, in a mild and melancholy tone, to show him his way to his apartment. This person—a young, handsome, gay Norwegian, and a favourite and humble confidant of his master—respectfully, but in profound silence, complied with the Monarch's request, and conducted him to his magnificent prison.

Not long after the wasteful and impolitic tour to England, France, &c., the Court went on a journey through Holstein and Sleiswick, during which the King and Queen paid a visit to Count Rantzau, at his principal country residence Aschberg.[1] The mansion was

---

[1] The family of Rantzau was one of the most celebrated in Holstein, not only for antiquity and the extent of their possessions, but for the number of warriors and statesmen they produced. The gardens at Aschberg were as much celebrated in that country as those of Stow in England. In the centre was a conical hill, perhaps an ancient tumulus, round which a spiral walk led to the summit. This mount was planted with ash trees; *berg* signifies a mountain, and the name of this county either gave its appellation to, or was derived from, this mount. On the top was a rural bower. From this mount there was a fine view over the lake of eight miles breadth, diversified by woody islands and picturesque shores. From the post road, a

neither very large nor magnificent. The old edifice was much in the style of gentlemen's houses in England of the seventeenth century. The new house, as it was called, was connected with the ancient structure, and consisted of a suite of four tolerable rooms on the ground floor and as many above: this building was allotted to the King and Queen and their principal courtiers, as Brandt, Struensee, &c. Amongst the females were the lady of General Göhler, and the wife of Counsellor Fabricius,[1] a gay, intriguing woman, whose husband was one of Struensee's confidential friends. Count Rantzau himself was the most finished libertine of his age; but even that experienced courtier saw with surprise the bold and altered manners of the young Queen, and the licentiousness that reigned amongst her female train. It was the opportunities that this Holstein journey, and the residence of the Court at his house, afforded to the Count of observing the conduct of Struensee and the Queen, that convinced him he had introduced an agent who would soon tower high above himself, and probably kick down the ladder by which he had been raised. His suspicions once awakened, he watched the proceedings of Struensee and the Queen, which, confirming his jealous fears to their utmost extent, soon eradicated every feeling

---

double row of venerable elms formed a noble avenue that led to the principal entrance. At a small distance was a tolerably good inn, where the domestics of the King and his Nobles lodged, and which, in summer time, was generally full of company from Lubeck, Hamburg, &c., who were attracted by the rural beauties of Aschberg.—EDITOR.

[1] This gentleman was possessed of very superior talents; he was Struensee's confidential adviser, whose fall involved him in ruin.

of friendship towards Struensee, and in it place implanted those deadly feelings of hatred which, at no distant day, led to the destruction of the incautious pair.

During the residence of the Court at the Count's mansion, he one day found means, in spite of the vigilance of Brandt and Struensee, to obtain an hour's conversation with the King. Count Rantzau knew his weakness too well to commit himself in any way. All he wished was to ascertain the state of the King's mind, who, pleased with the puerile amusements that were provided, seemed perfectly indifferent to everything else. Rantzau gazed on the emasculated being with looks fraught with more meaning than his words, and tears trickled down his furrowed cheeks. The King seemed affected; for a moment the former sensibility and vivacity of his character illumined his dimmed eye and pallid cheek. He seized the Count by the hand, and said: "You were a true friend to my father; you will never be an enemy to me." "Never, Sire! never will I hesitate to sacrifice my life in your defence!" Then, falling on one knee, he drew an antique ring from his finger, and put it on the King's, saying in a solemn manner: "This ring, Sire, was given me by your Royal father when I returned from Russia, and when, by fortunate exertions there, I was the humble means of averting a great calamity that threatened his throne; deign to wear this for my sake, and for your father's; and if ever your Majesty thinks yourself in danger, and you want the assistance of Rantzau, send this ring to me, and I will flee on the wings of affection and loyalty to your aid." Rantzau had scarcely wiped the falling tear away before the King, hearing footsteps approach, fell off at once into his idiot state, and running to a canine friend of his that was basking in the sun, took him round the neck, hugging him with ardour, and calling him his faithful guard. This uncommon dog was liver-coloured, of prodigious height and size; his broad chest showed all the strength of the English mastiff, his form the elegance of the greyhound. Such was the King's favourite dog, called "Gourmand."[1] Gourmand had a carriage for his sole use when the King travelled, and a lackey to attend him; he was served with food from the King's table, and was often fed from his Royal master's hand. In the midst of regal etiquette, Gourmand alone acted without restraint, though generally with distinguished decency; he would, when he pleased, stretch his finely-formed limbs on the same rich sofa where his master reclined, and then no one dared approach till he awoke. He was playful, docile, and incorruptibly faithful to his master; the only one of all the King's attendants of whom so much might be said with any regard to historical truth.

The partisans of Bernstorff, of Molckte, and of Juliana, in derision of Struensee's newborn honour,

---

[1] Gourmand, on account of his beauty and gigantic size, was presented to the King by a nobleman who resided at or near to Lubeck; after the fall of Struensee the King was deprived of his favourite dog, which was returned to the person by whom it had been presented. It is said that this dog leaped on and seized an assassin, who, at a masquerade in 1772, was there with a view to kill the King.—EDITOR.

dubbed this four-legged favourite of their Sovereign, Monsieur Gourmand, *Conferentie Raad*—*i.e.*, M. Gourmand, Privy Counsellor to the King. Such was the animal, and such the honours paid to him by Christian VII., to which he hastened almost before Rantzau had done speaking; a circumstance that led the Count to think that the King was apprehensive of 'danger, and fully comprehended the meaning of the Count's gift. It would be difficult to conceive a more distressing spectacle than that presented to a contemplative mind in the wreck of this gay young Monarch, now become an object of fixed aversion to his wife, and of secret scorn to his own menials. Enfeebled as he was in mind and body, he had yet sufficient consciousness to feel at intervals all the misery of his degraded condition, though he wanted resolution to quit those abhorrent vices by which it was produced. From this moment, till the fatal 17th of January, 1772, the King took no particular notice of the Count, but the ring kept its place on his finger. During the stay of the Court at Aschberg, Count Rantzau spared no pains nor expense to render his abode agreeable to the young Queen. Each day had its peculiar festivities and amusements; music, hunting, fishing, sailing on the lake, and rustic sports, which more than any pastime, pleased the imbecile King. The Queen, fully satisfied with the magnificence and respect with which Count Rantzau had entertained her —little dreaming of the share that her attentive host was to have in her approaching fall—gave him a superb snuff-box, richly set with brilliants, that had cost her husband a thousand guineas in London. Count Rantzau followed the Court in its progress. In his mind he anticipated more than all the sad results that flowed from the imprudence of Struensee; but, keeping these thoughts close and his countenance open, he eluded the vigilance of Struensee, Brandt, and even the lynx-eyed Madame Göhler. All the party, Rantzau excepted, were young and in the prime of life. They were all the willing slaves of voluptuousness, all engaged in amatory pursuits, and hence it is no wonder that an old experienced courtier, who felt himself thrown out by the instrument he had chosen to forward his own ambitious views, his malice sharpened by jealousy and desire of revenge, should be able to out-general the giddy, gay and wanton train, who filled the groves with music, love, revelry and song.

Of the rapid advancement of Struensee I shall say nothing, because the subject has been exhausted, and there is nothing new to say. I shall, therefore, gather together such particular facts that are nowhere else to be found, and which may possess sufficient interest, in the estimation of a tasteful reader, to atone for the want of historical importance.

From the time that Queen Matilda became the associate of Madame Göhler, Fabricius and other ladies of their gay cast, and after the influence of Struensee had attained that marked preponderance that was sufficiently potent to banish Bernstorff and Molckte to their respective estates, and to monopolize the exercise of sovereign power, the person of Matilda—her temper, manners, principles—all seemed to undergo a total and most disadvantageous change. Notwithstanding the daily exercise she took, either hunting or riding on horseback, Matilda grew extremely corpulent, and was become so much taller and larger than when she arrived in Denmark in 1766, that a person who had not seen the Queen for the last five years, would scarcely have been able to recognise her. Matilda, in her attire, was always gay and tasteful, and on occasions truly magnificent, adopting a medium between the fashions of London and Paris. Her complexion was exquisitely fair; and it was a disadvantage to her beauty that the fashions of the day obliged her to hide the colour and texture of her fine silver tresses under a load of powder and pomatum. Matilda looked handsome in any proper dress, and truly noble in her gala robes. In her common evening dress, she adopted that of the Court of Versailles. She had a bosom such as few men could look on without emotion, or women without envy; and she displayed more of its naked charms than strict modesty could approve, and far more than the Danes had ever witnessed in the preceding Queens—Sophia Magdalena, Louisa, or Juliana. Making no allowance for the progress of luxury and change of manners, the grave and illiberal censured the fair young Queen for that which delighted the young and gay. Matilda was a resolute and fearless horsewoman. It it believed that Struensee first led her to sit across her horse, like a man. No doubt this masculine habit, that was confined to the labouring farmers' wives and daughters, was adopted for security's sake, but it gave great and general offence to all the middle and higher classes of females. Perhaps her masculine and indelicate appearance, dressed in leathern small-clothes,[1] booted and spurred, riding across a horse, did her more injury in public opinion, amongst the elegant and cultivated of her own sex, than her undue preference of Struensee. A proof that, in an age of artificial delicacy, the want of morals may sooner hope for pardon than the want of decorum.

The Queen grew excessively fond of hunting; and the Court, in everything magnificent, kept up three establishments; and for each of those there was a separate uniform, on a very costly scale. The livery of which were as follows, viz.:

The uniform for the King's stag-hunt was a buff coat, light blue collar and cuffs, the coat trimmed all round with silver lace, scolloped; coat lined with blue; blue waistcoat, laced; leathern breeches, cocked hat, laced; black cockade.

The uniform for the hare-hunt was a green velvet coat and waistcoat, leathern breeches, brown top boots, cocked hat, green cockade.

The falcon, or hawk-hunt uniform was the most magnificent, being crimson velvet, with green cuffs and collar, trimmed with gold lace; leathern breeches, gold-laced cocked hat, green cockade.

When Matilda rode a-hunting she was dressed at

---

[1] In opposition to this want of candour, in which too many historians are apt to indulge, we need only take the testimony of living witnesses, who can vouch for her imprudent conduct and want of public decency on many occasions: a woman who could assume, and ride *en culottes* at the head of her guards, can, certainly, not be said to have many pretentions to female delicacy.—*Vide* "Wolff's Northern Tour," p. 81.

all points as a man! Her hair was dressed with less powder, and pinned up closer, but in the usual style, *i.e.*, side curls, *toupee*, and turned up behind; she wore a dove-colour beaver hat, with a deep gold band and tassels; a long scarlet coat, faced with gold all round; a buff, gold-laced waistcoat, frilled shirt, and man's neckerchief; buckskin small-clothes, and spurs. That she made a noble figure mounted on a majestic steed, and dashing through the woods after the chase, her cheeks flushed with ruddy health and violent exercise, may readily be conceded; but when she walked the charm was dissolved; her abdominal rotundity, and knees that turned too much inward, spoiled her figure, and gave her an awkward gait; the calves of her legs were of surprising circumference, her ankle large, her foot short and chubby. The King's dress was also a scarlet coat, buff waistcoat, and buckskin breeches; but so diminutive was his appearance, compared with his wife, that he looked like a stripling. Struensee dressed in the uniform of the hunts that he attended, and was the inseparable companion of the Queen, with whose person his robust figure accorded far better than that of her husband.

Although Struensee asserted, in his defence, that his only object was to promote union and affection between the King and Queen, it was notorious that the King was utterly disregarded; and that, even at table, the only place where they regularly met, seldom a word passed between them; and if they met in the galleries of the palace or elsewhere, they generally passed without speaking.

Matilda grew very despotic after the elevation of Struensee. Not only were all the attendants forbidden to speak to the King on pain of arbitrary imprisonment, but also to her son, the Crown Prince Frederick. It happened one day at Fredericksborg Palace, that the boy fell down, and cried out lustily. Struensee's favourite valet chanced to see him, and set the little fellow on his feet. Matilda and Struensee saw the transaction from the windows of the palace, and an officer was ordered by the Queen to send the valet to the Blue Tower, a civic prison near the long bridge where disorderly persons were confined. Thither he was sent, and there he found one of the English postillions, named William Smith, who, forgetting the Royal orders, had crossed a passage in the rear of the Queen's apartments leading to the stables. The Queen and Struensee were there, walking arm-in-arm, in deep conversation. For this breach of orders he was sent to the Blue Tower, on bread and water diet, which not suiting Smith's stomach, he wrote on the wall with a piece of charcoal, in English, the following couplet:

"The Queen, Brandt, and Struensee;
May the devil take all the three."

Smith broke prison, and ran away: Matilda then ordered a prison-room to be fitted up at Hirschholm Palace for the confinement of her servants. It happened once that a lackey entered a room on some occasion, when the Queen was there, expecting Struensee; enraged at the disappointment and exposure, she caused the poor menial to be imprisoned and fed on bread and water—a diet that might have been still more proper for herself. From these sources, in spite of the terrors excited by blue towers or strong rooms, various scandalous reports got in circulation, highly to the prejudice of the Queen and Struensee.

There are plenty of views of the great Palace of Christiansborg to be found, by any of which the plan of that huge and magnificent structure may be understood. It consisted of six stories above the vaults; three of those were extremely large and lofty, and dedicated to State purposes; three smaller stories ran between, not more than eight feet high, called the "Mezzanine Stories," where the State ministers and Royal attendants had suites of rooms; the Queen's apartments were in the grand (or east) front, on the second great story; the King's were on the same floor, but farther to the south; the Royal chapel formed another division of this vast palace; a lower structure, or wing, under which was one of the entrances to this huge structure, formed a continuation of the mezzanine story; Struensee's apartments were in the mezzanine story, opening into the grand passage leading to the Royal chapel, and next to the Queen's apartments; Count Brandt's apartments were on the same story, adjoining Struensee's, but next the chapel; from Struensee's bedroom there was a concealed staircase that led to the Queen's, by means of which, if he had not been surprised in his sleep, he might have escaped.

Struensee was never appointed tutor to the Crown

Prince, the child being only four years old when that favourite fell; but, young as he was, the Prince had an aversion to Struensee that could not be subdued; no doubt, in defiance of all precautions, the attendants had told him that Struensee was a bad man; nor could his mother make him call her favourite either Graaf (Count), or Excellentje, but always the "Doctor," and that with a tone of marked contempt.

Under Struensee's directions, the young Prince was treated in a very hardy manner; a companion was assigned him, a soldier's child, whose name was Edward; this boy was called a prince; he was dressed in the same plain uniform as the Crown Prince, ate of the same dish with him, and slept on the same mattress. This experiment was made with a view to repress, in his earliest years, those exalted notions of self-importance that had proved so fatal to his unhappy father; and it seems to have answered its intended object, as our present beloved King[1] is universally acknowledged as the least haughty or assuming of Sovereigns. Those pair of little men, the pseudo, and the prince-born, frequently contended for mastery. One day, when they had fought with greater fury than usual, Frederick asked Edward how he dared raise his hand against his Prince? "A Prince!" replied the other, "I am a Prince as well as you!" "Yes, but I am Crown Prince," rejoined Frederick, and fell upon him again when he had owned himself conquered. Matilda, hearing of this, had the little urchin sent for to her apartment, as well as his companion, insisting that he should beg pardon of Edward. Frederick refused to

---

[1] Frederick VI.

submit to her award, and the Queen, provoked by his stubbornness, beat him severely. He was conquered, but not subdued. As he withdrew, he turned his eyes resentfully towards Struensee, and said, " I'll go to the King, my father, and tell him, who shall send that nasty doctor away from you." By means of these severities, Matilda, in his days of infancy, lost his affections; so much so, that if he were very unruly, his attendants, perhaps as much from malignant feelings as ignorance, used to threaten to take him to the Queen! The probability, however, is, that to the system thus introduced, this Prince is indebted for the strength he afterwards acquired;[1] as previously he was a weakly, puny child; very cross and humorsome, continually crying; would not walk, but cried till he was carried; and even at two years old the attendants to make him quiet used to tell him, "Your mamma shall come to you." To get over these hindrances to his health and intellect, Struensee, with the approbation of the Queen, made a total change in the child's regimen: his food thenceforth was of the most plain and simple description, such as bread, rice, fruits, milk, vegetables, all cold; he was bathed in cold water two or three times each week; till at last, he would go of himself to the bath. The boys were very lightly clad; and the last winter had neither shoes nor stockings, nor fire in their room; everything was permitted that they could prepare or produce by their own power; if they cried for anything they desired, it was not given them, nor were they corrected, menaced, or coaxed; if

---

[1] *Vide* " Verantwortnung des Grafen Struensee an die Koniglicke Commission," pp. 97, 98, 99, &c.

they fell, there they laid till they got up by their own help; no one was to show any concern, or say anything about it; the Crown Prince and his comrade played together; in dressing and in eating they assisted each other; their apartment being free from anything whereby they could injure themselves, they were not disturbed whatever noise they made, and their solitary life soon reconciled them after their petty quarrels. Both were called by their Christian names only; they were accustomed to see strangers, by which means confidence and ease were acquired. His education was to commence in his sixth year, prior to which he was left to the effects of his own experience, temperate diet and exercise. They were mostly left by themselves, by which means the fear of darkness was removed, and the attendants were forbidden to play or converse with them. After the introduction of this system the Crown Prince was seldom ill, and, with the exception of one or two slight indispositions, his health was uninterrupted; he had the small-pox from inoculation, extremely light, and also the measles; he had acquired as much knowledge as could be expected from his tender years; could dress and undress himself without assistance, and go up and down the great staircase of the palace in a steady and careful manner, and was capable of everything that could be expected from a child of his years; his health was improved, his temper and bad habits corrected, and the utmost care taken that his infant mind should not be inflated with vanity by adulation and high titles, through which the morals of princes are so frequently vitiated in their infancy. It redounds to the honour of Struensee that his enemies, paying their court to the prejudices of the most illiterate and ignorant of the people, actually made this system a capital charge against him, falsely and absurdly affirming that it endangered not only the health, but the life of the Prince.

During the residence at Hirschholm Palace of Matilda and the Court, in 1771, a black boy, introduced by Count Brandt, was constantly with the King; the presence of this youth and the occasion of it gave rise to many strange conjectures. After the fall of Brandt and Struensee the young black was sent away and heard of no more. It was remarked that the boy never looked happy, and seemed anxious to keep as far from the King as possible. The dog Gourmand and this young negro were the chief associates of the King.

The Empress Catherine sent a beautiful young Circassian Princess, whom Potemkin captured with the Grand Vizier's tent at ——, as a present to Queen Matilda. She was placed in the Queen's apartments with the ladies of her chamber; after the fall of Matilda this young foreigner was sent back to the Russian Court; she was very wild and gay and about fifteen years of age.

At Hirschholm, Struensee generally breakfasted in the Queen's apartment. The table was spread with a profusion of dried meats, eggs, and other substantial food, as well as tea, coffee and chocolate. The Queen generally made a hearty breakfast.

Wherever the Court resided, it was a scene of sensuality in every shape. Before the Queen and suite set out hunting a hot luncheon was served up in the apartment called the Rose, where the great officers of

State, and foreigners of distinction, dined. This consisted, not of gewgaws, but of substantial dishes of meat, game, soups, fish, and pasties.

Struensee generally took his breakfast and luncheon in the Queen's apartment; sometimes, a dish of chocolate or coffee in his own room, but not frequently. The King was served in his own apartment, and was considered of little more .importance than his dog Gourmand or his negro-boy.

A few of the ladies followed the example of the Queen, dressed in the same uniform as the gentlemen, and rode across as they did; others, under a riding-habit, wore small-clothes and top boots, and sat sideways on their horses. Nothing could be more licentious than the Court of Matilda in 1770 and 1771; her palace was a temple of pleasure, of which she was the high-priestess: everything was found there calculated to excite and gratify sensual desires. A modest woman, or a sensible man, would have been laughed out of countenance. The Queen was not then, as heretofore, generally beloved; she grew harsh and imperious towards her women, who were mostly young voluptuaries—for with such Struensee and Brandt filled the Court, and, indeed, no respectable lady would be seen there. With these young, blooming, immodest women, the pampered domestics belonging to Queen Matilda, and to Counts Struensee and Brandt, used to associate. They, too, had their balls, masquerades, concerts and conversaziones, wherein decency or restraint were alike unseen. The vices of their voluptuous superiors were implicitly adopted, their manners aped, infirmities ridiculed, and their most secret transactions exposed.¹ Within three days of Matilda's being put to bed of the Princess Louisa, namely, on the 4th of July, 1771, she rode out on horseback; the horse plunged and kicked, till he backed into a dry ditch, when Matilda, sitting firm and undismayed, flogged and spurred the restive animal till she conquered, and rode home unhurt. She was delivered of a daughter ² at this palace, to which the Queen-Dowager Juliana and Prince Frederick stood sponsors, an act of courtesy intended by the former to lull the suspicions of her intended victims, for the indiscretions of Matilda were all reported to her, perhaps with exaggerations, and at this early period means were in contemplation to destroy Struensee, Brandt, and the rank and power of the Queen.

There was, perhaps, no Court in Europe, where more respect was shown to foreign Ministers, or their convenience more studied, than in Denmark. At Hirschholm, two days in the week, they dined at the King's, or rather, the Queen's table. On their return from the drawing-room to their respective apartments, they found a ticket on their dressing-table, specifying where they were to dine; some at the King's table, others at the Lord Chamberlain's, in the chamber called the Rose.

---

1 "The poor Queen of Denmark was certainly very imprudent. I learn she would even appear in full Court in breeches, and the Northern nations are rigid in the *bienséance*."—" Walpoliana," vol. ii. p. 93.

2 Louisa Augusta, who was married to the late Prince of Augustenburg.

The usual number that sat down to dinner[1] at the King's table was twelve, alternately five ladies and seven gentlemen, or seven ladies and five gentlemen. The King cut a wretched figure on these occasions: not so the Queen, who dressed very superbly, and made a noble and splendid appearance. The King and Queen were served on gold plate by noble pages; the Marshal of the Palace sat at the foot of the latter, the chief lady of the household at the head; the company, a lady and gentleman alternately, opposite to the King and Queen.

A table of eighty covers was provided every day in the Rose for the great officers of State, who were served on silver plate. At this table, Struensee, Brandt, their friends and favourites, male and female, used to dine. The courtiers paid Struensee as much homage as they used to pay to the King. His carriage was much changed: he grew haughty and imperious, more and more magnificent in dress and equipage; but was that to be wondered at? Where is the man who could endure such a flood of good fortune unchanged? A common mind may bear adversity with firmness; but show me the man that can conduct himself with humility and forbearance under a long course of the highest possible prosperty, and I will own he is great, truly great.

Long before the fatal catastrophe in which Count Rantzau bore so conspicuous a part, that nobleman strove to moderate the conduct of Struensee. Of the connection of the latter with the Queen he was at

---

[1] The dinner hour was seven o'clock.

no loss to guess; and he was well informed relative to the treatment of the King, for whose life he entertained serious apprehensions. The attendants, by their shrugs and shaking of their heads, spread reports more unfavourable than if they had openly told all they knew. It was reported in the palace that Brandt, intended to murder the King, in order that the Queen might be Regent during the minority of her son. Nor can I dismiss from my mind a belief in the reality of such a design having been entertained. Struensee had already committed the next greatest crime to murder. He was in possession of the sovereign power; of course, he wished to retain it, and he knew, as long as the King lived, he should be continually exposed to punishment. It is, therefore, consistent with human nature to suppose that he would rather consent to put a period to the animal existence of a wretched being who was politically and mentally dead, than see Matilda hurled from the throne, and himself consigned to the scaffold.

The letters written by Count Rantzau to Brandt sufficiently testify the reality of the suspicions of the former respecting the designs of the latter against the King's life. Of the intention to deprive the King of his life, the party accused was probably guilty; but of legal proof there was none. The law was shamefully strained; and if I cannot esteem Brandt as an innocent man in the moral acceptation of the term, he certainly was judicially murdered.

Count Rantzau expostulated with Struensee, as far as he judged it was prudent; if he had gone further, he would have been ordered to his estate, and, of course, been too far off the King to render him any assistance in the hour of peril. He was never friendly to the views of Juliana Maria; he would far rather have seen Matilda at the head of the Government, if she had not, in an unguarded moment, thrown herself and the sovereignty too into the hands of Struensee. Count Rantzau would have served the Queen if he had seen the least prospect of doing so effectually; but he was too cautious a courtier to venture his life and character in support of a man of so little prudence as Struensee possessed: and whose conduct, in the case of the mutiny of the Norwegian seamen, in 1771, confirmed the suspicions entertained respecting his total want of personal courage. He was then so vehemently alarmed that his pusillanimity made Matilda blush. Afraid of the approaching tempest, he implored the Queen to allow him to depart the kingdom, as the only means of saving his life or hers. She looked at him with ineffable scorn, and told him to flee from her whom he had deprived of character and friends and abandoned to the mercy of her foes. The bitterness with which she reviled Struensee on this occasion, and her constant opposition to his wishes of withdrawing, are supposed to have had considerable weight in producing the confessions, made after his arrest, that incriminated the unfortunate Queen. The haughty, violent temper of Matilda, whose mind was constantly perturbed, rendered her less amiable in Struensee's eyes than she, in their first private interview, appeared at Travendahl; and the want of courage in Struensee, made her, who was a heroine, look on him with contempt: so true it is that there can be no steady friendship that has its foundation laid in vice.

The Queen Dowager, Juliana Maria, now began to show herself again; her hopes once more revived; she saw with secret delight the embers of discontent glowing in every quarter of the kingdom; and if she could not procure the Crown for her son Frederick, now in his nineteenth year, she hoped, during the life of Christian VII., to attain the sole exercise of sovereign power.

She affected to feel the utmost commiseration for the King, and fear for his safety. Her agents industriously spread alarming reports as to the designs of "the Doctor's cabal," as Struensee's partisans were ironically called. She bore the most deadly hatred towards Count Rantzau; but finding he was violently enraged against Struensee and Brandt, Juliana employed her confidant, Guldberg, to sound him; giving the strictest charge to impress on the Count that it was was not for political power she was seeking, but to save the life of the King; and that she should advise the establishment of a Council, consisting of Count Rantzau and the old nobility, to govern the State. She never hinted one word as to any intention of proceeding criminally against Matilda. Juliana was an adept in dissimulation, and in this difficult negotiation she exceeded all former transactions of a treacherous nature. Neither Matilda nor her guilty favourite felt tranquil; it was impossible but that innumerable occurrences must have reminded her of her danger, and filled her conscious bosom with the most gloomy apprehensions.

When she travelled, or went out in the woods, Matilda was constantly attended by running footmen.[1] One of those gaudy appendages of Royalty detected Matilda and Struensee in a situation that admitted of no misconstruction.[2] Soon afterwards Juliana Maria paid an evening visit to Matilda at Hirschholm. She travelled by torchlight, and was attended by Chamberlain Blucher.[3] This was the last visit she ever paid Matilda, and its insidious object was, during the bustle occasioned by her arrival, to afford Blucher an

---

[1] They were usually apprenticed seven years, and performed astonishing feats of activity and strength, and would commonly leap a six-barred gate without touching. Queen Matilda would suffer them to run before her carriage all the way to Hirschholm, a distance of fifteen English miles, without rest; this they performed in two hours! Sometimes she would let them get up behind her coach, but not often. Their livery was very costly, with plates of gold in their caps. They had pensions when they grew old. Struensee had two, and ten other servants; he changed his liveries three times, as he was advanced; the last was green velvet. His running footmen wore buff jackets, sea-green scarfs, green velvet caps, with a plate of solid gold with Struensee's crest embossed on the front.

[2] "Of her (Matilda's) intimate connection with her favourite minister there seems not to be the shadow of a doubt. It was one of the chief articles in the impeachment of Struensee;—not denied by him, and partially confessed by herself. I have heard one of her pages assert 'that while playing in the knight's saloon in the palace, he accidentally fell against a concealed door in the wall,' (no doubt under the hangings) 'which, leading to a long passage, discovered the Queen and her paramour *tête-à-tête*, to their no small surprise and mortification.'"—Wolff's "Northern Summer," p. 81.

[3] A blood relation to Marshal Blucher. The then Chamberlain is, or recently was, living at Altena. An elderly gentleman, of this name and office, probably the same individual, is mentioned in the "Northern Tour," p. 98.

opportunity of gathering what information he could from treacherous attendants relative to the proceedings of "the Doctor's cabal." She stopped only a short time, but her behaviour to the reigning Queen was more than ever flattering and kind; yet, not four hours before, with well-dissembled sorrow, she had expressed her abhorrence of the utter depravity of Matilda, whom she affected to consider as a woman lost to every sense of honour and decency!

The Court lingered at Fredericksborg, apparently unwilling to venture into Copenhagen until the Regiment of Falkenskjöld[1] should have arrived, which was intended to have relieved the foot guards. Matilda and Struensee saw themselves beset on every side with the most pressing dangers. Their frequent consultations usually terminated in the hope of some favourable contingency removing the source of their apprehensions, but without being able to adopt any specific remedy.

Whilst dismay reigned in the palace of Matilda, confidence and hope enlivened the countenance of Juliana at Fredensborg. Count Rantzau had joined her party. The high rank, talent, and courage of Rantzau rendered the acquisition invaluable. They met in Copenhagen; Juliana having, to favour her machinations, entered the city before Matilda. After their first compliments were over, Juliana said:

---

[1] General Falkenskjöld, Colonel of the Regiment of Zealand, was a man of very arbitrary, haughty, and overbearing manners; he was about forty-five years of age, tall and well made; full six feet high. He lived in lodgings in Copenhagen.

"Struensee dabbles in half measures, and he will inevitably fall; he should have ordered me to reside at Fredensborg and have sent your Excellency to Aschberg." At this interview Struensee and Brandt were destined to destruction. The Queen-Dowager, however, pledged her word of honour not to attempt anything against the personal safety of the reigning Queen. As soon as Rantzau was gone, Prince Frederick, who had been very reserved during the interview, asked his mother how she could behave so friendly to a man towards whom her heart was filled with so much enmity? "Because I wish to ruin him," was her laconic reply.

That which accelerated the blow that levelled Struensee with the dust, was the ring that Rantzau had given to Christian VII. at Aschberg. It was returned to the Count by Colonel Kohler Banner. "The King has sent you this," said he, "and claims the performance of your promise." Rantzau seized the token, and laying his hand upon his sword, said to the Colonel: "Inform my King, if in your power, that my life and fortune are at his service." Count Rantzau was, in his heart, true and loyal to the King; Colonel Banner was a partisan of Juliana.

As the decisive moment approached, rumours of the foulest kind were circulated every hour, directed against Queen Matilda and her ministers. The life of the King was said to be in jeopardy, and Count Brandt was accused of beating and horse-whipping his Sovereign. Christian VII. was once the darling of the people; the licentious conduct of Matilda and her Court had lost her the respect of the best class of people, and rendered the lower class furious in their hatred of her and her devoted minion. She was called "The great w——," and Christiansborg "The great b——y house." All their former affection for their King returned; and even Juliana became in some measure popular, because in her they recognised the enemy of Matilda, Struensee and Brandt. How changed was the scene within six short years, when the cruel Juliana was execrated and driven into retirement, and the young and fair Matilda the object of love and reverence, and greeted with acclamation wherever she appeared. Yet was Juliana incomparably more guilty than the reigning Queen, since to her deadly malice the frailties and the vices of Christian were imputable; and if Matilda had had a man for her husband, possessed of common sense and a sound body, in all probability she would have gone through life without reproach or disgrace.

Although the accounts published in Germany and England are radically erroneous in many important particulars, yet the statement that the French and Swedish ministers warned Struensee of his danger from the machinations of Rantzau and Kohler Banner are perfectly correct.[1] But so well was Struensee aware of the rooted antipathy that Rantzau cherished in his bosom towards Juliana, that he could not persuade himself any possible circumstance could induce him to support her party; and without Rantzau's help, and as long as he remained master of the King's person,

---

[1] *Vide* "Latrobe," pp. 156, 157, 158

Struensee flattered himself his power could not be overthrown. The work so ably translated by M. Latrobe is also extremely unjust to the memory of Count Rantzau, with whose motives and character the author was evidently unacquainted, or determined to traduce. He even acknowledges that Rantzau, not long before the catastrophe took place, waited upon Struensee and remonstrated with him on the state of affairs, and that "Struensee met his arguments with objections; his protestations of candour with thanks; and his warnings with the usual smile of contempt of a short-sighted mind." Yet, he accuses Rantzau of a want of sincerity, and, to complete his own blunders, stigmatises him as a coward!

Count Rantzau's character for courage and generosity, the splendour of his name, and influence over the soldiery, far more than the example of either Kohler Banner or Eichstedt, determined the subaltern officers and troops to support an attempt that they were taught to believe was called for by their captive Monarch. Early in the morning of the 17th January, 1772, Rantzau showed them the ring that Kohler Banner had brought to him, and told them with powerful emotion when he had put that ring on the finger of their King. It was this circumstance that principally determined their conduct. Rantzau, seeing that their feelings were powerfully moved, sent a trusty messenger to Juliana to tell her to be prepared at two o'clock; and having posted the troops as he thought most prudent, he led a detachment into the interior of the palace to release the King and arrest the Queen Matilda,

Struensee and Brandt; whilst measures were taken to secure the brothers of Struensee and all his principal adherents who resided in the city.

An enterprise more hazardous could scarcely be conceived, and nothing but the consummate prudence, courage and address which Count Rantzau displayed on this trying occasion could have carried it into execution. The Count had pledged his word of honour to the King to hasten to his aid at the hour of peril; and his King had claimed the performance of that engagement; but his intellect was so feeble, and he was known to be so completely awed by the discipline to which he had long been subjected, that it was not at all improbable he should either totally forget, or disown, what he had done. In case of failure, an ignominious death awaited Rantzau; and if successful, he was well aware that it was too probable that the sovereignty that he was about to wrest for ever from the unsteady hand of the voluptuous Struensee would be transferred to Juliana. Count Rantzau did not risk himself by any communication with the troops till the moment of action had arrived. Juliana, like a tigress, was waiting in breathless anxiety the eventful moment. Kohler Banner and Eichstedt were employed in receiving the reports brought by Guldberg, and watching the residence of the rest of the destined victims. Matilda, Struensee and Brandt, exhausted by pleasure, had sunk into profound repose, from which they were to be awakened to behold the frightful abyss that yawned to receive them.

On the night of the 16th of January a ball and

masquerade was given by the Court. Matilda, magnificently dressed, and full of spirits, danced with Count Struensee, also with Prince Frederick, and conversed with his treacherous, black-hearted mother, who seemed more than usually civil and attentive. As soon as Count Rantzau appeared, the Queen-Dowager and her son watched intently every glance of his eye and every step he took. As he passed the King, Rantzau bowed, but did not offer to approach. The King laughed, began jumping about, and ran to his friend Gourmand, that lay stretched on a magnificent sofa. Patting him on the head, the King said aloud, " Min fortrorligste ven " (My most trusty of friends). Rantzau fully understood the meaning of this signal, and felt his confidence reassured; but again and again was his heart ready to burst as he looked at the Queen, at Struensee, at Brandt, and reflected on the horrors in which a few short hours would involve them. There was, however, no room for compromise or parley; the die must be cast, and he abide the issue. The ball was closed by the Queen and Prince Frederick. The Queen, attended by Struensee, retired to her apartments for the last time. Struensee must have gone to the Queen's room, for there his white bear-skin cloak was found a few hours after. She must have descended by means of the secret staircase to Struensee's apartment, where the guilty pair had their last *tête-à-tête*, and separated never to meet again.

The young Norwegian valet, whom Matilda had imprisoned in the Blue Tower for helping the Crown Prince to get up when he had tumbled, slept in an ante-room adjoining his master's, Count Struensee, and was lying on a sofa, waiting to undress his master. It must be supposed that at such a crisis this intelligent young man saw and heard enough to convince him that, from secret conspiracy or open insurrection, his master was in imminent danger; to which causes the singular dream he had at that critical moment was probably owing; for whilst the Queen and Struensee were enjoying the last few moments that fate allotted those guilty victims of unhallowed passion should pass together, the valet dreamt that he saw Godsckau, the State executioner, embracing Struensee, whose features bespoke the utmost horror and agony: presently he saw Queen Matilda dressed most magnificently, with Struensee by her side, seated under a canopy of state; then his wandering imagination carried him to the custom-house stairs, and he thought he saw the Queen Matilda, Struensee, Brandt, Lady Göhler, and the principal persons attached to the Court, approaching in a magnificent barge which, in a moment, went to pieces, and the persons in it seemed lost, or struggling with the waves; amongst them he saw Matilda, who screamed aloud, "Save me! save me! Struensee drags me down!" The young valet, full of horror, stretched out his arm to reach her amongst the wreck, when the bell above his head was rung. He suddenly awoke, his cheeks wet with the tears he had shed; his limbs still shook, and he trembled as he obeyed the call to undress his master. Just as he entered Struensee's room he heard the private door shut, and also the retiring step of Matilda, who had

8—2

just left the Count, who, surprised at the affright and dismay so visible on his face, said, "Ernestus! what ails you? what has alarmed you?" The poor fellow could scarcely speak till a flood of tears came to his relief. Apprehensive that he might faint away, Struensee took his hand and felt his pulse, which was high and throbbing; to compose which he took up a small silver-mounted medicine case that stood by the table, and gave the valet some drops in a glass of water, which presently revived him. The Count was still in the masquerade dress in which he had returned from the French theatre where the ball had been held, which was within the walls of Christiansborg. He looked remarkably well. His face flushed with health and pleasure, and his fine hair rather dishevelled. As the valet undressed him, he asked what dream had frightened him so much? Ernestus remained silent. The Count repeated his request; when, dropping the executioner and the Queen's exclamation, Ernestus told the rest. Struensee smiled, and appeared thoughtful; but presently he said, "You must go and see Mademoiselle —— in the morning; her handsome face will soon set all to rights again."[1] Struensee, as was his custom, after he had lain down, took his book in his hand to read himself asleep.[2] His valet, having a master-key, locked the door on the outside and retired to his own bed. His

---

[1] This was a gay young lady, belonging to Matilda's train, whose hair the young valet had dressed previous to her appearing at Court, and with whom Ernestus was supposed to stand in high favour.

[2] Pope's "Abelard" and "Eloisa."

sleep was, however, still perturbed and unsound; he thought he heard strange voices and the footsteps of many persons passing and repassing; at last he distinctly heard someone endeavouring to open, as it were with an iron instrument, the outer door of his room. His terrors now became realities; he leaped out of bed and approached the door to listen to those without; but, softly as he moved, his steps were heard, and in a low voice he was commanded in the King's name to open the door on pain of instant death. It is not wonderful that the young man, instead of alarming his master, obeyed this formidable summons, and gave admittance to his enemies. In an instant, but yet without noise or tumult, Colonel Kohler Banner,[1] dressed in full uniform (being red turned up with black), with two inferior officers, and Captain Dissentin, of the Norwegian Regiment, stepped within; two soldiers held each a cocked pistol to his head, and another pointed a sword to his breast; whilst the Colonel, bearing a wax taper in his hand, anxiously, yet softly exclaimed, "Have you awoke the Count?" "I have not." "You are sure of that? Remember, you are a State prisoner, and your life pays the forfeit if you tell me falsehoods." The Colonel then went to the door of Struensee's room;[2] finding it

---

[1] Colonel Kohler Banner used to pay the utmost homage to Count Struensee, and frequently assisted at his ministerial dinners. He was, at that time, the secret agent of Juliana and Guldberg. In his person he was about five feet ten inches high; middle aged; dark complexion, and cursed with a base and treacherous heart.

[2] Count Struensee's apartment was furnished in a style of regal magnificence; the mirrors were large and of the purest glass; the

fast, he said to the valet, "Have you a key?" "Yes, your Excellency, I have a master-key." "Then open the door as softly as possible." Ernestus obeyed, and Colonel Banner was the first who entered, the valet by his side; there were three inferior officers, each with a drawn sword in his right, and a wax light in his left, hand. The Count slept so soundly that he did not awake with all this noise and blaze of tapers. He was lying upon his right side, his head upon his arm. The book he had been reading lay on the floor. After a moment's pause, during which Kohler Banner stood gazing sternly on the unconscious culprit, he

---

most common utensils of silver, or silver gilt. The Royal suite of rooms above the Mezzanine story (*entresol*) were of extraordinary height, by which means the Mezzanine story (middle stories) were necessarily very low. Thus, Count Struensee's and Brandt's rooms were only eight feet high. Count Struensee's bedroom was hung with rich figured damask; the furniture of his bed and of the windows was purple velvet, richly trimmed with deep gold fringe; the canopy was formed in the shape of a Royal crown. Between his magnificent dressing-table and the foot of his superb bed, covered by the costly hangings, was a concealed door that opened to a staircase leading to the Queen's apartment, by which means, unknown to their attendants, they could visit each other. Struensee was particularly nice in his person and dress, and used the most costly perfumes profusely. His valet slept in an ante-room, through which lay the way to the Count's bed-chamber. The valet's bed furniture was magnificent, being sky-blue silk trimmed with silver lace and fringe; it was concealed by a superb screen. A bell was hung over this bed, the pull to which was in the Count's room. There was a secret closet in this room, also concealed by the hangings, in which Ernestus had presence of mind to throw some papers and other articles before he opened the door to Colonel Kohler Banner. After the execution of the unfortunate Struensee, the faithful valet found means to get into the room he had formerly occupied, where he found the papers safe; which, had they been discovered by his enemies, would have at once criminated more than one captive.

approached, and touching Struensee on the shoulder, awoke him to all the horrors of sudden and sure perdition!¹

His consternation may be much easier conceived than described. Suddenly he rose half up, and, wild with terror, said, "What's all this? In God's name, what is all this about?" Colonel Kohler Banner, in a loud and stern voice, answered him: "You are the King's prisoner; behold the Royal warrant for your arrest.[2] You must dress yourself without delay and come with me." "You will allow me to find clothes to dress with?" said Struensee. Banner then permitted the valet to go to his master's wardrobe, who hastily snatched a light blue morning frock, with round cuffs, that had been made in London, of Manchester velvet, and a waistcoat of the same;[3] but such was his confusion, he could not find any small-clothes, and

---

1 The Queen and Struensee returned to Christianborg Palace, where Juliana and all the Royal Family had apartments; and where, in case of an insurrection, they were likely to be taken or massacred. To save appearances they waited for Falkenskjöld's regiment, when General Eichstedt's dragoons and Colonel Kohler Banner's infantry regiment could have been removed; and then the devoted pair intended to have set out on a tour through the Duchies of Sleiswick and Holstein: the delay was fatal. Had their intentions been executed it might have proved so to the unfortunate Christian VII. —EDITOR.

2 The account translated by Latrobe is radically false in many important particulars respecting the arrest of Struensee; which errors have been successively copied into almost every work published since that time. Colonel Kohler Banner positively did not seize the Count by the throat, nor shake him; and he had in his hand the King's warrant for Struensee's arrest.

3 The unfortunate Count went to the place of execution dressed in these same clothes.

the Count was forced to put on the pair of pink-coloured breeches[1] which he had worn at the masquerade. It was a cold wintery morning, and his valet, who felt as much for his master as for himself, asked the Colonel to allow him to go, with a guard, to the Queen's room for the Count's fur cloak.[2] Captain Dissentin accompanied him, bearing a torch in one hand and a drawn sword in the other. Count Rantzau[3] and General Eichstedt[4] were there, with

[1] Jens Wolffe, Esq., Consul-General in London, was the chief of an opulent and long-established commercial firm, which was ultimately overwhelmed by national misfortunes that could neither be foreseen by their victims nor prevented. He was deservedly respected for benevolence of heart, public spirit, and high endowments. The Editor regrets having to notice the errors that through inadvertence have crept into the pages of such a writer. M. Wolffe collected his materials relative to the catastrophe in question full forty years subsequent to its occurrence. To that circumstance, and to the want of better information in his informants, the string of errors that appear on pages 84 and 85 are imputable. The story of Count Struensee reproaching his valet relative to a *pelisse*, and the *vriessche rok* (blanket coat), are totally groundless. If M. Wolffe were to make a further enquiry, he would be convinced of having been deceived.

[2] In Latrobe's translation it is implied that Struensee had been arrested and sent to prison before the Queen was arrested; but this fact proves the contrary, and that the Queen was first taken into custody.

[3] At this period (1772) Count Rantzau was about sixty years of age; his features were good; complexion florid; and when young, he must have been very handsome. He had a slight cast in his eyes; he was nearly six feet high; his hair had become grey through age, but to hide that unyouthful mark the old beau used black pomatum (pomatum thickened with hair-powder burnt black). His manners were highly polished. When he arrested the young Queen he had on a scarlet surtout lined and trimmed with fur; a commander-in-chief's regimental coat beneath, red turned up with buff; his under dress was silk.

[4] General Eichstedt was merely a creature of Juliana's; he

several inferior military officers bearing swords and tapers in their hands. Rantzau, and all the officers, were uncovered. His appearance denoted excessive mental agitation. Probably his mental sufferings were as intense as those of his Royal victim. The Queen, who appeared almost as tall and robust as the Count, was standing with her back towards him, and one of her women was then lacing her stays. When the Queen heard the well-known voice of Struensee's valet she turned towards him and said: "Tell your master to emulate his Queen, and repel insult with scorn and defiance." Her face was greatly flushed; her features distorted with rage and grief, and her fine tresses, all in disorder, floated round her bosom, reaching below her waist; her female attendants looked like pale pictures of despair. The valet gazed mournfully; he was about to reply, when Count Rantzau fiercely exclaimed: "Silence! if you speak, you die!" The young man, dismayed and confounded, bowed humbly to the Queen as he was hurried back to his master, whom he found dressed, and greatly agitated. Perceiving that his valet had nothing on but his shirt and small-clothes,[1] he said to

---

had not one bright or amiable trait in his character; but was coarse in his manner, and, speaking comparatively, illiterate. In his person he was rather short and stout; about forty years of age; arbitrary towards all beneath him; towards the Queen-Dowager, her son, and Count Rantzau, fawning and servile. He lived in 1772 in the Kol Torvet. He commanded the regiment of dragoons, a company of which escorted the unfortunate Matilda to Cronenborg Castle.

[1] The anxiety shown by Count Struensee relative to his valet was occasioned by seeing him stand nearly undressed on a cold

Colonel Kohler Banner: "Why is my poor servant thus kept naked? In God's name, let him have his clothes." Upon which he was permitted to dress; and whilst Colonel Banner and his officers were hurrying Struensee to the guard-room, where Brandt had already arrived, the valet contrived to take up his master's gold English repeater, his ring and brooch, both of diamonds of great value, the gifts of the Queen,[1] and also the purse that the Count had laid on the table near his bedside, containing about eighty gold ducats; those he secured, as he thought, for the benefit of his master. In a few minutes he was called below. There he saw the guard-room blazing with tapers, and the two State prisoners, who were kept separate. Presently two hackney coaches drove up to the door. Struensee, accompanied by officers armed with loaded pistols and drawn swords, was put into the first coach, and Brandt into the second. Escorted by a strong party of dragoons, the cavalcade proceeded from Christiansborg Palace, over the Hoëy Bro (High Bridge), along the Stora Stradet, Kongens Nye Torv, and Norgen Gaden to the citadel. Here the two prisoners were confined in

---

winter's morning. Perhaps it was this circumstance, imperfectly remembered, that led to the mistakes that are mentioned in a preceding note. It was a striking feature in this sad spectacle, that a valet half-dressed went to the chamber of the Queen and saw her in the same state, her room full of military officers.

[1] The repeater was of the most superb and costly kind, set round with a double row of brilliants; with the chains and seals it was worth three hundred pounds. The diamond ring and brooch cost fifteen hundred guineas!

separate rooms belonging to the officers, and two officers, who were relieved every two hours, were constantly in the room, and two sentinels outside the door. During their progress to the citadel through the principal parts of the city, Struensee wept, wrung his hands, and showed the utmost grief and despondency, whilst the companion of his misfortunes, though not the witness of his weakness, Count Brandt,[1] displayed that high spirit which never forsook him, not even when Godsckau, the executioner, laid his hands upon him to mutilate his body and take his life.

---

[1] Count Enevold Brandt was descended from a noble, though not a titled family. He was a far superior character to Struensee, and if he had been the favoured lover in all probability he might have avoided the fate that befell his friend Struensee, whose greatest misfortune was his being a foreigner. Count Brandt, in person, was moderately tall, lightly made; a fine military figure; he was greatly marked by the small-pox; his eyes, hair, and complexion dark; lively and gay to an extreme; he dressed with great elegance; was munificent and generous; a general lover, and the idol of the ladies of Matilda's giddy Court. The portrait given in the "Conversion of Struensee" is a wretched performance, not at all resembling the animated and voluptuous original.

CHAPTER VII

Critical situation of Juliana Maria, Count Rantzau and the other conspirators—The courage of Queen Matilda —Cowardice of Struensee—A singular riot: its source developed—The execution of Brandt and Struensee.

IN the arrest of the Queen, Count Rantzau had occasion for all his fortitude and presence of mind. Difficulties beset him every step he moved. When he reached the King's bedroom, the glare of the tapers alarming him as he awoke, seemed to drive all recollection of Rantzau from his mind, whilst the sight of the Queen-Dowager and her son called to the King's remembrance that inbred dread and hatred which he had ever felt towards them. He turned, with marks of fierce resentment and strong aversion, from that insidious and cruel woman then kneeling by his bedside. Count Rantzau saw the peril he was in, and the alarm of the Queen-Dowager and her son was such that they seemed petrified with horror. The Count motioned them to retire from the bedside; and then, approaching, he told the King that he had obeyed his orders, and rushed to his assistance. "My death, Sire," said he, "which will be the sure result of your indecision, concerns me less than the fate which may befall your Majesty after I am gone." Weak and irresolute, the King kept saying: "What can I do? what can I do?" "To save your life, Sire, you must order Struensee and Brandt into arrest." After a few minutes' pause, during which he repeated the same ejaculations as before, the King signed those instruments that Guldberg[1] had prepared. The destiny of the reigning Queen had occasioned long discussions between Juliana Maria and the Count; the former being eager to proceed against her with every possible severity, whilst Count Rantzau as firmly refused to have anything to do with the business if the Queen-Dowager acted as though personal aggrandisement and the gratification of vengeful feelings were the only objects she had in view. Finding Rantzau resolute, the Queen-Dowager assented to everything that he proposed, being secretly determined to humble him as soon as he should have

---

[1] M. Guldberg, then about forty years of age, was to Juliana, perhaps, what Struensee was to Matilda; but Juliana was an arch dissembler, and Guldberg was steady and discreet. Like Struensee, he was of plebeian extraction, and the son of a Norwegian clergyman—he had served in the church at Roeskild. He possessed many good, and some amiable qualities, which, joined to his learning and talents, procured him the appointment of tutor to Prince Frederick, son to Juliana; a step that led to the confidence he afterwards enjoyed with that Princess. He was devoted to study and business. During Struensee's short-lived greatness, M. Guldberg was a frequent visitor, perhaps a treacherous guest. After the fall of Struensee, he rose upon his ruins, and became a minister of State. It was rather singular that he married two sisters, the daughters of a miller at Fredensborg. After his dismissal, on the 28th of March, 1784, by the son of Matilda, he was allowed a pension of 4,500 crowns per annum, and remained high steward to his patron, Prince Frederick.

put it in her power. Guldberg, Eichstedt and Kohler Banner, like zealous partisans, supported the wishes of the Queen-Dowager; and they urged Count Rantzau to consider the destruction that Queen Matilda might bring upon them all if she were left at liberty. Nor did they forget to urge the danger there was of Matilda falling a victim to popular fury, as soon as Struensee and Brandt, with their cabal (as these conspirators called the partisans of Matilda), should be overthrown. Rantzau gave these arguments due consideration; and, partly to prevent Matilda from assisting her favourites, and no less for her own personal safety during the hurricane that was approaching, he at last agreed to her arrest and temporary confinement.

To bring the King to this point was necessary to their safety; but, also, very likely to be refused. Rantzau insisted that the Queen-Dowager and her son should accompany him to the King's apartment. This was done to prevent that guileful woman from sacrificing him to her safety in case of failure; and her hated presence had the effect already described. It was probable that Christian never loved Matilda, and quite certain that he feared her more than any human being besides. When, therefore, Rantzau presented the warrant for the arrest of the Queen, he took every possible pains to convince the wavering and irresolute King that the temporary arrest of his consort was as requisite for her safety as for the safety of the State. Christian threw the paper from him with considerable emotion; and if at that moment Matilda had appeared in his presence, there is no doubt but the guards would have led the Queen-Dowager and her son, Rantzau, Guldberg, Eichstedt and Kohler Banner, to the dungeons intended for their foes: but she, at whose glance the puerile King would have drooped his head, was absent, and the soldiers laid down their arms. After long hesitation, and after his fears had been awakened of her being torn in pieces by the infuriated populace, the arguments of Rantzau prevailed, and the fate of the unhappy Queen was sealed. These were the real causes of the arrest of Queen Matilda, whose personal conduct under the dreadful reverse that awaited her is detailed with tolerable correctness in the German work that was translated by Latrobe, and which created so strong a sensation in Great Britain.

The Queen, like the Cherokee Chief, though overpowered was not subdued. The King had kept them dallying so long, that Rantzau was afraid daylight would appear before he should be able to get the Queen removed. Matilda heard him say to Eichstedt: "We must make haste, it will soon be day;" and turning suddenly upon him, in a firm and emphatic manner, she said: "Miserable man, well may you dread the light! The deed of this night will for ever blacken your fame. Your fall will quickly follow mine. My errors will be obliterated by my sufferings: the fair and the brave, the mild and the virtuous, will shed a tear over my sad destiny; whilst thou shalt perish unpitied, and be followed to thy tomb with execration. March! detested, hoary-headed traitor! lead me to my dungeon. Lead me anywhere, so that mine eyes are spared thy hated presence."

The Count heard her with profound silence, and laying his hand on his bosom, said aloud: "Madam, your reproaches I do not feel, because I know I do not deserve them. I was called by my King to come to his aid; and so may God judge and deal with me, as I speak truth when I aver my bosom is free from revenge, and filled with ardent wishes for your Majesty's present safety and future happiness." Scarcely half dressed, and wrapped up in a large *roquelaure*, looking with a stern indifference on the surrounding officers, she descended to the gate, where a coach and four, surrounded by a strong body of dragoons, was waiting to escort her to Cronenborg Castle. Count Rantzau, bareheaded, attended her to the coach. Just as she put her foot on the steps, the enraged Queen, as her last benediction, struck the Count a violent slap with her open hand on his cheek, exclaiming: "Take this, thou accursed traitor; and remember, this treason shall cost thee thy head!" The Count, who must have felt very uncomfortable, made her a profound bow as the door was closed, and said, loud enough to be heard by all around: "I am no traitor, Madam. I fear God, I love and honour the King, and wish your Majesty a good journey." The word of command being given, the escort set off. An officer with a drawn sword sat opposite to the Queen, who looked round her with a smile of contempt, mingled with despair. The light of numerous torches, the glare of brandished swords, the prancing of the steeds, the rattle of the coach, above all, the spectacle of a young Queen thus treated, formed a subject interesting to the painter or the poet, and never to be forgotten by those by whom it was beheld. When this high-spirited woman first entered the vast portals of that stupendous structure that now, partly shrouded in darkness, frowned on her fallen fortunes, how little did she dream of this terrible reverse! As the escort passed the portals of Copenhagen, her heart began to sink, that heretofore had been sustained in that terrible scene by pride and indignation. When she passed Hirschholm Palace, she was observed to wrap her face in her large veil and *roquelaure;* her bosom heaved, and in spite of her efforts, she sobbed audibly, and clasped her hands together. The only consolation her misery received was the vicinity of her infant daughter, for which she was indebted to the firmness of Count Rantzau, whose sufferings and mortifications endured this day were scarcely to have been indemnified, even by the Crown of Denmark.[1]

---

[1] The following account of the Queen's conduct is taken from the translation of the work of an anonymous German author beforementioned:

"Count Rantzau and Colonel Eichstedt went with some officers to the apartment of the Queen, who, alarmed by the noise in her ante-chamber, called her women, and in the paleness of their countenances read their fear. She enquired what had happened, and was at length told that Count Rantzau, in her ante-chamber, demanded to speak with her on the part of the King. She expressed in the most affecting manner her grief, her apprehension that she was betrayed and ruined, and her resignation. Then, acquiring fortitude, she went half-dressed to Rantzau, who read the order of the King, which she heard with firmness and without interrupting him.

He felt dissatisfied with himself. The bitterness of the Queen's taunts, as well as her prophecies of his speedy fall, sank deep into his mind. The wretched imbecility of the King; the fawning demeanour of the crafty and selfish Juliana; the vague and uncertain prospect of any good, either to his King or country, arising from the fall of Struensee; and the horrid doom which awaited the captives, tended to shake his mind and depress his spirits with gloomy presentiments.

To the King showing himself from the balcony of

Being still unable to give credit to it, she read it herself, without betraying any mark of fear, and Rantzau entreated her obedience to the order. 'An order,' said she, 'of which, perhaps, the King himself knows nothing, or which has been obtained from his weakness by the most horrid perfidy. No! to such orders a Queen gives no obedience.' Rantzau, with a severe air, replied that his commission would permit no delay. 'No such order,' said she, 'shall be executed against my person before I have spoken to the King. Let me go—I must, I will speak to him!' At these words she advanced towards the door, but was withheld by Rantzau, who changed his entreaties into menaces. 'Wretch!' said she, 'is this the manner of a subject to his Queen?' The fierce and irritated Rantzau gave a significant look to his officers, of whom one, more daring than the rest, advanced towards the Queen. She tore herself from his hands, and called loudly for help, but no person came. At length, being alone and defenceless, in the midst of armed men, this unhappy Princess, transported with rage, ran to a window, and would have precipitated herself from it, but she was withheld. They endeavoured to carry her away, and she defended herself till her strength and recollection failed. When she recovered herself and perceived no means of escaping, she yielded, and was allowed time for dressing; after which she was conducted to the carriage which took her to the Castle of Cronenborg."

By comparing this with the preceding particulars, the reader will be able to form a correct judgment of the conduct of Queen Matilda and Count Rantzau.

his palace to the burghers of Copenhagen, Count Rantzau had no objection; but to see him parade the city, accompanied by Juliana and Prince Frederick; to hear a hired rabble shout in honour of that woman and her son, filled his mind with disgust. Now that the danger was over, the Queen-Dowager. soon let Count Rantzau know that there were individuals whose counsel had much more influence with her than his. This was particularly exemplified by Juliana Maria persisting in exhibiting the impotent King in gala dress, decking him with the richest jewels, accompanied by her perfidious son, who was thus exposed for several hours, bowing from his state-coach to the shouting mob on either side, in whose clamorous shouts the name of Prince Frederick was insidiously blended with the King's. Against this act of malignant indecency, Count Rantzau in vain protested; six hours had not elapsed before that nobleman felt that all his fears were likely to be realised. In his heart he regretted the too ardent zeal with which he had devoted himself to save a King who was not worthy of esteem or respect.

Whilst this indecent farce was acting, Guldberg and Juliana had prepared another source of humiliation to the fallen Queen, and of gratification of that fell spirit of hatred and vengeance that would perhaps have led Juliana, if opportunity had served, to have washed her hands in the heart's blood of Matilda. It was chiefly by the machinations of Guldberg that the city was filled with the most foul and outrageous violations of truth respecting the licentiousness of

Matilda's Court, which was certainly too gross to be defended, though it fell infinitely short of the exaggerated picture spread by a cloud of base emissaries hired by her enemies. What peculiarly marked the quarter whence they flowed was that the King was no less the object of abuse than the Queen; and whilst the latter was called the "W——e of Babylon," the "Scarlet w——e," and other gross and opprobrious epithets, the King was accused of being addicted to the worst of propensities. It was affirmed that, to keep him quiet whilst Struensee had his Queen, Brandt provided him with the means of gratification! Such were the scandalous tales circulated amongst the vulgar to weaken their attachment to the King, and rouse their passions and prejudices to the utmost pitch of fury. When the events of the night became known, the city was suddenly thrown into rage, confusion, and dismay. The inhabitants flocked in multitudes towards the King's palace, and as those reports were rapidly circulated through the country, thousands upon thousands soon rushed to the city, increasing the uproar and confusion. When the arrest of Queen Matilda and her partisans was fully understood, the air rang with the opprobrious epithets bestowed on her name. The most fierce and dangerous of the rioters were the sailors and their wives, and the vulgar inhabitants of St. Anna's quarter towards the Oster Port. They seemed in a manner organised and led by persons whose motions they obeyed. "Now the great b——y house is purified," said the ringleaders, "let us proceed to the purification of the city." Lists of names and places of abode were immediately handed about. The mob divided itself into masses, and attacked and gutted every house of ill-fame and the apartment of the poorest prostitute in the city; acting so methodically, that if there were only a single room inhabited by a courtesan, they seized her goods and broke the doors and windows, without injuring the other rooms or any other property. The leaders openly sold to the best bidder what they could of the plunder, and divided the proceeds; the rest they burnt in heaps in the different open spaces of the city. When they had completed this mischief, of which Juliana was the authoress, being full of drink and courage, they took it into their heads to march towards the citadel to demand the prisoners; and but for the firmness of Count Rantzau, under the vile pretext of fear and incompetent power to resist, their vengeance would have been saturated with blood, and the most unpopular prisoners given up to their fury. The Count rode boldly amongst the maddened rabble; told them that strict justice should be done, but that the cannon of the citadel should be turned on them if they dared to persist. Such was the fury that animated the savage, prejudiced multitude against the Queen, whose safety would have been very precarious if she had not been sent away.

During the first day of his imprisonment, Struensee seemed stupefied; he did not eat; he drank only a little wine and water; he wept, but not excessively until he saw his valet enter, whose captivity called a flood of tears to the relief of his master's bosom.

The Count, to whom no one was permitted to speak, was so overcome by the honest grief depicted in the face of his young valet, that he took him by the hand, kissed his cheek, and said: " Poor fellow! I intended to have provided for thee; I delayed it too long, not wishing to lose thy services; and now thou art the companion of my prison! Can'st thou forgive me for this?" The young man, affected to a degree of intense sympathy, sobbing and crying like a child, threw himself at his master's feet, and, embracing his knees, said: "Oh, God! Oh, God! If I had not opened the door my beloved master might have escaped"![1] The officers who were present could scarcely refrain from shedding tears. At last, Struensee, a little relieved, raised the poor fellow from his suppliant posture, and took, at his persuasion, a cup of coffee. The officers not understanding German, Ernestus told the Count, whilst resting his head on his knees, that he had secured his gold repeater, diamond pin and brooch, and also his purse, which he slipped into the Count's hand; that Count Brandt was in the next room, the Queen sent to Cronenborg,

---

1 There appears some uncertainty as to this point. If the secret staircase led to the Queen's rooms the Count would inevitably have been seized there; if it led to a gallery or passage communicating with the grand suite of rooms, in that case he might have escaped from the palace, but not from the city.

Mr. Wolffe, in his interesting work, states that "The Queen endeavoured to make her escape through a secret passage, but on her arrival at the outer door, to her great mortification, found it guarded by sentinels." *Vide* " Northern Tour," p. 95. This sentence confirms the preceding accounts as to the existence of a secret passage, but affords no further elucidation as to where it led.

the Count's brothers and friends all under arrest;[1] that his papers, as also his property, were seized; and lastly, he mentioned the riots of which he had been informed. The Count was dreadfully agitated at this news; and yet he did not expect better. The purse he contrived to hide in the bed. The watch and jewels he bade his valet keep. Fearful lest his valet had no money, Struensee took up the purse to give him a couple of ducats; when, owing to its slipping, he was detected—a fact the officers dared not conceal. The commandant, a lame, short old man,[2] soon came, and very unceremoniously searched the Count and

---

[1] General Falkenskjöld was thrown, in the depth of a Northern winter, into a narrow and damp dungeon, where mutinous or disorderly seamen were usually confined. Some friend presented a petition to Prince Frederick, praying that the Colonel might be removed to a prison less unwholesome. The author whence these particulars have been borrowed[*] attributed to Prince Frederick the following sarcastic and inhuman reply—namely, "A man who has fought against the Turks ought to be sufficiently hardened to bear any situation." There was a double sting in this reply; Falkenskjöld having served in the recent expedition against Algiers, which had totally failed, and thereby greatly exasperated the public mind against the principal officers concerned. The malice of Juliana and her partisans was particularly bitter against this officer, who was firmly attached to Struensee, and who would have prevented this catastrophe if his regiment had arrived in time.

Lady Göhler, with the General, her husband, was taken to the citadel and guarded by officers placed in their room; she was shortly afterwards removed from the citadel and kept close prisoner in her own house.

[2] When Count Struensee was delivered as a State criminal to the commandant, the former said in a mournful tone of voice, " I suppose this visit is totally unexpected by you?" "Not at all," replied the uncourteous commandant; " I have been for a long time past constantly expecting your Excellency."

[*] "Latrobe," p. 208.

took away the money. He then rummaged the valet, and thus obtained the valuable gold watch that the Count purchased when in England, the diamond brooch, a present from Matilda, that cost five hundred guineas, and a ring that cost one thousand guineas. Such was the magnificent spoil that thus casually fell into the hands of the colonel-commandant, Von Hoben, a coarse, unfeeling man, and an obsequious creature of Eichstedt's. Whether it was done to insult or gratify the Count, a silver-gilt chamber-pot and wash-hand basin were brought from his stately apartments, forming a striking contrast with the humble furniture of his present abode, and still more so with that to which he was soon removed.

The commandant, addressing the Count, told him that orders were given to allow him four shillings sterling per diem, and two for his attendant,[1] and that an orderly-sergeant was in attendance to fetch what he wanted. Then, turning to the valet, he said, "You have told the Count of the riots, as well as handed him a purse of ducats; now, mark what I say, if during your confinement and attendance you tell the Count anything whatever—*even if it rains*— you shall be sent to Gluckstadt, condemned to perpetual slavery and chains. As the Count is ignorant of our mother-tongue, and you can speak German,

---

[1] Mr. Wolffe asserts: "An officer remained with him during the time of his confinement, and only half-a-dollar was allowed for his daily sustenance." In this he was misinformed. The sum allowed the Count proved fully sufficient to the decent supply of his wants. It was equal in Copenhagen, at that period, to twenty shillings in London, in 1812.

you are to use that language, and loud enough to be heard by the sentinels outside; and care will be taken that the officers on guard shall also know German." It was owing to Rantzau's interference that the valets of the two Counts were confined in the same prison with their masters, with, liberty to wait on them. He was afraid they would otherwise be exposed to continual indignities, if not to private torture, to prevent which he obtained this indulgence, a privilege which ceased when judicial proceedings were begun, and when those priests were obtruded on the captives who were the abject tools of Juliana and Guldberg, who carried to their employers the confessions extorted from the prisoners, and operating on the frighted imagination of Struensee, led him to accuse and criminate the Queen.¹ To complete their

---

1 The work published in England in 1776, entitled "The Conversion and Death of Count Struensee," by the Reverend Mr. Munter, and that of Count Enevold Brandt, by the Reverend Mr. Hee, convey the most abject idea possible of both those individuals. The priests, by whom it was compiled might, in their private characters, be respectable. It would, however, be credulous indeed to believe, if they had not enjoyed the *confidence* of Juliana and her adherents, they would have been selected on that occasion; and if they had been men of unbending integrity, they never would have been chosen. These extraordinary confessions must be regarded as an *ex parte* statement that, previous to publication, underwent the revision of Struensee's bitterest enemy. Many of the facts bear a stamp as if they were wrung from him by torture, others by the hope of pardon. Whilst the *trial*, if such it may be termed, was going on, these priests visited the prisoners; and it is reasonable to suppose they received their instructions from the Minister of Police, and shaped their questions accordingly: they passed alternately from the office of the Attorney-General to the prisoners, and *vice versâ*. As to Mr. Munter, the admissions and innuendoes

tender mercies, they published in their accounts of his conversion such monstrous confessions that, if they could be believed, would prove Struensee to have been the most depraved, dastardly and base of recorded villains.

Under the new regulations, discourse became irksome; but the presence of Ernestus, who was lodged in a room below the Count, was still a great relief. The second night, about midnight, the valet heard heavy steps ascending the stairs, and a clank, as of a heap of chains or fetters thrown on the floor above his head. This disturbance filled him with terror, for his fears foreboded that those irons were for the Count; and he expected, with fear and trembling, the same treatment. Presently he heard the sound of hammers, as if riveting on the fetters! In about half-an-hour the noise ceased, the persons descended, and passed his door without stopping. This was some relief, but the thoughts of his master's fate kept him awake and in tears till the morning, when his slumbers were dis-

---

contained in his share of the work represent Struensee as the most filthy of depraved sensualists; whilst Mr. Hee, who was selected by the Bishop of Harboe to visit Count Brandt, writes thus (p. 274): "*The third confession was of such a nature, I dare not mention it, though it concerned his soul.*" The imagination being left to revel in an infinity of horrible conclusions, was likely to content itself with this, that however bad it might conceive the Count to be, it would still fall short of his guilt! This was, indeed, pursuing the victim beyond the grave; and if Mr. Hee's motives were to do the utmost possible injury to the memory of Count Brandt, he unquestionably adopted the most certain mode of attaining it. This, however, is a conclusion that it would be illiberal, and perhaps unjust, to insist on.

turbed by dreams of the Count being beheaded and quartered.

When he was permitted to leave his own room, he went with a heavy heart to the Count. The looks of the sentinels, who sorrowfully shook their heads, confirmed his apprehensions. Struensee strove to conceal his disgrace, covering his face with the bedclothes; but this could not last long, and when the eyes of the master and man met, they seemed equally affected; both looked pale and haggard, and their eyes were swollen by crying. The valet saw with horror and dismay that the Count was chained to a massive iron staple driven into the wall, which passed through a swivel fixed to a thick ring that encircled his right ankle and his left wrist, and so short as barely to admit him to reach a night-chair that stood at the foot of his bed, or sit on the bed's side, the staple being fixed opposite the centre of the bedstead. The valet, from excess of grief, could scarcely speak. Seizing Struensee's hand, he kissed it with respectful affection, and bathed with his tears the iron ring that encircled his master's wrist.[1]

Man is the most docile of all animals: he accommodates himself to all situations, and the most painful privations! Horror-stricken as was this unhappy voluptuary when first he saw his limbs enchained, in the course of a couple of days his

---

[1] The Count hurt the wrist of his right hand by a fall from a horse, and always afterwards wore a black ribbon round it. It was on that account the ring was fastened round his left wrist. Count Brandt was chained from his left foot to his right wrist

grief subsided, and he strove to relieve himself as much as possible by adapting his position to the length of his chain. He also began to take his meals with something like an appetite. He breakfasted about nine, off coffee, rolls, tops and bottoms, and biscuits; at one he dined, took a glass of light wine, and a cup of coffee; drank tea about five or six o'clock, and perhaps ate a biscuit or two; he took no supper, but drank a glass of port wine and water. He was always very abstemious as to wines and spirits; at least, after he was placed about the King. His meat was cut by his valet, so that he might eat it with a silver fork or spoon, not being permitted to use a knife, lest he should commit suicide.

The Count was supplied with provisions by a French *restaurateur* named Mareschal, who lived on Reverentz Gaarden, Konung's Nye Torve: everything was most carefully examined before it was served up; even the bread was cut open, and the napkins shook and held up to the light.

For the more secure confinement of the Count, or (more correctly defining its object) for his greater punishment, he was soon removed from the officers' barrack to a room in the vallum, behind the church, a small, low, square room, with one small window in the corner, and scarcely fourteen feet square; the walls were bare; a stump bedstead, a bed of the meanest kind, a table, close-stool, a stove, and two chairs for the officers formed the miserable furniture of this gloomy place; but even here, as if to tantalise his memory, the silver-gilt chamber-pot and washing-basin were allowed him. He was now chained more closely than before, so much so that it was with difficulty he could reach the night-chair or sit upright on the side of his bed. This was the act of Juliana, who more than once, after the valet was dismissed, gratified her malice by viewing in disguise the wretched victim of his own folly, and her treachery!

Without a moment's notice the valet was dismissed; nor was he allowed to speak to, or take leave of his master! The Count was so much affected by his loss that he was at first quite inconsolable; it was even reported that he tried to destroy himself by forcing the silver fork down his throat. Immediately after this, the priests and lawyers commenced their operations, working alternately on the hopes and fears of the unhappy man, who was partly persuaded by his treacherous spiritual visitors, and no less impelled by the horrid tortures with which he was threatened, to accuse the Queen of having first seduced him, concealing nothing that ever had occurred between them. This act of cowardice, that did not save himself, gave the finishing blow to the slender hopes of the Queen: the triumph of Juliana was now complete; her exultation knew no bounds, and had not fear restrained her, she would have brought both the Queen and the Count to trial for adultery and treason. The trial of Count Struensee sufficiently proves how greatly the law was strained to reach him; as to Count Brandt, whatever criminality attached to his motives, no act of high treason was proved, and his sentence remains an indelible stain and disgrace to the jurisprudence of Denmark.

Count Struensee, too late, saw and deplored the weakness into which he had fallen in making unreserved confessions to priests, who, however sanctified their manners, were selected and sent to him by his mortal enemies. He saw that the hopes of mercy insidiously held out were false and illusive, and intended only to entangle him deeper and deeper; many a time he filled with dismay the officers who guarded him when, furiously clanking his chains and grinding his teeth, he cursed his own baseness and the perfidy of his enemies. At last, seeing nothing but an ignominious death before his eyes, without any means of avoiding it, he collected the scattered energies of his mind and wrote, on a limited quantity of paper, chained as he was, his defence, entitled, "Verantwortung des Grafen Struensee, an die Königlicke Commission" (*i.e.*, "The Reply of Count Struensee to the King's Commissioners"). It contains thirty pages of close letterpress; and, if it fails to justify the conduct of Struensee, it shows the weakness of the proofs that the commissioners had been able to assemble, and the gross absurdity of many of their charges. The efforts of the Count to relieve the Crown vassals from the accursed yoke called feudal services were construed as an act of high treason[1] against the sovereignty,

---

[1] "Dass, im fall jemand sich unterstehen würde, etwas auszuwürken oder an sich zu bringen, welches auf ein oder ander weise,

because, forsooth, by relieving the oppressed and degraded farmers and labouring poor, the sovereign power must be diminished; and by the Act that conferred the sovereign power on Frederick III., it is declared an act of high treason in anyone who should, by any means, directly or indirectly attempt to deprive that King or his successors of any part of the sovereign power! Thence, according to this atrocious doctrine of the Crown lawyers of Denmark, that glorious undertaking, the fulfilment of which has since immortalised the memory of Count Bernstorff was an act of high treason in Count Struensee!

---

der absolute herrschaft und souverainen macht des Königszum nachtheil und Schmälerung gereichen, betrachtet, und diejenigen, die dergleichen erworben oder erschlichen haben, als Beleidiger der Majestät, und als solcke, welche die Königlicke monarchische gewalt und hoheit gröblich angetastet, gestraft werden soller."—*Vide* " Urtheil in Sachen des Generalfiscals, wider den Grafen Struensee," p. 121.

By this formidable and elastic article of the capitulation made by the wise burghers of Copenhagen with Frederick III., it is declared an act of high treason if, at any future period, any person should by any means attempt to diminish the despotic power of the Crown! Under the sanction of this law, Struensee rendered himself liable to the death of a traitor by every act of political reformation that he introduced.

M. Suhm,* in his letter addressed, in 1772, to Christian VII., after glancing his eye at the despotism of Denmark, thus defines the boasted freedom of us English, viz.:

"Thus will Denmark become the land of liberty, of unlimited power, of peace, plenty, and security beyond even that of England; where, although self-interested and servile ministers cannot prevent the voice of the people from being heard at the foot of the throne, yet, by their influence, they prevent its effects, and cause those who are the interpreters of public grievances, and who stand forward in so upright a cause, to be thrown into prison."

* Counsellor of State.—*Vide* " Wolffe's Northern Tour," p. 89.

Queen Matilda was in a manner annihilated when the confessions of Struensee—every page signed with his well-known hand, and couched in the most offensive terms—were laid before her.[1] Struensee's want of fortitude decided her fate. Count Rantzau was at first incredulous. When a copy was handed to him, he saw at one glance that the Queen Matilda would be divorced and banished, and Juliana remain sole mistress of the field. He cursed the pusillanimity of Struensee, and his own folly and precipitancy; for it could not escape him that the day must soon arrive that should terminate in disgrace his own career.

Struensee had many amours on his hands, and many a ruined female too late bemoaned her fate. He had several illegitimate children, for none of whom could he make the least provision, not a single dollar of all his property being left him. His brothers afterwards provided for those children, principally in Prussia.

Ernestus, the valet, strove in vain to obtain an interview with his master previous to his execution. Pleased with his fidelity to Struensee, Count Rantzau took him into his service, treating him in a manner peculiarly kind. As the fatal day approached, the young man appeared more and more affected, growing seriously worse, which did not at all tend to cheer the spirits of his new master, who remained in his

---

[1] The account published in Germany in 1788, and translated by Latrobe the next year (p. 242), accuses the King's commissioners of having signed the name of Carolina Matilda to her confession: a charge altogether improbable, as they were possessed of superabundant evidence to establish every fact it contained. Sir John Carr copied this little embellishment into his "Northern Summer."

house on the 28th of April when the dreadful sentence was fulfilled. He used every argument in his power to tranquillise the mind of the faithful Norwegian, whose fixed sorrow seemed too violent to admit of consolation. The heaviest calamities are, however, lightened by the hand of time, and youth is the season when grief is soonest forgotten: within about a week after the execution, a wish once more to behold the face of his lamented master led him to the place where his mangled remains were exhibited,[1] and

---

[1] Mr. Coxe, ed. 1802, vol. iii., p. 1, gives the following account of this horrid scene, viz.:

"I visited the spot where Struensee and Brandt were executed on the 28th of March (*April*), 1772. The scaffold was constructed near the east gate of the town; and they were conducted to the spot in two separate carriages, through an immense concourse of people. They arrived at the place of execution about 11 o'clock. Brandt first alighted, and mounted the scaffold with a slow step and undaunted mien: he heard his sentence read, and saw his coat of arms broken without expressing the least emotion; he then prayed for a few minutes, and spoke a few words to the people. When the executioner approached to assist him," (undress) "he said to him with firmness, yet not without mildness, 'Stand off! and do not presume to touch me.' Without any assistance he pulled off his pelisse and prepared for his fate. He first stretched out his hand, and bade the executioner do his duty, without shrinking from the blow; it was struck off, and his head severed from his body almost in the same instant; his body was then quartered.

"During this dreadful scene, Struensee remained at the bottom of the scaffold" (in a coach, the priest conversing and praying with him) "anxiously expecting and dreading his own fate. His whole frame trembled when Brandt's blood gushed from the scaffold, and he was so agitated that he could not walk up the steps without help. He said nothing, and permitted the executioner to assist him in taking off his cloak. Instead of imitating the serenity of his fellow-sufferer, he started up several times before he gave the signal, drew back his hand, which was shockingly mangled before it was cut off, so great was the shock his sensibility received that he fell senseless on the earth, in which state he was found; and after he revived and was carried home, he was confined for a week to his room. From that period his grief wore off, but whenever he recollected

and was at last held down by force whilst the executioner beheaded him."

Such is Mr. Coxe's relation of Struensee's last moments, and it is to be hoped of his last sufferings; but it contains a few errors that are excusable in describing what had happened several years before. Godsckau, the executioner, was bred a surgeon, and articled to his trade; wore a sword, and was not held infamous; the axes he used were very sharp and heavy; he had two by his side covered in bags. Struensee was really convulsed, and therefore could not hold himself still; his face and right arm were of necessity placed in the cavities purposely cut into the block to receive them; the executioner's assistant held the hand by the fingers, and the head by the hair: it were no wonder if the headsman was a little nervous; but the hand was struck off at a blow; the axe was fixed tight in the block; he seized his other, and the neck of Struensee being very short, part of his chin was cut off; it is probable he was insensible before the fatal blow was given. The two Counts were taken to the scaffold in their irons; and, as both were executed on one block, Struensee had the horrid task to perform of laying his face and hand in puddles of the yet reeking blood of his dearest friend, whose mangled remains lay spread around! A stronger mind than Struensee ever possessed might have been totally unhinged by the dreadful scene before his eyes.

The executioner having disembowelled the bodies, cut off their private parts, and divided the trunks each in four quarters; the entrails, &c., were thrown into tubs placed on the scaffold to receive them; the heads, and right hands, and bleeding quarters, were then exposed to public view as they were conveyed all through the city to the field at the opposite extremity, where they were to be left to rot, or be devoured by the fowls of the air. For each body, four stout balks were, at equal distances, driven in the earth; a taller pole was fixed in the centre; the entrails, &c., were buried in a hole dug at the foot of the central pole; on the top the head was fixed, the pole being forced up inside the skull, through which a

the sufferings of the Count and of Queen Matilda, whom, beyond any other witness, he could have criminated, it inspired him with melancholy, and often cost him the silent tribute of a tear.

---

spike was driven to make it fast; the hand was nailed to a piece of board placed transversely below the head; a cart or waggon wheel was fixed horizontally on the top of each of the four posts or pillars on which a quarter of the body was exposed, made fast to the wheel by chains of iron. In this manner were the bodies of the two Counts disposed of; and such was the horrid spectacle presented to the eyes of the valet when he reached the dismal place. Its effect on his nerves is already mentioned; but Juliana is said to have gone to glut her insatiate malice with the sight. It was rumoured, though it is almost too horrible for belief, that she said to Guldberg, "It is not quite complete; the head of the * * * * is wanting to make it so." The place where the bodies were thus exposed was that on which the scavengers emptied all the filth of Copenhagen.

CHAPTER VIII

Character and conduct of Count Rantzau—His disgrace—Benevolence of Matilda—Gratitude—Lex talionis—Sensibility and gratitude—A fascinating mistress—Visit to Zell—A fair penitent—Reconciliation of Matilda and Rantzau—Their deaths.

WHILST the sovereignty was in reality possessed and exercised by Juliana Maria, taking warning by the fate of Struensee, she suffered the Council of State to be re-established, which, with the exception of Count Rantzau, was composed of persons devoted to her views. The members consisted of the elder Counts de Thott, d'Osten and Rantzau; de Schak Ratlau, and Colonel (now General) Eichstedt. The King soon found his condition was not bettered; he changed keepers, and that was all, and was deprived of some gratifications (and perhaps properly enough) that he received under the reign of his consort.

Juliana took care that the day and hour, and every horrid feature of Struensee's execution, should be made known to Queen Matilda, who generously pardoned the man that had betrayed her, imputing his conduct to the effects of torture. She passed that day in her bedroom, with no other company than her infant, now doubly dear to her desolate mother; and during the rest of her life, though the name was never heard to pass her lips, she is said, at her palace in Zell, to have devoted its anniversary to fasting and prayer. There is no doubt but her fall wrought a thorough reformation in the mind of Matilda, that was tainted by only one crime, and that one flowing from the criminality of others rather than the innate depravity of her own heart.[1]

---

[1] Latrobe (p. 247), speaking of the Queen, says, "Her sensibility rendered her capable of feeling her misery in its utmost extent; and the expressions in which she depicted the excruciating apprehensions of her mind to her counsellor Uhldal, fully showed with what acuteness she felt them."

P. 268.—" On the 27th of May, two English frigates and a cutter arrived at Helsingor (Elsineur), and on the 30th the Queen left Cronenborg. The last moments which this amiable Queen spent in the Danish dominions were distressing in the highest degree. She was now under the necessity of parting from her only comfort, the only object of her affection" (untrue and improper), " her infant daughter, and of leaving her in the hands of her sworn enemies. She fondly pressed for some minutes the babe to her bosom, and bedewed it with a shower of tears; she then attempted to tear herself away, but the voice, the smiles, the endearing motions of her infant were chains that irresistibly drew her back. At last she called up all her resolution, took her once more into her arms with the impetuous ardour of distracted love, imprinted on the lips of the babe the farewell kiss, and returning it to the attendant, she exclaimed, 'Away! away! I now possess nothing here!' One of the King's boats carried her to the first frigate, and the squadron (commanded by Captain Macbride) saluted her on coming on board, and set sail for Stade, whence she was to travel by land to Zell. Unfortunately the ships were detained by contrary winds, and she had still, for a whole day, the distressing view of the country which to her had been the source of so many misfortunes. The next day a favourable wind enabled the fleet to proceed.

" Thus ended this memorable revolution, which is certainly one of the most extraordinary political events in the history of any

In spite of the remonstrances of a certain great Power, the enemies of Matilda persevered in proceeding to divorce her from the King. It admitted of no very favourable construction that the King, her brother, did not send for her home to his own Court, instead of ordering her to fix her residence at Zell—a city, the birthplace of her unfortunate ancestor, who was immured so many years in the Castle of Aller. It was a measure better calculated to lead an erring woman to reflection and amendment than to restore a dubious character in the estimation of the world. Matilda fell the victim of an ardent constitution, and a debauched, impotent, and depraved husband, whilst that detested and detestable step-mother, whose life from the first

---

country. The Princess, who thereby lost the most exalted situation that birth or fortune can bestow, deserved a better fate. Truth cannot deny, nor judgment approve, her errors; but the heart must allow that she had the justest claim to pity and indulgence. Her sensibility and the circumstances into which she was thrown were powerful enemies to a susceptible mind, whose very excellencies led her into danger. After her first error, the good qualities of her own heart hurried her into the embarrassments in which she was involved. The warmth of her disposition led her to take the first step upon the wrong path; she was too much infatuated to be immediately conscious of it, and she had proceeded too far before she discovered her mistake. The discovery alarmed her, and she strove to measure back her steps; a thousand obstacles opposed her return; she felt herself too weak to overcome them; her first efforts were ill-judged, and only led her deeper into error; her mind was exceedingly distressed, to alleviate which became her only study. Dissipation offered her the readiest assistance; and, with the activity of mind peculiar to herself, she grasped at everything that might have a tendency to banish reflection from her bosom. Since that dreadful moment when the veil was torn from her eyes, when she was awakened from her trance, and a long and severe punishment inflicted, her conduct is her best defence with the

year of her arrival in Denmark was but one tissue of criminal intrigues and intended murder, was permitted to triumph and descend to the tomb unpunished, although universally detested.

The ignominious confessions of Count Struensee, however extorted, mortified Rantzau no less than they delighted Juliana. I state that which Rantzau himself declared when I affirm that his sole object in arresting the Queen was to prevent her from rescuing Struensee, and to save her from the machinations of Juliana, who, artfully working on the prejudices of the very lowest of the people, might have found means to have destroyed her by a popular insurrection. The riots that took place in the city immediately after the

---

humane, susceptible, and the virtuous. Cronenborg witnessed in this Princess the most sincere repentance, the most tender maternal affection, the noblest sympathy with her unfortunate friends, and the most heroic resignation to her cruel fate. Zell afterwards saw in her the purest virtue and piety, the sweetest affability, the most compassionate heart, and a degree of fortitude in her distressing situation which shed a soft and tranquil lustre over the evening of her life." Such is M. Latrobe's translation, which in places I have altered, being sure he mistook the meaning of his German original. He mentions the evening of Matilda's life! Matilda perished ere its meridian, by an infectious fever. At Zell she paid liberally for intelligence as to her children; and she had waxen figures dressed like them, which she addressed as if they were her children. Matilda fell a victim to her gratitude. A running footman, named Alexander Stuart, who had attended her in Denmark, and whom her enemies could neither suborn nor intimidate, was seized with a putrid fever. She respected this man on account of his fidelity and attachment. Insisting on seeing him, the generous woman caught the dire infection, and died a few days after poor Stuart had breathed his last.

arrests of the 17th of January, 1772—riots that were intended to insult and degrade the character of Matilda —afforded incontestible proofs that the apprehensions of Count Rantzau were not chimerical. Rantzau, no less than Juliana and her cabal, was determined on the overthrow of Struensee and Brandt, after which Rantzau fully intended to have restored the Queen. It was his untoward fate to succeed in every step that militated against that greatly unhappy lady, and to fail in everything that was kind and gracious in his intentions towards her.

Count Rantzau found himself thwarted in every project that he thought would be of use to his country, and forced to acquiesce in plans that he knew to be founded on private interest. He was compelled either to be the slave of Juliana and her cabal, or to oppose her when he knew opposition would not avail. Previous to the arrest of Struensee the Count entertained serious thoughts of effecting a radical revolution in Denmark, tearing up the feudal system by the roots, and establishing a representative Government on the model of that of England. This subject had often been discussed between him and Struensee; and if he could have induced Struensee to have considered him (Rantzau) as the head of the patriotic party, for which his high rank, great possessions, talents and experience so well fitted him, the attempt would have been made; but the Queen ruled the King, and through him the realm; Struensee ruled the Queen, and was *de facto* the Sovereign of Denmark: blinded by pride, fired by ambition, he

———, 1772————— that were
———— the character of Matilda
———— that ——— apprehensions
———— chimerical. Rantzau, no
——— cabal, ——— determined on
———— and Brandt, after which
——— to have restored the Queen.
———— to succeed in every step
———— greatly unhappy lady, and
———— was kind and gracious in
——— her.
———und ———— thwarted in every
———ght ———— be of use to his
——— to acquiesce in plans that he
——— on private interest. He was
——— be ———— ——ve of Juliana and her
——— h——— ———— he knew opposition
Previo——— to the arrest of Struensee
——— se———— thoughts of effecting a
——— Den———— ———— ——— ———— ——dal
———, and establishing a ——— ——————
——— model ———— of England. This
——— been dis———ed between him and
he could have induced Struensee
him (Rantzau) as the head of the
——— which his high rank, great
———d experience so well fitted him,
———— been made; but the Queen
———rough him the realm; Struensee
——— was *de facto* the Sovereign of
———, ———, fired by ambition, he

COPENHAGEN
FREDERICKSBORG PALACE, NEAR

cut with Rantzau, followed his own crude suggestions, and perished as we have seen. Instead of addressing anonymous letters to Count Brandt, and useless remonstrances to Count Struensee, if Rantzau had demanded an audience of Matilda, warned her of her danger, and as the only honourable and safe means of providing for her safety, had proposed such a revolution, it is very probable he would have succeeded; and then that glorious measure was sure to have been carried; for what could a few impotent nobles have done against the united power of the Crown, the army, and the people?

With many fine qualities, Count Rantzau had great vices: ambition worked to the full as powerfully in him as in Struensee; and in his morals he was equally relaxed; he became jealous of Struensee; he thirsted for revenge; to obtain which, in defiance of the dictates of common prudence, he coalesced with his mortal foe, and the very worst woman in Denmark. In that coalition the Count betrayed a degree of weakness that deprived him of all claim to sympathy; Struensee fell the victim of his own egotism and vanity, Count Rantzau of his own defective policy.

The banished and repudiated Queen was scarcely seated in her melancholy residence at Zell—far away from her friends, her children, and every earthly pleasure—and the features of the unhappy Struensee were yet plainly distinguishable, grinning horribly and ghastly above the waggon wheels on which was exhibited his black and decaying quartered body, when that stroke which Rantzau foresaw, and Matilda foretold, fell upon Count Rantzau.

The Dowager-Queen had already secured a majority of votes in the Council in favour of appointing her son Regent of the kingdom during the minority of the Crown Prince Frederick; but still, without Rantzau's concurrence she dared not risk the undertaking, the real object of which was, of course, her own aggrandisement. The artful calculator conceived that Rantzau had so completely committed himself by his arrest of Queen Matilda that he must by necessity succumb, and forward her views, whatever they might be.

On the approach of summer, the Danish Court, which, after the fall of Matilda, became austere, formal and gloomy, removed from the winter palace in the capital to Fredericksborg. Juliana then took possession of Matilda's State rooms, and made her minion Guldberg the occupier of those where Struensee had so often revelled in a flood of voluptuousness.

Her chamberlain, Blucher, took a note written by Juliana, and dictated in very flattering terms, requesting the attendance of Count Rantzau the next day, to spend the day and pass the night at that palace.

The Count ordered his *vis-à-vis* and four, a change of linen and clothes, and attended by his Norwegian valet, drove to the grand entrance, dressed *en gala*. The moment his name was announced, Prince Frederick went to the head of the grand staircase to receive him, and whispered in his ear that his mother wished to speak to him before the drawing-room commenced; he went through the Prince's room to the Queen-Dowager's; there he found General Eichstedt, General Kohler Banner, and that able statesman, Guldberg.

The Queen-Dowager received the Count, as indeed did all present, with distinguished homage; presently the Prince withdrew, looking very significantly on Rantzau, and telling him he hoped on his return to learn that he might rank his excellency amongst the number of his particular friends—casting his heavy eye on his mother's creatures, who, of course, bowed most obsequiously and profoundly. The task was left to Guldberg to explain to Rantzau that, to preserve the internal tranquillity of Denmark and command the respect of foreign States, the gentlemen then present, and others, considering the lamentable imbecility of the King, and the tender age of the Crown Prince, had applied to the Queen-Dowager to prevail on her son to accept the office of Regent; but ere they proceeded further, they wished to obtain His Excellency's sanction.

The blood rushed in a torrent to the old Count's face, his eyes flashed fire, and eyeing the speaker with fierce disdain, he said, "Never, whilst Rantzau wears his sword! You are all guilty of more treason against the King," said the Count, looking sternly at the persons who were present, "than what was proved against the scoundrel Struensee: henceforth let my name be erased from this cabal, and if you dare to proceed, this sword shall chastise your disloyalty and presumption." Eichstedt, Banner, Rantzau, all rose together, and their hands, as if instinctively, were laid on their swords; the crafty Queen turned pale as ashes from rage and fear; Guldberg rushed between the angry nobles, exclaiming, "For shame, gentlemen! in the Queen-Mother's presence is this decorous?" At his request, Eichstedt and Kohler Banner, humbly begging forgiveness of Juliana, seated themselves; Rantzau, too, apologised to that woman, whose malice, had her power been correspondent, would have transfixed him to the earth, or severed his limbs like those of Struensee. But if the Count was fiery and open, Juliana could be cool and reserved. She therefore affected to rebuke Guldberg for his presumption, affirming with the utmost effrontery that she knew nothing whatever of the measure alluded to, and felt truly sorry that the Government, in its present state of weakness, should lose the support of one of its firmest pillars. This ironical and satirical speech conveyed to Count Rantzau the acceptation of his dismission from the Council of State.

Count Rantzau then withdrew, visibly and violently agitated. To conceal the tears he could not repress, he kept wiping his face and complaining of the heat of the drawing-room. His valet, Ernestus, with evident marks of concern, noticed the angry frown that ruffled his brows, and would, if he had dared, have asked what had disturbed him. The Count read his thoughts in the expressive features of his valet, and said, "There is nothing the matter, only it is so d——d hot. Go, my friend; order a dragoon to overtake my coach, and bring it back." Ernestus turned pale at this order, for he knew the Count had been invited, and had designed to spend the day and night at Fredericksborg. He obeyed in silence, half suspicious that the Count's head sat but loosely on his shoulders. The *vis-à-vis* drew up; the Count leaped in; Ernestus followed. The whole way home the Count kept complaining of the heat and wiping his face. When he arrived at his palace he undressed, and had recourse to his constant solace in trouble, *i.e.*, his pipe.[1]

This was the last time that ever Count Rantzau was at Court in Denmark. The next day a gentleman of the Court—Major Harboe, of the Horse Guards—came to the Count, ostensibly to propose an accommodation, but in reality to sound his feelings, and, if possible, ascertain his future views. They took chocolate together, and had a long conference. The Count was too experienced a courtier to be entrapped by a shallow young man like this, and the latter, unable to induce the Count to make a confession, in all probability substituted one of his own fabrication; at least, the events that followed indicated as much.

The disgrace of Count Rantzau was soon spoken of by the whole city, and generally with satisfaction, for he had the singular adroitness to offend every party in the State, without forming one of his own. The

---

[1] The Count was excessively addicted to smoking, and very particular in everything relating thereto. His meerschaum pipes (mounted in gold and silver) were of the costliest kind; his tobacco was procured from Cadiz. He frequently smoked himself to sleep, his large pipe, secured from letting any fire fall out, resting on ribbons above his head, and the tube in his mouth. He would at times smoke in the night. One pipeful of tobacco lasted two hours. A silver tinder box, &c., stood by his bedside, ready to renew his pipe if it chanced to go out.

rumours respecting his ill-treatment of Queen Matilda were fed by exaggerated statements from Juliana and her partisans, by which means the character of the Count was most unmercifully treated, particularly by the ladies. The courtiers no longer sought his notice; his ante-chambers were no longer crowded by humble supplicants, but, in the midst of a crowded city, he felt himself in solitude and alone.

After the visit to Fredericksborg Palace he stayed but a fortnight in Copenhagen, and that period was principally employed in arranging his pecuniary affairs, and taking leave of his mistresses. The children of Count Rantzau Rastorff were the heirs to the entailed estates; and the Count, with all his levity, was anxious that his tenants, to whom he had ever been a mild and indulgent landlord, should not be oppressed, nor, after his decease, be deprived of their honest earnings that during his life-time they might have acquired.

Love, war, and State intrigues had alternately engaged the Count's attention from his earliest days of manhood; and so docile was his genius, he could follow the three pursuits at once with as much intensity as if one alone engaged his attention. The last object of the Count's amours in Denmark was a fine young actress, Sophia Livernet, who was the first female dancer at the Opera. He was wooing this young damsel just as his head was full of the great undertaking he meditated against Counts Struensee and Brandt. The father of his favourite was a tailor residing in the city, to whom she was very liberal. As she lost her engagement by accepting the addresses of

Count Rantzau, the old nobleman settled a competent annuity on her parents to protect them from want in their old age, whilst he conferred sufficient wealth to render Sophia independent, the interest of which he secured to her during life in the Bank of England Stock, with liberty to dispose of one moiety by will. The other moiety he gave her to use as she pleased.

The girl was not more than eighteen when this old nobleman found means to gain her affections. Her character stood the first of any young actress on the stage; she was neither insolent nor wasteful, and, in point of personal beauty, there were few could boast of brighter charms. In stature she was of a graceful height, without being tall; her face oval, features of the Italian cast; her complexion was remarkably clear, and her colour so blooming that she never used rouge; her eyes were a brilliant black; her lips thin, rosy, and finely formed; her teeth small, white, and even; her tresses a dark auburn; her neck and bosom were of the finest form; her motions graceful, and her disposition good and affable. Such was the young girl whose first public attachment was to a man of sixty years of age. Her subsequent conduct indicated that her respect for the Count was not founded on mercenary principles alone. Miss Livernet's quitting the stage gave offence to Queen Matilda, to Struensee, and Brandt, and a message was sent to the Count to require her re-appearance. He sent word that Miss Livernet resided in his hotel, and if they wanted her, there she was to be found. The Queen, haughty and irritable, was for sending an officer to take her by force; but Struensee and Brandt, who knew the Count better than the Queen, dissuaded her from taking any steps by which they might make an irreconcilable enemy of that enterprising man. Such was the brief history of Sophia Livernet, who, at the time of the Count's difference with the faction whom he had set up, was living with him in the Princens Palace, a still greater favourite than his pipe, which is saying a great deal, considering the strength of his attachment to that source of humble pleasure. But there was this difference between the one and the other, namely, that he forsook his mistresses when the bloom of youth and beauty forsook them, and often long before; whereas the longer he smoked his meerschaum pipe, and the older it grew, the more beautiful and valuable it became in his eyes.[1]

His affairs in the metropolis being finally settled, the Count, leaving Miss Livernet in his hotel, accompanied only by his favourite valet, Ernestus, went by water first to Elsineur, and thence to Warrenborg, a small town on the Baltic.[2] During the passage he seemed absorbed in thought. The sight of Cronenborg Castle brought the remembrance of Matilda and her sufferings to his mind; and

---

[1] This really is the case with those pipes; the rich clouded colour for which they are chiefly prized by amateurs, arising from the internal heat, managed in a peculiar way to produce that effect.

[2] In the map of Zealand in Mr. Coxe's "Travels," vol. v., p. 84, there is no such town as Warrenborg noted; there probably exists some mistake as to the route taken by the Count from Copenhagen to Corsoer.

whether it was her fate or his own—for he felt he was going into perpetual banishment—he again complained of the heat, and wiped a tear from his eye. A tack made by the skipper close to Copenhagen afforded the Count a view of the mangled remains of Struensee and Brandt. The Count was startled at the sight; his features denoted horror and surprise. "Put about instantly," said he sternly to the skipper; "do you think I want to look at the remains of those men?" Unconscious of offence, the skipper humbly stated that he must first gain the point of land ahead. Ashamed of his weakness, the Count flung him a ducat and went below, where, leaning his head on his hand, thoughtful and abstracted, he sat silent and motionless. The skipper was by birth a Norwegian, and finding that the Count's valet was his countryman, he showed him the ducat, saying, "What made your master startle at the sight of the limbs of Struensee and Brandt, and order me to put about, when, without reaching the Ness, I could not get on with this wind?" The valet shook his head, and made no reply. The skipper continued, "Perhaps the old gentleman is not right in his head; or may be, all is not right here?" laying his hand on his heart. "Had he any hand in bringing those men to that dreadful end? If he had, the Lord have mercy upon him; I would not have their blood on my hands—not for all the ducats in the world!" Ernestus looked the old man in the face attentively, and said in Norsk, "Are you not Peter Nielsen, who rescued the King from the sea when he was Crown Prince?" "Aye." said the blunt old man, "that man am I. The villain Brockdorff,[1] I believe—God forgive me if I wrong him—intended he should be drowned. King Frederick, of blessed memory, gave me a handful of money, and ordered I should be provided for; but I never had any provision till the good young Queen chanced to hear that I had once saved her husband's life. Heaven bless her, and be her guide and protector!" said the grateful seaman: "she sent for me and made me tell her all about it, which I did in my homely way. The beautiful Queen shook her head, as much as to say, I know who was at the bottom of this; so did I, too, but I didn't say so. So then she bade her woman tell me I should be provided for when the King, who was then in England, came home; and she shook me by my coarse hand, and made her baby put its little hand into mine to thank me for having saved its father's life; and she gave me money, for I was

---

[1] "During the life of King Frederick V., the Royal party were often entertained by a water frolic upon that part of the sea which lies immediately behind Fredensborg. The present King (Christian VII.) in one of those expeditions was more wild and disorderly than usual; neither entreaties nor remonstrances could prevail on him to be quiet. One of the gentlemen of the household, Brockdorff by name, whose manners were in general not the most polished, threatened to throw the young Prince into the water unless he behaved more decently; and, taking him by the arm, he was really unfortunate or awkward enough to throw him overboard. The Prince was immediately saved, but he never forgot the circumstance; and ascribed his misfortune to a design of his step-mother upon his life, in order to raise her son, Prince Frederick, to the throne. This suspicion grew up with him, and it was in vain to attempt to persuade him to the contrary."—LATROBE, p. 276.

very poor through sickness and bad luck, and soon after the King returned I was indeed sent for to the palace, and the King himself took me by the hand; but it seems His Majesty thought I was provided for. Count Struensee was there, but he was no Count then—happy, mayhap, if he had never been. He was then the King's German doctor. I could speak a little German, and he told me I was to have a hundred dollars a year for life, so that I need never work or go to sea again. I fell on my knees to thank the King and Queen, and told them that I should die if I was not to work nor go to sea. They smiled when they heard this, and the King said, 'Old man, thou shalt not die if I can save thee.' So then Doctor Struensee—God bless his soul! and may his sins be forgiven him—said, 'A gift of a small vessel would be more useful.' 'True,' said the Queen, 'he shall have a vessel, and the pension too.' This very yacht was the Queen's gift. Now, have not I and mine a right to pray for my benefactress?" Ernestus was so much affected, he could not reply. Of the circumstance he had often heard Struensee speak, but the man he had never seen; and now that Count Rantzau was fallen in disgrace, the vessel bestowed by the Queen wafted him from the shores he was doomed to tread no more. The wind was now right aft; the mate was at the helm, the Count yet below; the old skipper and the young valet were standing forward; of course the sound of their voices was borne away by the breeze. The heart of the young man was so full, he could no longer conceal that he had been the favourite valet of Struensee; that he was now in the service of Count Rantzau, who was the nobleman by whom his packet had been freighted.

The old man was deeply affected at this discovery, for he knew not before the name of his freighter. "Well, indeed, might his conscience twinge him at the sight of those men's limbs!" said the skipper, indignantly; "but how came you to take service with the sworn enemy and destroyer of your late master?" "I lost my all when I was torn to prison; I gave no evidence against the Queen nor the Count; and thus I was left destitute and unpaid. Count Rantzau is a generous and good master; and hearing that I had been faithful, and wanting a valet, his excellency hired me; and a kind, indulgent master I have found him." "God be praised," said the skipper; you did not disgrace your honest parents, whom I well knew at Bergen. Many a cup of good wine have I drunk in their cellar; and blessed be His righteousness that is now bringing disgrace and punishment on the destroyer of my benefactors. "Take this ducat," said he, "and return it to the Count, and tell his excellency all I have in the world I derived from those whom he destroyed." "You mistake the Count's character," said Ernestus. "No, I mistake him not," rejoined the blunt old man; "and if you will not carry the ducat back, why here it goes (throwing it into the sea)! It would bring a curse on me and mine if I were to keep it." The skipper then began a long argument to persuade Ernestus to quit the service of the Count; and the valet was no less zealous to convince the skipper that he had formed too unfavourable an opinion of him; so that when they reached Warrenborg the opinions of both were still the same. The skipper promised to be silent and discreet as to the quality of his passenger, except the Count should avow himself; and having received the freight, which the skipper made a vow should be given to the poor, and never blended with his honest money, they took leave of each other.

The Count did not find his spirits revived by his valet's telling him, in reply to a demand why he seemed so melancholy, the singular conversation he had had with the old skipper, suppressing only the hearty maledictions bestowed on his master. The Count seemed more surprised than pleased at this adventure. "Did the old fellow know me?" said the Count. He was answered in the negative. "I am sorry for it," said he, "for I should have wished to have tried his attachment and his avarice. I flung him a ducat because I had spoken cross to him. Perhaps he would not have accepted it had he known Count Rantzau was the donor?" "He flung it in the sea as soon as he learnt it." "What!" said the Count sternly, "this after telling me he knew me not?" The valet then told the whole story from beginning to end. The Count was deeply affected at this proof of strong aversion. "I am already," said he, "an outcast from society—a wanderer like Cain; every man's hand is held up against me!" For an hour or two he continued very melancholy, till a buxom girl coming in his way, Matilda, Struensee and his own self-banishment seemed forgotten in the ardour with which he paid his addresses to the rosy young rustic. From Warrenborg the Count travelled in his own equipage (that arrived by another vessel) by land to Korsoer, where he crossed the Great Belt, landing at Nyborg, whence it is four German or sixteen English miles to Odensee,[1] the capital of Funen, and formerly a Royal residence.

---

[1] The execrable tyrant, Christian II., was buried in a church in this town. The brief account given of him in Mr. Coxe's "Travels" is so very interesting that the translator thought he should rather please than offend his readers by inserting it as a note in this portion of the "Secret History of the Court of Denmark":

"John ascended the throne in 1481, on the death of his father, Christian I.; and in 1497, renewing the union of Calmar, obtained the crown of Sweden, which the Swedes, however, did not long permit him to enjoy. He died on the 12th of February, 1513, having on his death-bed admonished his son, Christian II., admonitions which had no effect on a breast already corrupted by power and impatient for dominion. John would have acted more wisely had he endeavoured to render the infant mind of his son capable of receiving the impressions of virtue, and had not shamefully neglected his education—a crime highly reprehensible in a father, but unpardonable in a Sovereign who is, perhaps, rearing a tyrant for his subjects and entailing on his country a series of evils for which he is himself chiefly accountable. Historians agree in representing John as a wise and prudent Prince, inclined to peace, but enterprising in war, and as generally moderate and humane—admitting, however, that he perpetrated, occasionally, acts of violence and cruelty, derived from a species of melancholy madness that preyed upon his mind and at times deprived him of his senses.

"His son, the cruel and unfortunate Christian II., is entombed near his father, under a plain gravestone, somewhat raised, but without inscription. He was born at Nyborg, on the 2nd of July, 1481, and evinced, in his youth, symptoms of a lively genius and good understanding, which, if properly cultivated, might have rendered him the ornament, instead of the dis-

The Count hired a furnished house about five miles from that small city, where he lived perfectly retired, seeing no company whatever except the farmer's daughters, who brought him fruit. When his sensual fits came on he ceased to moralise; those subdued, he was again the sentimental philosopher and stern reviser of an ill-spent, oft lamented, but never amended life.

It was not to be expected but most of those florists and fruit-girls who visited the house of the Count should prefer as a sweetheart a fine young fellow, scarcely one-and-twenty, to a Count of sixty,

---

honour, of his country. The young Prince was entrusted to a common burgher of Copenhagen, and afterwards removed to the house of a schoolmaster, who was a canon of the cathedral. In this situation his chief employment consisted in regularly accompanying his master to church, where he distinguished himself beyond the other scholars and choristers in chanting and singing psalms. He was afterwards consigned to the tuition of a German preceptor, a man of learning, but a pedant, under whom, however, he made a considerable proficiency in the Latin tongue. From this humble education Christian imbibed a taste for bad company, and was accustomed to haunt the common taverns, to mix with the populace, to scour the streets, and to be guilty of every excess. The King at length, informed of these irregularities, reproved him severely; but as the Prince had already contracted habits which were grown too strong to be eradicated, these admonitions were too late. He feigned, however, contrition for his past behaviour, and again won the affections of his father by his military successes in Norway, and by an unwearied application to the affairs of Government.

"During the first years of his reign, which commenced in 1513, his administration was in many respects worthy of praise; and the excellence of many of his laws has induced Holberg to affirm that, if the character of Christian II. was to be determined by his laws, and not by his actions, he would merit the appellation of Good

although he might, barring unknown contingencies, be able to trace his pedigree up to Charles the Great, or the greater hero Oden, or carry in his arms three-score and ten quarterings. Ernestus, delighted and

---

rather than of Tyrant. Happy would it have been for himself and his people had he continued to reign on the same principles!

"At first, all his enterprises were crowned with success. He abridged the power of the Danish nobility, and exalted the regal prerogatives; he obtained the crown of Sweden by conquest, and was even proclaimed hereditary Sovereign of that kingdom. A prudent and temperate use of these advantages might have ensured him a long and undisturbed possession of the throne; but his natural disposition, now freed from all restraint by prosperity, hurried him to the perpetration of the most flagrant acts of tyranny. The dreadful massacre of Stockholm, in which six hundred of the principal nobility were put to the sword under the semblance of law, and amid the rejoicings for his coronation, exhibited such a striking instance of his malignant and implacable character that, on the success of Gustavus Vasa, the spirit of resistance diffused itself rapidly from Sweden to Denmark, where he had exasperated his subjects by repeated oppressions and the confidence which he placed in the lowest and most worthless favourites.*

* The first of these favourites was the infamous Sigrebit, mother of the King's mistress, Divike. This artful woman, who was a native of Holland, and had kept an inn at Bergen, in Norway, even after her daughter's death retained such power that she might be styled Prime Minister. She was the only channel of favour, transacted all affairs of importance, had the care of the finances, superintended the customs of the Sound, and had, in a word, acquired such a wonderful ascendency over the infatuated monarch that her influence was attributed to fascination. On the King's deposition, Sigrebit was so much detested that, from apprehensions of the popular fury, she was conveyed in a chest on board the vessel which carried Christian from Denmark. Holberg adds: "She consoled the King for the loss of his crown by assuring him that, through the Emperor's interest, he could not fail of being chosen Burgomaster of Amsterdam." The particulars of this woman's life, subsequent to her escape from Denmark, are not known.

The other favourite of Christian—no less infamous than the former—was Nicholas Slagelbec, originally a barber of Westphalia, and recommended to the King by his relation Sigrebit. He rendered himself so useful to Christian by his sanguinary advice at the massacre of Stockholm, and by being the instrument of his cruelty, that he was rewarded with the Archbishopric of Lunden. Not long afterwards, however, the King threw on his favourite all the odium of the massacre, and sacrificed him to the public vengeance. The unfortunate victim was first racked, and then burnt alive, exhibiting a melancholy example of what little confidence is to be reposed in the favour of a tyrant.

gratified, thought again of the fair ladies in the gay Court of Matilda. Both master and man seemed to have lost all mournful recollections, when suddenly an event occurred which reminded the Count how

---

"In 1523 Christian was publicly deposed by the States of Denmark, and the crown transferred to his uncle, Frederick, Duke of Holstein. This deposition was neither the consequence of Frederick's intrigues nor of party spirit, but occasioned by the just and universal detestation which pervaded all ranks of people, and had more the appearance of a new election on the demise of the Crown than of a revolution which deprived a despot of his throne. Christian himself was sensible of the general odium, and, though by no means deficient in personal courage, made not the least effort to retain possession of the throne which he had often dishonoured. Quitting Copenhagen, he repaired to Antwerp under the protection of Charles V., whose sister Isabella he had married. After many delays and solicitations at the different Courts of Europe, he at length collected, by the Emperor's assistance, a fleet and army, with which he invaded the Danish dominions; his attempts, however, proving unsuccessful, he fell, in 1542, into the hands of Frederick I., and was consigned a prisoner to the Castle of Sonderborg, a strong fortress in the Isle of Alsen.

"The place of his confinement was a dungeon with a small window, admitting only a few rays of light, through which his provisions were conveyed. Having entered this gloomy cell, with a favourite dwarf, the sole companion of his misery, the door was instantly walled up. Even the horrors of this situation were aggravated by the death of his only son John, who expired at Ratisbon in the fifteenth year of his age, and on the same day on which his father was taken prisoner. The premature decease of this accomplished Prince, whom he tenderly loved, and on whom he rested his sole hopes of enlargement, reduced him to a state of despondency. After much anxious solicitude by what means he could convey intelligence of his dreadful situation to his daughter, the Electress Palatine, and to the Emperor Charles V., the King prevailed on the dwarf to counterfeit sickness and solicit his removal from prison for the recovery of his health. If successful, he was to seize the first opportunity of escaping from the Danish dominions to the Court of the Electress, that

just his first conclusions were, namely, that if he did not go into voluntary exile, he should be banished by regal power.

About five o'clock one morning a Royal courier arrived at the Count's door, announcing the approach

---

she might engage the Emperor to intercede with the King of Denmark for some alleviation of her father's sufferings. The dwarf accordingly feigned sickness, was transferred to the neighbouring town, eluded the vigilance of his guards, and made his escape; but was overtaken at Rensburgh, scarcely a day's journey from the Danish confines.

"Christian, frustrated in this attempt, and deprived of his faithful associate, lingered for some time in total solitude, until an old soldier, worn out with the fatigues of war, offered to share the King's imprisonment. This veteran, being immured in the dungeon, amused the Royal prisoner with various anecdotes on the different princes and generals under whom he had enlisted, and by describing the expeditions and battles in which he had been present; and, as he had served from his earliest youth, was a person of much observation, and by nature loquacious, he assisted in relieving the *tædium* of Christian's captivity. Nor did any event, scarcely the loss of his son, more sensibly affect the deposed Sovereign than the death of this soother of his misery, who expired in the dungeon.

"After a confinement of eleven years in his original cell, Christian was at length removed, through the intercession of Charles V., to a commodious apartment in the same castle, provided with suitable attendants, and indulged with the liberty of visiting in the town, attending Divine service in the public church, and hunting in the neighbouring district. Yet even this change of situation, which had been so long the sole object of his wishes, could not make him forget that he was still a prisoner, the recollection of which affected him occasionally to such a degree, that he would suddenly burst into tears, throw himself on the ground, utter the most bitter lamentations, and continue for some time in a state approaching to insanity. However deservedly odious Christian II. may have appeared in the former parts of his life, yet his subsequent sufferings raise compassion; and it is a pleasing satisfaction to every humane mind that he

of a nobleman from the Court; and almost before Ernestus was dressed, Major Harboe arrived. "I must see Count Rantzau immediately," said the Major. "His excellency is not up." "Then you must conduct me to his bedroom." "Ho! ho!" thought the valet; "the guards are behind to take away the Count,

---

recovered from his despondency and acquiesced in his fate with perfect resignation.

"In 1546, after a confinement of sixteen years and seven months in the Castle of Sonderborg, he was conveyed to the Palace of Callenborg in the Isle of Zetland, a place to which he was particularly attached. Christian III. repaired in person to Assens, received his fallen rival with great marks of attention, and promised him every comfort which could tend to alleviate his situation. These unusual honours, joined to his removal from a place where he had experienced so much misery, and the prospect of again inhabiting his favourite palace, excited transports of joy, and he compared himself to a person recalled from death.*

"Being conducted to Callenborg, he had the satisfaction of finding these promises religiously fulfilled. He survived this happy change ten years, and his mind was so softened by adversity that, old as he was, his death was hastened by affliction for the loss of his benefactor Christian III. He died on the 24th of January, 1559, in the 78th year of his age and in the 36th from the period of his deposition." †

* "Quibus ille non secus animo exhilaratur, *ac si morte extractus, novam lucem intueretur.*"—"Cragii Annal. Christ. III.," p. 324.

† In 1808, amongst a great number of loose paintings not usually exhibited to strangers, there was, in the museum in the King's palace at Stockholm a full-length portrait, large as life, of Christian II. To the best of my recollection the unhappy man was depicted in the garments he had on when, in 1553, he was exhumed, if the expression is allowable, from his dark and dreary dungeon at Sonderborg Castle. His aspect was wild, savage, and gloomy; his habiliments all in tatters. In Mr. Wolffe's "Northern Tour," p. 18, there is a representation of him, dressed in Royal robes and wearing the Order of the Elephant. Allowing for the difference of age and costume, the features appear the same in both representations, from which it is fair to infer it is a good likeness, as it unquestionably is a beautiful engraving. The story of Christian's amour with the fair Dyveke, daughter of Madame Sigrebit, is given at large in Mr. Wolffe's entertaining work. Mr. Coxe (vol. v., p. 181) mentions a striking portrait of Christian II. amongst the pictures of the Danish Kings that were exhibited in the Palace of Fredericksborg.

and, perhaps, myself also!" There was no time for deliberation or delay; the valet, therefore, with fear and trembling, introduced the Major to Count Rantzau in his bedroom. The Count awoke in an instant; and, in the most careless and indifferent manner, told Ernestus to go below, and stay there till he was called; then, without rising, but courteously asking the Major to take a chair, he said, "Now, sir, please to explain the meaning of this unexpected honour?" The coolness of the Count a good deal disconcerted the Major, who began to apologise for the unpleasant errand on which he was arrived. "Pho!" said the Count, "do not mince the matter, man! but tell me, has His Royal Highness the Prince Regent sent for my head? Am I your prisoner?" "That depends," said the Major, "on the answer your excellency pleases to give to these despatches," handing a packet to the Count, who, in a careless way, broke the seal, and running his eye over the contents, without deigning a reply, rang his bell for his valet, to whom he said, "Order out horses and carriages immediately; I am going with Major Harboe to my seat at Aschborg; lose not a moment in getting my carriage ready, and do you follow me, after paying my bills, and bring with you all my luggage." He then ordered coffee and refreshments to be prepared for himself and the Major, and desired that the Royal courier might be hospitably entertained. The cool and tranquil carriage of the Count filled Major Harboe with amazement, not unmixed with chagrin. As they sat at breakfast together the Major said, "Your Excellency sees the alternative—

perpetual banishment from Zealand and Funen, or compliance. Is the alternative not worth a little deliberation?" "Not the delay of one moment," exclaimed the Count; "were this stupid head of mine the object of your journey, instead of my immediate departure for Aschberg, you would have found me just as ready to have submitted to the stroke, rather than submit to set my lawful Sovereign and the Crown Prince aside, and declare Prince Frederick Regent."

The Major could scarcely refrain from smiling at the satirical tone and manner in which Count Rantzau alluded to the gross blunder he had committed. Finding him inexorable, the Major dropped that subject, and the discourse took a different turn; on the part of the Count it was free and unembarrassed, whilst Major Harboe laboured under evident restraint and embarrassment. He had the temerity, however, to remind his host that it was probable, when his excellency arrested Queen Matilda, he little expected he should so soon be surprised in his turn, before he was out of bed, by an order of perpetual exile. The old nobleman told the insolent courtier that he presumed the honour of being the bearer of such a message had in some measure blunted his sensibility. Touched by this reply, he earnestly entreated the Count's pardon, which being granted as soon as asked, and the breakfast over, the Major was surprised to see the carriage drawn up to the door and the Count ready to depart. They crossed the Little Belt that day and slept at Hardersleben. At the end of the next day's journey they reached Sleiswick, and on the third, totally unawares and unexpected, they arrived at Aschberg. As soon as they had got within the castle, the Count bade the Major welcome, and invited him to remain as long as suited his convenience. Although some persons might have taken this as a polite hint, that the sooner he departed the more pleasant it would be, the Major construed it literally, thanking his host with much ceremony, but said he should remain only a day to rest himself. The Count ordered a noble entertainment to be served up in the State rooms. His domestics wore their State liveries. The table and sideboard were covered by massive pieces of plate, curiously wrought, that different monarchs had presented to the illustrious warriors whose achievements rendered the name of Rantzau so renowned in history. His wines were exquisite, and whilst they dined a crowd of rustics, dressed in their best apparel, waited on the Count to welcome him home. A bevy of fine healthy girls brought him nosegays and baskets of their choicest fruits, and the lawn being thrown open, opposite to the magnificent room where the Count and his guest were sitting, they witnessed the affection and gaiety of heart with which a numerous and happy tenantry hailed their lord's return.

The following morning Major Harboe took a formal leave of Count Rantzau, who, just as he mounted one of the finest chargers in the Count's stud, asked him if he had no message to send to the Queen-Mother. "None!" said he; "except you please to tell Her Majesty what a delightful spot Aschberg is, and how its lord was received." Nor did the Major forget to report the enthusiasm with which the old nobleman was hailed by the soldiery on his journey, particularly by the veterans who had served under his command, by whom he appeared to be idolised. It was this popularity with the army that induced the Queen-Mother to court his support with so much earnestness, and the same feeling prevented their instituting any legal process whereby his ruin might have been completed.

The unexpected arrival of Major Harboe at Odensee, and the sudden departure of Rantzau, prevented the latter from apprising Miss Livernet of this affair previous to his setting off for Aschberg. When the Count hired a furnished house for himself, he took a smaller one for his mistress, sending his valet, under the name of Kruger, to Copenhagen, to request her return with the messenger. Ernestus reached the Princens Palace unobserved, and found Miss Livernet well in health and delighted with the message, and not a little uneasy on her protector's account, who was extremely unpopular in the city and anathematised by the Court, his fall and banishment having excited vast surprise and little commiseration. The reigning party were generally disliked, but they were also feared, and with that *respect*, which they shared in common with Satan, they were forced to be content. Miss Livernet and her waiting-maid returned with Ernestus, under the name of Mr. Kruger, to Odensee, and shortly after her father and brother followed. The Count was rather embarrassed with this addition to his suite, and asked his mistress if her father was a member of the Burgher-guard? "Yes, my lord, a sergeant." "Most excellent," said he; "then he shall wear a sergeant's uniform of my regiment!" Thus the old tailor was metamorphosed into a Holstein sergeant; but the good folks in the neighbourhood soon conjectured that he was more obliged for the Count's favour to his daughter's beauty than his military services. The brother of Miss Livernet was a capital dancer; but her connection with Count Rantzau reached him, and he was discharged. Being apprehensive of a persecution, or desirous of billeting themselves upon the Count, the father and son followed their daughter and sister to Odensee.

Such was the state of affairs on Count Rantzau's sudden departure. Ernestus knew he was to escort Miss Livernet to Aschberg, but he had not received any directions respecting her father and her brother. He, therefore, suggested that they should embark in a vessel then ready to sail for Lubeck, which city was only a few hours' ride from Aschberg, and there await further orders: Miss Livernet's maid preferring a sail through the maze of islands, or the company of the younger Livernet, went by water to Lubeck; and Ernestus had the felicity of escorting the beautiful young mistress of Count Rantzau from Odensee to Aschberg. The weather was delightful, the journey picturesque, the travellers young and pleased with each other. They did not reach Aschberg quite so soon as the Count expected; but they assured him that so many horses had fallen lame, wheels had come off, and accidents had happened, that it was astonishing they arrived as soon as they did!

They found the old Count in high glee, his castle full of company, and nothing but feasting and revelry talked of as they approached the vicinity of Aschberg. The Count gave the reins to magnificence and pleasure. Balls, concerts, masquerades, and rural sports succeeded each other, at which not merely the nobility in the neighbourhood assisted, but the wealthy sons of traffic from Hamburg, Altena, and Lubeck. Such revelry and sober dissipation had never been seen before, except on Matilda's recent visit, and Aschberg seemed more to resemble the country palace of a favourite minister of State than the forced residence of a banished man.

I have not spared the Count's vices. They were great and numerous. I ought not, therefore, to omit his virtues, amongst which his generosity held the foremost rank. He might have been regarded as a model of what a landlord should be if he had not employed his fascinating manners, his polished address, his rank, and his gold to corrupt the wives and daughters of his vassals. From his earliest youth he had given himself up to amatory pursuits. It was said of him by the ladies of Hamburg that the Count could never be forgotten at Aschberg as long as the lineaments of his face were discernible amongst his vassals.[1]

He was delighted to see his farmers dress and live better than their neighbours. With all his errors, and

---

[1] This formed the blackest trait in the character of Count Rantzau. He carried vice and profligacy into the cabins of his poor illiterate bondsmen. It could scarcely be called seduction, for those who yielded were little better than his slaves.

the vast power that his high rank and the accursed feudal system gave him, he was never known to oppress his tenants, or sanction any act of fiscal injustice towards them.

He possessed several lordships besides Aschberg. He caused all his vassals to be apprised of his ensuing departure for a distant country, never to return; and also that it was his wish, before he went away, to secure all his tenants in their present possessions by granting them long leases, which, by the payment of a very moderate fine, might be renewed. He forgave all arrears to those who were poor or had large families, increased the farms of those who had too little land, and, to encourage them to plant fruit trees and timber, he covenanted that, at the expiration of their lease, if their lords would not purchase at a fair valuation, they might remove the trees. As a Count of the Roman Empire, he possessed the power of life and death over his vassals; but, as a man, he abhorred the brutal and degrading system. He held a local court of justice at Aschberg, not to enforce those odious rights, but to ratify and confirm all the grants he had made, so that his successor should not have it in his power, were he so inclined, to harass or oppress them. This solemnity over, he gave his vassals a general invitation to his castle; he had temporary sheds erected for their reception. He gave them such substantial feasts as the English barons are said to have displayed in days of yore. Tents and marquees were provided for the accommodation of the higher classes; a rustic fair was held, that was crowded with bands of music, players, and vendors of all sorts of bagatelles. Such was the last splendid *fête* which this magnificent nobleman gave ere he took his last leave of his native home.

These festivities over, the Count packed up the massive family plate that had accumulated for centuries. The heavy frames of solid silver were taken from the large Venetian plates of glass that adorned the State apartments. The valuables of all sorts were removed, great part of which he sent to Hamburg to be converted into cash, and the funds remitted to Amsterdam and Paris. One of his last labours was to examine his papers, and destroy those he did not wish to be seen. This was a painful task; for it brought once more under his eye the warm and grateful epistles written by the unhappy Struensee, when he looked up to Count Rantzau as his friend and patron. The sight of those papers touched his heart; nor could he help feeling remorse now that time had abated his resentments, and he was about to go into perpetual exile. If the firm texture of his mind had not been his shield, he must have dreaded an assassin in every stranger, as scarcely a day passed when the Copenhagen post arrived that he did not receive anonymous letters couched in the most opprobrious terms, and threatening him with death! These, whilst he lived in the midst of his tenants, he totally disregarded; but it struck him that he might be pursued abroad by assassins employed by Juliana or her cabal, who might be glad to be rid of one who knew so much of their wickedness; he therefore determined to travel *incognito*, and, if possible, remain unknown.

Just before he set off from the spot where he drew his first breath, he called his valet before him, and asked, had he any objection to travel with him to France and Italy, promising to provide for him in his will if he accepted his offer, and conducted himself as he hitherto had done. Ernestus readily agreed. The Count had already made Miss Livernet independent; and he gave her the offer of quitting, or going into exile with him, telling her, as he wished to travel really *incognito*, if she accompanied him, it must be in man's attire. The Count was agreeably surprised to find that her only fears were that she should be left behind. Understanding that the Count had sold his plate and other valuables, the generous girl offered him back, not only the money he had given her, but all that she had saved as first opera-dancer. The old gentleman pressed her to his bosom, gave her a hearty kiss, and told her that all he wished was her company, if agreeable; and as to the sale of his plate, he did it to save the purses of his vassals.[1]

After he should have arranged his affairs at Amsterdam, the Count intended to assume the name of Breitenburg,[2] and that Miss Livernet should pass as

---

[1] Amongst the measures adopted by Count Rantzau to promote the future welfare of his vassals, it appears singular he did not at once emancipate them. Perhaps he feared if he did so it might have been construed as sedition by his political enemies, and thus have injured the peasantry.

[2] There is, or was, a castle of that name not far from Itzehoe which formerly belonged to the Counts Rantzau, and was formerly their principal residence.

his nephew. He also designed to leave Aschberg privately; but the anxious vassals kept such vigilant watch that, touched by their affection rather than influenced by pride, he set off in his State carriage and liveries, attended by his numerous tenantry on horseback and foot, amongst whom there was scarcely one but really felt regret at the Count's departure. When he arrived at the confines of his estates the doors of his coach were opened to admit those who pleased to take a personal leave, when a scene ensued as would be difficult to describe, the grateful creatures embracing the Count's legs and knees, kissing his hands, and bedewing them with their tears. Full two hours were passed in this melancholy ceremony. Many fell on their knees by the roadside to pray for blessings on their generous protector; and when at last the cavalcade proceeded, the grateful rustics stood uncovered till a turn of the road excluded any further view. Such were the honours spontaneously paid to Count Rantzau by his vassals on his going into perpetual banishment.

Shortly after the Count had arrived at Hamburg he was insulted by a Danish officer, who was in hopes that he might thereby promote his interest at Court. The Count was, however, so much respected by the burgomasters, who had not forgotten the services he rendered their city when seized by Frederick V., that the officer was arrested, escorted to the gates of Altena,[1]

---

[1] "Al-te-na!" (*i.e.*, "much too near") said a Danish King as he surveyed the spot whereon Altena was afterwards built. The King spoke in reference to Hamburg, to which exclamation the name was owing.

and forbade to return whilst the Count remained in Hamburg. Notwithstanding this protection by the ruling magistrates, and the popularity excited by his recent and past hospitalities, Count Rantzau perceived, wherever he went, that his appearance excited hostile feelings. One morning, when the Count felt more than commonly low and desponding, his young valet said, after much hesitation, "I am afraid what I am about to tell your excellency may displease you; at all events I know too well it will give you pain. It relates to a solemn promise I made to my late master: may I proceed?" Count Rantzau coloured. Ernestus thought he was angry, and stopped speaking. The Count, who was daily becoming nervous, struck by the solemn tone and manner of his servant, felt the blood rush to his furrowed cheeks, and seeing the effect it had on Ernestus, with the greatest mildness he encouraged him to proceed. With his eyes full of tears, and, in a mournful tone of voice, Ernestus thus obeyed: "As we are now out of Denmark, and not more than a day's journey from Zell, I could not reconcile it to my conscience to fail in the performance of a sacred and voluntary promise. I am sure you harbour no resentment against the dead, and your excellency has often in my hearing expressed respect and commiseration towards the Queen." The Count nodded assent, holding his left hand across his eyes. "Upon my first interview with my master after our arrest, I was, of course, violently affected, and not at my own captivity alone. He was sitting on the side of his bed, his head resting on his hand, looking the image of despair. My presence seemed to revive him a little. He called me to him, embraced me, and, resting his burning forehead on my shoulder, he kissed my cheek! I was so affected, I sank down at his feet, in which posture, in a few minutes afterwards, I handed him his purse. Whilst he leant and wept over me, he slipped from his bosom a miniature picture given him by the Queen. It was her own likeness as she arrived in Denmark. The Count whispered softly in my ear, 'If I escape death, preserve this for me; if I perish, as I expect I shall, convey it to the Queen.' I put it in a private pocket in my waistcoat. When I was searched it was not found. Here it is," said Ernestus, handing to the Count a portrait, painted, I believe, by Reynolds, mounted in gold and set with brilliants. The Count looked at it with strong emotions: respect, commiseration and remorse were visible in his countenance. He turned pale as death, whilst the cheeks of Ernestus were covered with tears. The Count gazed mournfully on the portrait for a minute or more, and then exclaimed: " Unhappy lady, I solemnly take God to witness that if my treatment of you was harsh, my motives were merciful; but thy maledictions are fulfilling! Already I am thrown down by those whom I set up! Like thee, Matilda, am I in exile. Thy fall excited the warmest sympathy; mine, universal satisfaction. To avoid the finger of public scorn, or the less poignant stiletto of the assassin, I shall be reduced to lay aside my name. Even my ashes shall find no sepulchre, except in a foreign land. No sculptured stone must tell whose bones rest there, or execrations will pursue me even beyond the grave;

and perhaps my remains, torn from the tomb, may, like Struensee's, be scattered and devoured by the fowls of the air!" Never, at any previous moment, had Ernestus seen the Count so extremely agitated. Some minutes elapsed ere he spoke to Ernestus. At last, in a subdued tone, he said to his weeping valet, "Go, liebe karl,[1] leave me, and return when the bell rings." It was a full hour before he was called. The Count was calm, but his countenance bore more legible marks of the mental sufferings by which his bosom was rent. "You told me," said he, mildly, "it was a portrait of the Queen; but you did not name the little cherub whose likeness is concealed within the crystal, under the crown and cipher wrought of the Queen's hair?" "I did not know of any such thing, your excellency," said Ernestus. "Then see it now, my poor fellow," said the Count. "I am sure it will present an object that will touch thy susceptible heart." He then moved a secret spring, and the astonished young man saw a miniature of the young Princess Louisa Augusta, her celestial features dressed in smiles and surrounded by budding roses—the likeness so strong, so exquisitely drawn and painted, that its freshness, animation, and delicacy seemed almost to equal the beautiful and innocent original. "It is the face of a cherub delineated by the pencil of an angel," said the Count. "Then that angel was the Queen, your excellency; for I well remember one morning, as I was dressing the Queen's

---

[1] An expression answering in English to "my good fellow" if addressed to an equal it means "my dear fellow."

hair,[1] that Lady Göhler asked to see the likeness of the young Princess, and I am sure this is it; but it was not set." "How do you know it was painted by Queen Matilda?" "Because on Lady Göhler saying it was executed in a manner superior to the best style of any professional artist, the Queen replied, 'If an artist loved his infant as tenderly as I love mine, natural affection would prompt him to excel himself.'" "Then it is hers indeed," exclaimed the Count, "and I am weary of existence! I am half-inclined to go to Zell, hand this precious relic to the Queen, and end in her presence a life that is insupportable!" The remainder of that day he spent in his chamber, and told his valet to be ready to set off for Zell the following morning. Alarmed at his expressions, Ernestus went to the fair Livernet and told her confidentially what had passed that moment between him and the Count. She shook her head, and said, "Depend on it, ——" (calling him by his surname), "the arrest of Queen Matilda will lead to the death of the Count. I know his heart is secretly a prey to the most deadly anguish. With all his faults he is generous, munificent and kind. He has been outwitted by a fiend. I agreed to travel with him because, in the first place, I really respect him, and would not

---

[1] Ernestus was reckoned the first friseur in the Court; and often dressed the Queen's hair if her hair-dresser, M. Andreas Burchas, were indisposed. Struensee was extremely particular as to his hair, which he wore dressed in the same manner as the Queen's. His toilette was magnificent; and he was profuse in the use of the richest and most costly perfumes: in every point he was an epicure and voluptuary.

appear that mercenary being that was solely attracted by his rank and high estate, and who fled when adversity fell upon him. I have witnessed paroxysms that have made me shudder. In those moments I have found myself able to subdue his rage and recall his reasoning powers. That forms a second cause why I have agreed to accompany the Count in his undefined travels, and in the disguise of a man." She might have added a third, more potent, perhaps, than either, *i.e.*, her secret attachment to Ernestus, whose handsome face and figure and kind disposition had made a complete conquest of her heart.

Miss Livernet felt more uneasiness than she chose to express. Her confidence in the discernment of the blue-eyed Norwegian was not small. She went with a palpitating bosom to the Count; and suddenly assuming a gaiety that was a stranger to her heart, ran smiling into his room. She found him with a pistol in his hand that he appeared to be loading. His looks were wild and haggard. Turning his glaring eye-balls towards the door, he asked her sternly how she dare approach unbidden and without notice? Instead of reply, she rushed to his bosom, and throwing her arms round his neck, entreated him to leave Hamburg, and not risk his life by a duel with that wretched parasite who hoped for *éclat* and preferment as the reward of his insolence. "Your character for courage, my dear Count," said the artful pleader (who marked the intended suicide, but glanced only at a duel), "is too well established to suffer by your refusing to meet every desperado who may dare to challenge you."

The Count, deceived in thinking Sophia Livernet was deceived, suffered her to return the pistols to the case whence he had thus taken them. Kissing off the tear that glistened in her bright eyes, the volatile old nobleman forgot, in the caresses of that fascinating girl, the dreadful purpose he had in view when she entered; for, goaded to desperation by the storm of passions that raged in his bosom, he had in a frantic moment seized his pistols, and if his faithful guardian had not drawn the charges from his pistols when he returned to his quarters the night before, his own hands had terminated his existence.

The accomplishments of Miss Livernet were not confined to her graceful dancing; she had a sweet voice, and was enthusiastically devoted to music. A pedal harp stood in the room, and some music books lay strewn on a table. She took her seat at the harp, and played some plaintive German airs, accompanied by her dulcet voice, that drove away the melancholy which had filled the Count's bosom, who was a votary of Apollo as well as of Venus. Fascinated by the skill and pathos of the fair girl, the enraptured nobleman clasped her in his arms, and said, with vehemence, "Sophia! thou art dearer to me than all my possessions beside! Say, my beloved, how can I recompense thee? Speak boldly, for were it to make thee Countess Rantzau, I would not refuse!" Smiling at his gallantry, and, perhaps, exulting in the power of beauty and music, she said, "Promise me, then, on your word and honour, never more, be your trials what they may, to think of suicide." The Count was amazed. In a moment he recollected the circumstance of his pistols being unloaded when he thought to have found them charged; and he felt that to her vigilance he was indebted for his life. For some moments he was unable to speak. At last he said, in a solemn tone, "I promise thee, noblest of women, never to raise my hand against my life; and if you will accept that hand, thou shalt be my countess."

Sophia thanked him for the first part of his promise, and with ineffable sweetness told him she would rather possess his love as his mistress than run the risk of being despised as his wife. "Reflect, my lord," said she, "on the ridicule and disgrace you must encounter were you to marry me, and have a *tailor* for your father-in-law! I should be cursed as a wicked, cunning jade; and, ten to one, if you died first, your heirs would find means to annul the marriage and strip me of my fine title! No, my dear Count, I dare not venture to become your wife. Only yesterday morning, dressed as a country girl with a basket of flowers, I followed among three or four blooming lasses into your august presence. Because I had changed the colour of my hair, rouged my cheeks, and learned my *plaat Duitsch*[1] pretty well, my sagacious lord did not know me! yet you gave me the preference, kissed me till I trembled for my rouge, and told me to be at the back door at eight o'clock; and here, your excellency, are the necklace

---

[1] The language spoken by the country people who live in the vicinity of Hamburg is called *plaat Duitsch*, *i.e.*, low German.

and the ear-rings that you then gave me." The Count could scarcely believe his eyes. "What the devil does all this mean?" said he. "Were you indeed the flower-girl whose bewitching eyes and well-formed bosom caught my attention?" "Yes, indeed, my lord, I am that very girl over whose virtue you thought to triumph by tempting her avarice. As your mistress, my lord Count, I can bear these *youthful* sallies; but, as a countess, I should, perhaps, trouble you with complaints or remonstrances. I might say, if at twenty years of age I were content with a lover of threescore, I could not tell why my husband required a dozen flower-girls to attend his toilette every morning, and should soon offend you; and shall, therefore, never accept the honour of being your countess!" He laughed heartily at her lively wit. No longer thinking of Matilda, the portraits, or of suicide, he that day gave himself up to the fascinating girl who stepped a minuet more gracefully than any woman in Denmark, and to please the Count, exerted her talents to the utmost. She put on the costume in which the day before she had beguiled him of his trinkets! She sang, she danced, she played; she encouraged him to smoke. He drank a whole bottle of Château Margaux. At last he sang some favourite duets with his attractive mistress, and, giving the reins to dalliance, swore that he was still the happiest man alive, and never more would suffer the blue devils to get the upper hand of him! In the course of the evening he told her of that secret she already knew from Ernestus; and the tenderhearted girl, as she surveyed the portraits, dropped a tear on the highly-wrought trinket. She strove, however, to suppress her emotions, and, in a careless tone, said, "You see I could deceive your excellency. Shall I carry this precious picture to the Queen? She will not recollect one whom she never saw except in a ballet." The idea pleased the versatile Count, who, within the last twenty-four hours, had experienced the pangs of the fellest remorse and the thrilling delights of refined sensuality. Looking archly in her face, he said, "Shall Ernestus attend you? I know you have a good opinion of that youth, and perhaps would rather be his wife than my countess?" The playful girl parried this unexpected hit by saying that, next to his lordship's company, none other would be more welcome. Ernestus was delighted with the charge. He dressed himself in a handsome suit of mourning. Miss Livernet arrayed her lovely person in the picturesque habit of a wealthy Hamburg merchant's daughter, and they set off on their destination time enough to reach it ere night. They crossed the dreary tracts of sand, and having arrived at Zell, they went to the principal inn. After having taken some refreshment, the young travellers, full of the interesting objects of their mission, went to reconnoitre the present residence of Queen Matilda, in whose praise the people of the inn were profusely lavish; and not less so of their execrations against those who had occasioned her misfortunes. "It is well the Count is not here, Ernestus, to hear this," said Miss Livernet. "It is well, indeed," the young man replied; "I often shudder at hearing such terrible things as are said of him at Hamburg, particularly by the English." " I wish," said Sophia, " our dear Count was safe out of Hamburg, for I think he would not be in as great danger anywhere else." Ernestus shook his head, and said the presentiment on his mind was that he would come to an untimely end. Just as Ernestus said this, the guide who went before them made a halt, and told them they were arrived near the palace, and asked if he should enquire for anyone within ? This intelligence arrested their discourse. They saw they were arrived at the outskirts of the town, and that before them appeared a large fortification surrounded by a broad moat full of water. All was still and silent. Dark masses of building appeared to rise within above the ramparts. All they heard, save their own voices, was the heavy tread of a couple of sentinels upon the drawbridge. The moon burst forth in great splendour as a dark cloud passed away, and for a few moments showed the form of the palace before them. It appeared old, decayed and gloomy. " In what part of this pile does the Queen reside ? " said Ernestus. " In the square building in the centre. It was once a very grand palace, before the last Duke surrendered the Duchy of Zell to his brother, George I., King of England." " Grand palace ! " said Ernestus ; " and is this the residence of her who was mistress of Christian-borg ! " " You are a Dane," said the guide ; " do you wish to see your Queen ? She is very fond of seeing her subjects, particularly if they bring her any news of her children." " Then, sir, we have news she will be glad to hear," said Miss Livernet. Ernestus then asked the guide what Danish attendants the Queen had with her? "Not many, I should hope," said the Hanoverian, proudly; "but here comes one who can tell you more!" As he said this, Stuart came up, and, in a tone of pleasure and surprise, said, "My God! is it possible! is this not Ernestus?" The meeting was alike unexpected and agreeable. Ernestus told him that the lady with him was from Hamburg, and invited Stuart to their quarters. The two domestics had, of course, a world of questions to ask and answer, and the result was, that after Stuart was made acquainted with the purport of their journey, he advised Ernestus not to appear unless the Queen enquired for him. "She has now," said he, "become tranquil, resigned, and in some measure reconciled to her condition. The sight of you may make all her wounds bleed afresh; let, therefore, Miss Kruger see her first, to give this valued present. If the Queen asks to see you, this lady will say that you are near. A cousin of hers, a Princess of Saxe-Gotha, is now with Her Majesty. They are just returned from a tour to see the Castle of Ahlden, about twenty miles distant, where the wife of George I. was confined so many years. Neither the country, nor the castle, nor the sad history connected with it are calculated to cheer her spirits. You would scarcely know her, so greatly is she changed; and this visit, though it will please her, will, I know, almost break her heart. Come you to-morrow morning about nine: I will tell her that a lady from Hamburg wishes to see her alone and on very particular business." Then, looking kindly at Sophia, the faithful domestic said,

"You need no better passport, madam, than your own beautiful face."

Sophia Livernet, dressed in her Hamburg costume (which was rich and highly becoming), was at the portal of the palace at the appointed time. Stuart was there waiting. He conducted the fair stranger through various apartments that bore evident marks of past grandeur and present decay. In one that was furnished in the modern style he asked her to wait whilst he went to announce her arrival.

He returned instantly; and such was the agitation of the Queen and her eagerness to see this fair stranger—of whose beauty and graceful demeanour Stuart had spoken so highly—that she met her near the door of her breakfast-room. In the kindest tone of voice and benignity of aspect, the graceful Queen encouraged Sophia to speak without fear or reserve.

In this interview Miss Livernet was no actress. Her intelligent countenance showed that her bosom laboured with some important secret. Her modest look and respectful demeanour were pledges for the sincerity of her goodwill towards the august personage she had the honour of beholding. The Queen was struck no less by her beauty than with the elegance of her form and the propriety of her carriage. Had she been bred in a Court she could not have shown more true politeness. Taking her by the hand, Matilda said to her in German, "Stuart tells me you come to bring me tidings of my children. Do not keep me in suspense, but tell me, are they well? How is my dear boy and my darling Louisa Augusta?" As the

Queen spoke, Sophia dropped on one knee. With her head half-averted, not to disturb Her Majesty with too rude a gaze, she gently held towards her the miniature of her child. The moment her eye caught the well-known portrait of her infant, she exclaimed, "Heavens, it is my Louisa! Where! when! how did you procure this portrait? Tell me, ere my heart bursts with expectation." "It was given by a deceased nobleman to his valet, and by that person consigned to my hands to be delivered to Your Majesty." "A thousand and a thousand thanks, sweet girl, for the precious gift. See how the innocent smiles at her unhappy mother! Never whilst I have life shall this dear image be parted from my bosom." During this time the beauteous stranger remained kneeling. Presently the Queen, whose emotions nearly overpowered her, exclaimed, "Forgive me, young lady, for suffering you to remain in that posture; let a grateful mother thus thank you for the most welcome gift that you could have brought—my babes alone excepted." Saying this, she raised her to her bosom and kissed her cheek; then, leading her to a chair, the Queen commanded her to be seated, and she showed the truest sense of politeness by instantly obeying.

The Queen shed tears in profusion—they relieved her full-fraught heart. She kept kissing the picture of her infant with more real devotion than ever the most zealous Catholic felt for the relic of a deity or saint. Then, looking wistfully at Miss Livernet, she said, her lips quivering as she spoke, "How did this escape the lynx-eyed vigilance of my destroyers? Where is the valet? Ah! what a dreadful hour that was when last I saw him! My heart has since had many trials, and this is not the least painful. I am now," continued she, "a veteran in sorrow, though so young in years. Fate has crowded into the last ten months of my life more misery than, if spun out to the length of a century, might have embittered every hour!" Then, adverting to Ernestus, she said, "He must have run great risks in saving this for me. I wish to see him—and yet, perhaps, I ought not, on account of the recollections it will occasion." Fixing her eyes on the young stranger, Matilda suddenly exclaimed, "Surely I have seen your face before. Were you ever in Copenhagen?" "I have been there, madam, and have had the honour of seeing Your Majesty at the Opera." "Ah!" said she, rapidly, "that is it. You resemble a favourite dancer belonging to the Opera." Matilda then asked if Ernestus was still in Denmark? and was told he was in Zell. "I respect his delicacy in sending the portrait by a female," said the Queen; then taking from her side a gold watch and superb appendages, gave it to her fair guest, saying, "Accept of this as a memorial of my esteem. Before you leave Zell I wish to converse with you again; and should you ever stand in need of a friend, you may reckon on me as one who will never fail you. Tell Ernestus," said she, "I will see him two hours hence." The Queen then rose, and her fair guest, in a lowly posture, with equal grace and reverence, kissed her offered hand; Matilda

13—2

saluting Sophia on the cheek. Stuart then conducted Miss Livernet to the apartment of Madame ——, a lady of her household, who kindly pressed her to take refreshments, discoursing with her in the most affable manner, while Stuart went to prepare Ernestus for the approaching interview.

The valet felt infinitely embarrassed on account of being in the service of Count Rantzau. He had not been candid enough to tell that circumstance to Stuart, and he was indecisive how to act, and half-inclined to conceal it. He was undetermined till after he found himself in the presence of his Queen.

Matilda received him seated on a sofa. She turned her head aside, covering her fair face with a handkerchief; her whole frame shook, and she appeared almost suffocated with painful feelings. Full ten minutes elapsed ere she became sufficiently composed to ask him questions, and the valet, not less agitated, could scarcely reply. Her first questions were about her children. Matilda looked much disappointed when she learnt that he had no recent intelligence to give. She then commanded him to relate his own adventures. In a tremulous tone he narrated the leading incidents that had occurred. After several questions of inferior interest—waiting, as it were, to acquire firmness to put *that* which had its fibres entwined in her heart's core—Matilda, in a manner indescribably touching and mournful, said, " I have been told that recourse was had to actual torture to force *him* to accuse me. Tell me, Ernestus, without duplicity or reserve, do you believe that my merciless and unrelenting enemies really had recourse to an expedient so wicked and so terrific?" Her head was bowed down as she asked this question so important and so painful. Her fair bosom rose and fell, undulating from intensity of feeling; her voice, scarcely audible, was tremulous and subdued. From her fine eyes tears of shame, sorrow and remorse fell copiously; and though the most vivid recollections of the lost, fallen, guilty Struensee filled her whole heart and shook her lovely frame, though his *name* quivered on her lips, her tongue gave it not utterance. Full of sensibility, and weighed down by emotions almost too powerful to be sustained, Ernestus, in a manner peculiarly solemn and emphatical, embraced this opportunity to do justice to the unhappy Struensee, by saying, "Yes, gracious Queen, I do most firmly believe that my late unfortunate master was actually tortured by the application of thumb-screws before he could be wrought on to act as Your Majesty's enemies desired; and he was menaced, if he refused, with the cruellest tortures to which a human being could be subjected." As he spoke, Matilda raised her drooping head, her mental suffering evidently abated and her sorrow soothed by this communication. The Queen clasped her hands, and, with mild composure, exclaimed, "I forgive him! with all my heart, I forgive him! and I hope that God will forgive him also! Count Rantzau treated me very harshly; but he had a desperate undertaking to accomplish, and I provoked him to the utmost of my power. I am endeavouring to forgive him also. He was once my friend. I hear that he has fallen into disgrace—is banished to his estates—and is now at Hamburg. The cause of his disgrace is variously stated; perhaps you can tell me the real cause?" "That I can, my gracious Queen. The Queen-Mother, Juliana, General Eichstedt, General Kohler Banner and M. Guldberg were all agreed to make Prince Frederick Regent during the life of the King, my Sovereign, and of the Crown Prince. Without the concurrence of Count Rantzau they dared not make the attempt. The Count, madam, conceiving that the King and the Crown Prince might both be set aside, or that something bad might befall them, sternly refused his assent. He reproached those persons who had proposed and seconded the measure as being traitors to their King and country: this, Your Majesty may believe me, was the immediate cause of Count Rantzau's disgrace and exile!" The Queen heard him with amazement; incredulity was marked on her fine, sorrow-stricken features. "What!" said she, "do you tell me that he who tore me from my palace, my husband and my babes, who has blasted mine honour and destroyed my peace of mind for ever, has been the saviour of my husband and my son, and for their sakes braved the resentment of that cruel woman who reigns in my place?" "It is true, my gracious Queen; all this has Count Rantzau done!" Matilda, with strong passion, exclaimed, "Incomprehensible man! if this prove true, I can forgive him all the injuries that he has done me! Not long would my sweet Frederick live if his cruel uncle were once declared Regent! But are you not deceived?—how did you acquire the knowledge of those important facts?" "From the Count's own lips, gracious Queen. I attended his Excellency in his carriage as he returned in disgrace from the Palace of Fredericksborg. He exclaimed, 'I have twice saved my King and country in the hour of peril; I will save it a third time!'[1] He never returned to Court again. Towards my unfortunate master he generally expressed hatred, but of Your Majesty he has ever spoken with the utmost respect." The Queen paused for a short time, and, in rather a hasty manner, said, "How came you, who appear to deplore your late master's wretched fate, to take service with Count Rantzau?" To this question Ernestus replied by telling the truth, to which he was tempted by the altered manner in which she spoke of Count Rantzau. The Queen said, "My inclinations would have led me to take you into my service, but for the constant recurrence of things I wish for ever to banish from my memory." She sat absorbed in thought; at last she said, "The facts you have communicated to me give a new phase to the part that Count Rantzau has acted, and it helps to forward my wish to tear from my heart all animosity against him; yet, detesting, as I know he did, the disposition of the Queen-Mother, how was it possible, without becoming her confederate in my ruin, he could ever think of coalescing with her? Tell me, without reserve, what you know on this subject." Ernestus hesitated, and

---

[1] These were the Count's words as he left the palace. He alluded to the hand he had in the fall of Peter III., by which the invasion of Denmark was averted, and next to the arrest of Count Struensee.

remained silent. "Do not feel any dread of hurting my feelings. Tell me his real motives, if you know them." "I verily believe, most gracious Queen, that Count Rantzau knew that a plan was in agitation to take the life of the King!" At these words the tears burst from her eyes; she wrung her hands, and, appealing to the Almighty, declared her ignorance of any such intention. "It must be," said she, "an artifice of the Count's to cover his malicious designs." The valet was again silent. "Am I to think," said she, in a tone of agony, "that you believed him? Did you ever hear or see anything to induce you to think that any such design existed?" "If I must reply, it is, and it has for upwards of a year past been my opinion, that if the two Counts had not fallen as they did, the King would not have long survived. Count Rantzau, madam, ever felt tenderness and compassion towards Your Majesty, and I sincerely believe it was to save Your Majesty's life he had you removed from Copenhagen!" This avowal evidently wrung her heart; she gave vent to her feelings in a shower of tears. "Oh, God!" said Matilda, "in what a fearful labyrinth have I been entangled! I am, and ever shall be, wretched; but what would have been my state if such dreadful designs were really cherished and had been executed! You have been," continued the Queen, "too often a witness of my errors for me to hesitate thus to humble myself before you. When you return to Hamburg, tell Count Rantzau that I thank him for his efforts to save my son and his Sovereign; and tell him, too, that with my whole soul I fully and freely forgive him." Ernestus could not contain his satisfaction at this noble conquest of herself. "I believe in my heart, madam," said he, "that the Count has never enjoyed one happy hour since that fatal day. Your generous forgiveness will restore peace to his bosom and take a mountain from off his mind." She then entered into an enquiry as to the circumstances of Ernestus, and told him in all cases of adversity to apply to her, presenting him with a purse, that she told him was the work of her own hands, containing a hundred guineas. He had then the honour of kissing her hand, and took his leave

When he repaired to Stuart and Sophia, his looks showed how powerfully his mind had been agitated; nor did he keep them long in suspense. "Thanks be to God," said Ernestus, fervently, "the dear Queen has forgiven Count Rantzau, and has authorised me to assure his Excellency of her full and entire forgiveness! How greatly," said he, "is the Queen changed! her sufferings have indeed not been lost on her. The sedate and melancholy cast of countenance that she has attained renders her beauty more striking, she is much less corpulent, and altogether her appearance is infinitely improved." "Did the Queen name Struensee to you?" said Stuart. "Never once," replied Ernestus. "She spoke of him, but his name never passed her lips." "Nor have I heard her name the guilty and unfortunate man," rejoined Stuart, "since her residence here, where, without flattery, I can affirm she is idolised by all who witness her piety and tranquil resignation."

During the absence of Ernestus, Sophia explained to his friend his present situation with Count Rantzau.

The rest of this day they spent in seeing Zell and its vicinity. On the following morning Miss Livernet was ordered to attend the Queen, who asked her many questions respecting Count Rantzau, saying, "I cannot help thinking that you have moved in a higher sphere of life than your present costume, graceful and becoming as it is, announces." "I can endure dissimulation no longer. I am not, indeed, my beloved and injured Queen, what I seem to be, nor worthy to appear in your august presence; but I come with a heart filled with love and reverence towards you!" The Queen looked earnestly in her face, and with a smile of the truest benevolence said, "At last I recognise in you Mademoiselle Livernet, whom Count Rantzau induced to leave the Opera! I really thought I knew your fine features the moment I saw you; and now let me bid you welcome in your proper name." From this generous girl Matilda learnt enough fully to convince her that Rantzau was truly penitent for all the indignities he had occasioned, and that to his unshaken fidelity her son probably owed his life; "for," said she, "not only did Count Rantzau enter his protest in the Journal of the Council of State, but he sent a copy to Stockholm and London, and to each of the leading nobles in Denmark, the Duchies, and in Norway." The Queen was so pleased with these proofs of attachment to her husband and her son that she conquered her resentment so completely as to write to the Count, assuring him of her entire forgiveness, thanking him for his recent exertions in favour of her beloved Frederick and his father, and adding, if he wished to retire to Great Britain, she would write to London to prepare the way for his being received.

The first and the last anxiety of this amiable penitent (for such she really was) related to her absent children. Sensible of this, and willing to pour all the consolation into her bosom that was possible, Mademoiselle Livernet related to the young Queen the adventure that befell Ernestus with the skipper, old Peter Nielsen, who took the Count in his yacht from Copenhagen to Warrenborg. The Queen recollected the circumstance, and commanded Sophia to proceed, who then told Matilda that she thought this old skipper would be the most secure channel whereby to receive, from time to time, authentic intelligence of her children. The Queen eagerly embraced the idea. Miss Livernet wrote to a confidential friend of hers—a lady who was related to the head nurse of the young Princess—to meet her at Hamburg, assuring the Queen that she would not go till everything should be arranged to secure to her a regular correspondence—"till time and circumstances permit Your Majesty once more to meet your children and re-ascend your throne." "Oh, if that happy day should ever come! But," continued Matilda, mournfully, "it cannot be! I am fallen, fallen, never to rise again!" Such were the last emphatic words on that subject spoken to Miss Livernet. When Ernestus and his fair companion returned to Hamburg they found the old Count very impatient, and not a little under the influence of "the blue devils," not knowing what construction to put on their long stay; but when his beauteous mistress told him in what manner they had been received, and when she handed to him the brief but comprehensive letter written by the well-known hand of the Queen, he kissed it with a devotion and gratitude scarcely less ardent than Matilda's caresses of the portrait he had returned. "Now," said the Count, "I can brave the finger of public scorn, and the dagger of the assassin; I can live tranquilly, and meet death without terror."

The joy and agitation of the Count was extremely great. Sophia felt towards him a strong and grateful friendship; she flattered herself that he might give up his romantic project of travelling to Italy *incognito*. She felt deep aversion to assuming male attire, and therefore strove with all the blandishments of which she was mistress to induce him to accept Queen Matilda's mediation, and retire to Great Britain. The Count heard her with silent attention, and smiling, said, "You have not, my Sophia, duly considered the subject, or you would never advise Count Rantzau to insult, by his presence, the Sovereign whose sister his hand hurled from a throne to a prison." The fair pleader was silenced, and the tour southward persevered in. But when Sophia told him of what she had promised the Queen, it appeared to give him very great satisfaction.

In less than a fortnight Peter Nielsen and his yacht arrived at Hamburg, bringing the lady to whom Miss Livernet had written. What pleased that kind-hearted girl most of all was the animated and correct likenesses recently taken of the Crown Prince and the infant Princess Louisa Augusta.

Sophia's friend had always commiserated the Queen's sufferings. She had lost her children when young, by shipwreck; therefore she entered the readier into the plan of correspondence proposed by the Count's generous mistress. Sophia scarcely allowed her time to rest before a carriage was ordered, and, attended by Ernestus, set out again for Zell. Their arrival was announced by Stuart. Those whose situation it has been to be separated from their infants whom they loved with intense affection, never perhaps more to behold them, may guess—for I cannot describe—the emotions of Queen Matilda on seeing the pictures of her children, taken within a few days of reaching her hand! This arrangement, that was made on a just and economical plan, was continued undiscovered till the death of the Queen, and formed one of the greatest alleviations that her sorrows received.

When Peter Nielsen heard from Ernestus of the reconciliation that had taken place between the Queen and Count Rantzau, and found that the correspondence of which he was to be the medium was known to him, he condescended to take the Count's hand and tell him he could now indeed believe he had become a repentant sinner, and he hoped he "would save his soul alive." The Count took his coarse compliment in good part; and, everything being arranged, he soon afterwards set out for Amsterdam, attended by the accomplished Miss Livernet, who daily grew more and more dear to him as her various excellencies displayed themselves, and also by his favourite valet, Ernestus, intending in that metropolis to hire servants who should know nothing of his rank or country.

The MS. from which these pages have been copied closes at this period, *i.e.*, the autumn of 1772. The further destiny of the fair Dane and faithful Norwegian is unknown; but the Count, notwithstanding his reconciliation with the forgiving Matilda, fell by the hand of an English officer at Avignon,[1] who had sworn to avenge her fall. He was buried in that city.

The errors of the Queen were obliterated from the bosom of every gentle and cultivated member of society, as well as from the minds of the benevolent illiterate. Never was self-conquest more complete, or reformation more perfect. She fell at last a victim to her own sensibility: poor Alexander Stuart fell ill of an infectious fever; she was admonished by her physicians not to see him or go near his apartment; she disregarded their advice, went to look once more at her faithful servant, caught the dreadful disease, and died within a few days after him.

Such was the melancholy and untimely end of a Princess who was, in her most censurable moments, an object of pity and indulgence, and whose strong and incessant efforts to atone for a single error displayed the noblest virtues that adorn the human mind. Had her days been spared till her gallant son broke the fetters of Juliana and her crafty son, and drove them into a forced retirement, she would no doubt have been recalled to participate of his power and press once more her children to her bosom.

---

[1] Said to be Captain O——, who accompanied Matilda to Denmark, and held a commission in the Danish horse-guards.

Remarks on the preceding Danish MS.

At the close of a narrative abounding with such extraordinary incidents as the preceding, tinged, as it unquestionably is, with an air of romance, the translator of that manuscript, and author of the subsequent portions of the history of Sweden and Denmark, feels it his duty to express his opinion as to the degree of confidence that he places on its veracity. He fully and unequivocally credits every particular relative to the rise and progress of Struensee's fatal amour with Queen Matilda, the subsequent licentiousness of her Court, the particulars of the arrest and behaviour of Struensee, the rankling envy, insatiate malice, and aspiring ambition of Juliana Maria, and the strict accuracy of the motives and adventures imputed to Count Rantzau. In short, the chief points on which he feels any doubt are those which attribute the meditated murder of Christian VII., when a child, to Juliana, and the almost incredible assertion of her having so totally lost sight, not merely of her dignity, but even of her sex, as to have had recourse to those atrocious means to destroy his physical and intellectual powers that are imputed to her. The peculiar features of the secret history connected with Gustavus III. and the birth of the ex-King of Sweden are correctly stated. On this side the water, national prejudices have weighed, and still weigh heavily, against Juliana; but the more serious the charges adduced, the stronger and more conclusive should be the evidence. The translator would have expunged those passages from

...n if those charges had not, in Latrobe and others, been long since before the world. ...certainly are plausible, and that is all that ...admits of his saying. Between the servile ...y, nay, the idolatry of her partisans,¹ and the

---

¹ "The following extract is taken from a letter written in German, and afterwards translated into Danish and French, by one Mr. Helfried, for the express purpose of promulgating Struensee's disgrace, to whom he owed his rise and fortune, which letter was addressed on this occasion to the King of Denmark, by Mr. Suhm, conseiller de conférence."—*Vide* Wolife's "Northern Tour," pp. 16-90.

"Blessed be Juliana! and extolled the name of Prince Frederick! Thanks to all good patriots who, from pure motives, tore the bandage from thine eyes, that thou mightest see clear, who avenged thee and thy kingdom, who risked their lives for thy deliverance, and who restored thee to thy true and genuine power! In truth, it was high time, for I saw the citizen draw his sword against his fellow-citizen, and those who were otherwise peaceable were urged on to murder. Perhaps in a few days thy residence might have fallen a prey to the all-devouring flames, and Denmark and Norway, that wish for nothing more than the happiness of their Kings, might have been reduced to despair. Look now, O King, at the joy that sparkles in the eyes of thy subjects; regard and reflect on their spontaneous gladness.

"Our blood shall flow for thee, for Juliana, for Frederick! Who does not praise and honour that dangerous, that honourable night which broke our chains and caused us to become again a people? Glorious, eventful night! future Homers and Virgils shall sing thy praise. As long as Danish and Norwegian bravery shall live, so long shall the fame of Juliana and Frederick endure—but not increase, for that is impossible."

For such readers as may not have seen any work explaining the fate of those persons who were arrested with Queen Matilda, an extract is subjoined containing the requisite information, viz.:

"Madame Von Göhler was released from her confinement in her own house, but ordered never to appear at Court. Rear-Admiral Hansen was deprived of his seat at the Board of Admiralty. Lieutenant-Colonel Hesselberg and the Diplomatic Counsellor Sturz were ordered to live in a small town in Schleswig, the former upon

CHRISTIAN VII

After the painting by Angelica Kauffman

frightful portrait drawn of her in the preceding manuscript, it is difficult to decide as to the real character of Juliana. That she was a woman of aspiring ambition, eager and ardent in her wishes for regal sway, and an adept in political intrigues, cannot be successfully denied. The conduct of Matilda and Struensee sanctioned the violence adopted to snatch the reins of government from their feeble hands. And that if Juliana could, she would have set aside the succession of the present King, may be safely admitted. And if Count Rantzau had not, by his resolute

---

a stipend of 300, and the latter of 500 dollars. Lieutenant Aboe was *acquitted of every charge against him*, and banished the realm for the term of two years. The Counsellor of State, Willebrandt, and the Royal physician, Berger, were banished the metropolis, upon a stipend of 300 dollars each, and the latter was ordered to spend the remainder of his life at Aalborg, in Jutland. There remained still three prisoners upon whose fate the judges could not speedily decide: these were General Göhler, Colonel Falkenschjold, and the First Commissioner of Finance, Struensee. The sentence pronounced upon the first served as a specimen of what the others might expect. This brave warrior was deprived of his post, his rank and his pay; was banished the islands of Seeland and Fühnen and the Duchy of Schleswig, and reduced to an annual stipend of 1,000 dollars, *because*, according to the very words of his sentence, *he had given cause of suspicion*. The spite of Prince Frederick dictated the sentence of Colonel Falkenschjold. he was deprived of his command and of his post as Royal Chamberlain, and banished for life to Münkholm, a fortress situate in the most northerly part of Norway, where he was allowed only half-a-dollar a day for his subsistence. He was twenty-seven years of age, and no crime could be laid to his charge but his friendship for Struensee. Struensee, the Commissioner of Finance, who, after the execution of his brother, had been thrown into irons, was obliged to petition for his release, upon which his papers and effects were restored to him; but a promise was exacted from him that he would never write or speak upon the revolution."—LATROBE, pp. 254, &c.

conduct, as a member of the Council of State, frustrated the plan formed in 1772 of naming her son as Regent, in all probability the present King would never have ascended the throne. With all these faults on her head, Juliana must still be regarded as a woman of very superior capacity. Weak monarchs are generally seen surrounded by ministers of feeble intellects; they appear to feel a sort of instinctive envy and unconquerable dread of the proximity of ministers gifted with great and powerful minds; yet Juliana Maria selected as her ministers none but men of superior capacity, and judging of her by *the company she kept*, the result is favourable. If her character had been so excessively depraved, would Count Bernstorff have accepted a place under her? These remarks, the author thinks, are requisite to liberate the minds of his readers from the very unfavourable impression the preceding chapters are calculated to produce, ere he proceeds with the original memoirs that follow.

CHAPTER IX

The Danish Court after the fall of Struensee—Wise and dignified conduct of George III.—Memoir of Count Andreas Petrus Bernstorff—A celebrated tourist quoted, and censured—Violation of the Danish flag—Source of that abuse—Its consequence—The armed neutrality of the Northern Powers—Count Bernstorff retires—The Crown Prince Frederick seizes the reins of Government—Count Bernstorff restored.

THE Protestant interest of Europe, the commerce and politics of Great Britain, and perhaps the personal feelings of our King, combined their influence to produce the Royal marriages that took place in the year 1766 in Sweden, Denmark and Holland. But that powerful influence, which the Cabinet of London might reasonably have expected from the marriage of the King of Denmark with the Princess Caroline Matilda, was lost through the frailty of that unfortunate and ill-advised Queen. The evils resulting from the indiscretion of Matilda did not fall exclusively on her own head, nor on her partisans in Denmark, but extended itself to the political and commercial relations of her native land. It was more honourable to the gallantry and generosity of the British public than to its justice or discernment, that the nation appeared readier to avenge the indignities suffered by Matilda than to investigate the merits of her cause. The youth, beauty and sufferings of this dethroned Queen excited the most powerful sympathy. Vengeance, sudden and terrible, was denounced against Juliana and all those who had been concerned in Matilda's supposed unmerited disgrace. The King (her brother), who was the most competent judge, proved by the line of conduct he adopted on this delicate occasion how he estimated that of his young and unfortunate sister. Far from availing himself of the popular fervour to seek vengeance for the gratification of wounded pride or unjust resentment, George III. contented himself with stemming the torrent of persecution in Denmark and rescuing Matilda from the hands of her enemies. Instead of endeavouring to bolster her reputation by receiving her into the bosom of his family and Court, he condemned the fair culprit to a penance sufficiently severe and humiliating in fixing her future residence at Zell. He did not, however, from motives of State policy, abandon Matilda in the hour of deep and bitter affliction; nor would he suffer family pride to hurry him into measures by which the interests of his people might have been materially injured.

After the dethronement of Matilda and the death of Struensee, it required all the talent of Juliana and her party to keep the wheels of Government in motion.[1]

---

[1] It is mentioned in the "Annual Register for 1772," that a Count Wolingsky had his tongue cut out, on account of words he had used reflecting upon the conduct of Christian VII. and Juliana. No such event happened in Denmark.

The finances were in the utmost disorder, trade at a standstill, and Norway in such a state of popular ferment, on account of an obnoxious poll-tax, as threatened a general revolt. The moral state in which Matilda left her Court is already shown. Juliana banished those sirens whose licentious revels had rendered it unfit for the presence of a modest woman, and restored the ancient formality and etiquette: by which means, all that it gained in character and stateliness was lost in attraction. The elegance, the graceful ease, the voluptuousness of Versailles, all suddenly disappeared; and German etiquette, stiff, formal and graceless, arose in its stead. If Juliana restored the demi-barbarity of ancient German grandeur, she occasioned a greatly beneficial reduction of expense in the Royal establishment. On the morning of Matilda's arrest Juliana caused a confidential note to be delivered to each of the foreign ambassadors, stating the grounds on which those who had done the deed were prepared to justify their conduct. It was scarcely possible, even for the cold bosoms of calculating statesmen, to avoid a powerful sympathy excited for the fate of this illustrious woman, whose gross aberrations had unfortunately tended to bias and silence her most natural advocates. When Struensee confessed a connection it was as vain for him to deny as to expect mercy from its avowal; and when the sentence of divorce, founded upon that confession and other incontrovertible evidence, was completed, all the foreign ministers attended, dressed in deep State mourning, at Christianborg, to receive an official copy of the evidence, and also of the sentence pronounced against the Queen. From that hour, the name of Matilda was erased from the Church Service of Denmark, and she ceased to be the wife of its wretched King. These humiliations it was not in the power of the King, her brother, to avert; but his influence preserved her rank as a Queen, stopped the promulgation of the sentence, and his ships of war conveyed Queen Matilda from her melancholy prison in Cronenborg Castle.

Whilst this awful process was carrying on, Juliana strengthened herself and adherents by conciliating the opinion and securing the sanction of foreign Courts, and particularly those of St. Petersburg, Berlin and Versailles. The favourite minister of Frederick V., the great Count Bernstorff, who was banished the Court at the instigation of Struensee, lived long enough to hear of the fall of the unfortunate minion, but died within a month after the receipt of that welcome intelligence. His nephew, Count Andreas Petrus Bernstorff, who has since immortalised his name in Denmark by executing several great and useful projects, was selected by Juliana to fill the important office of Minister for Foreign Affairs. A wiser choice it was not in her power to have made. He was known to possess in an eminent degree high mental endowments and gentlemanly manners. Educated under the eye of his uncle, and amidst the splendour of a magnificent regal Court, he could scarcely avoid being a finished courtier and profound politician. To introduce this celebrated statesman, we insert a brief memoir of him, taken from Mr. Wolffe's "Northern Tour."[1] This appointment had the most beneficial influence both at home and abroad, conferring strength, respectability, and the promise of duration on the new Government. He rendered himself popular with the Northern Courts by the care he took to preserve and increase the Danish Royal Navy, as well as to increase the commercial marine. The fall of Matilda,

---

[1] The liberality displayed by Jens Wolffe, Esq., author of the "Northern Tour," so frequently quoted, encourages the belief that he will not complain of the whole of his brief memoir of Count Bernstorff appearing in these pages.

CHARACTER AND POLITICAL CAREER OF COUNT BERNSTORFF, LATE PRIME MINISTER OF DENMARK.

"Nichts kann einem Sterblichen gluckseligeres begegnen, als wenn er in guten Tagen einer von den beglückten Menschen, und in bösen, einer von den grössten Männern ist."
No greater blessing can befall a human being than in good times to be a fortunate man; in bad, a great man.

Count Andreas Petrus Bernstorff was born at Hanover, on the 28th of August, 1735. From his earliest youth his character was mild, benignant, kind and endearing to all around him. His natural flow of spirits was misunderstood by his tutor, Munther, under whose care his father had placed him, with the view of imbibing the first rudiments of education; he was checked and corrected by the severity of a man whose scholastic ideas being chiefly confined to theoretical knowledge, knew but little of the human heart. Emancipated from the rod of this instructor, he appears, in his fifteenth year, to have been placed under the tuition of Leischnig, a man of considerable talent and experience. With him, he entered deeply into the study of history, theology, and the living and dead languages. In 1752, he went with his brother to Leipzig, where he became acquainted with the poet Gellert, whose friendship was a source of infinite use and gratification to him. Led on by an insatiable thirst for knowledge, and a wish to become personally intimate with characters eminent for their abilities or rank in life, he now prosecuted his

and the discussions to which that event gave rise, created a strong anti-Britannic spirit in Denmark. The exterior forms of amity, though faded and relaxed, still remained, but the spirit of harmonious peace had fled. The Danes whom pleasure or commerce led to visit England, were overwhelmed by popular execration. The English who visited Copenhagen, from the sailor to the gentleman, carried with them the most inveterate

---

travels into foreign countries. He made some considerable stay at Dresden and Gottingen, At Geneva he acquired a perfect knowledge of the French language, which was of infinite service to him in his diplomatic career. He then went to Italy, where he commenced an intimacy with M. de Chauvelin and the Duke de Choiseul, the French Ministers at Turin and Rome, as likewise with the Abbé Barthélemy, the renowned writer of the travels of Anacharsis. With the latter, and a celebrated artist, he studied the antiquities and the fine arts. During this journey he fulfilled the earnest wishes of his uncle (the great Bernstorff, who afterwards retired from the Ministry during the reign of Struensee), and determined to enter into the Danish service. In 1756 he quitted Italy, and returned through Trieste, Vienna and Dresden to Hanover. After staying a short time under the parental roof, and being in vain solicited to fix his residence there, he went to Paris, where he remained six months; thence he crossed over to England, and was intimate with Admirals Hawke, Anson and others. Here he followed the pursuits of agriculture, a study for which at all times he had a strong propensity, remaining some time in Norfolk; after this, he returned through Holland to Hanover.

Bernstorff's first *début* in affairs of State was an appointment in the German Chancery, where his uncle presided, who seemed determined to encourage him in the attainment of some degree of eminence in the line of politics and diplomacy. When the old Count Bernstorff was Minister to Frederick V. he had an opportunity of furthering the object of his wishes; and during several successive years his nephew's advancement was rapid and certain. In 1766 Frederick V. died, and a cabal was formed for the purpose of ruining the credit of the Minister in the eyes of his successor, Christian VII.,

prejudices, not merely against the Queen-Dowager and her son, but the nation itself. The British periodical Press lent its powerful influence. An elegant writer—though a most illiberal and prejudiced tourist [1]—contributed on his return, by the publication of his tour, to feed and perpetuate an injurious enmity that a wise and liberal writer would have strained every nerve to extinguish. The coolness and reserve with which the

---

which, however, had the reverse effect: the Count not only refuted the charges brought against him, but had the Order of Dannebrog conferred on him, together with the gift of an estate near Copenhagen. At that time the farmers were in a state of bondage, and subject to the feudal laws, which rendered them totally indifferent to the cultivation of lands; the owner and peasant equally suffered under these unwise and barbarous regulations. Count Bernstorff was foremost to abolish this system of slavery. As a philanthropist he could not behold with indifference the wretchedness of these poor people, in a country which Nature seemed to have formed for the comfort and opulence of its inhabitants. He wished to be considered the benefactor of a free and wealthy race, rather than the lord of

[1] " The Prince (Frederick) has received no other mark of bounty from Nature or fortune than Royal birth. He is very much deformed, and this personal imperfection has gained him the appellation of 'Richard III.' among those who do not love the Court, though it undoubtedly originated among the English."

"*As to Prince Frederick, Nature, it is said, has very completely disqualified him for affairs of gallantry.*" A more judicious, instructive and entertaining traveller, namely, the Rev. William Coxe, visited Denmark in 1779, and was presented to this Prince, and Sophia Frederica, *his wife!* It showed no small degree of magnanimity in the Royal pair to admit an English tourist to a private audience. What reparation could Mr. Wraxall make for the propagation of a scandal that went to throw on his consort the suspicion of being an adulteress, and to assert the illegitimacy of her children? It was a cruel and a cowardly attack, disgraceful to the author, and injurious to the character of his country.—*Vide* " A Tour, &c.," by Mr. Nat. Wraxall, pp. 52 and 54, 3rd edition, 1776.

English were received at Court, and the mistrust with which their steps were watched, were indignantly felt and complained of; but those persons forgot they had expressed nothing but hatred and contempt, and almost openly strove to excite discontent and revolt. There can be no doubt that English *hauteur*, and English prejudice had a powerful tendency to mature that antipathy which paved the way for the accession of Denmark, in 1780,

---

slaves. Believing their misery to arise from having been oppressed by hard labour, he resolved to abolish their system of partnership in enclosures, and to place them in such a situation that they might expect to reap the fruits of their individual industry. To effect this, he parcelled out the lands in suitable lots, and prevailed on his tenantry to throw dice for the choice, encouraging them by presents to move their residences to the ground which fell to their share.

Count Bernstorff expended from his private purse in settling and giving permanency to this arrangement, 7,000 dollars; but the sum was well applied, and he found himself amply repaid by the hilarity which soon accompanied the labours of these poor families, whose welfare he had taken so much pains to ensure.

The grateful peasants, some years afterwards, erected a plain marble monument by the side of the high road in honour of the Count.

In 1770 the old Count Bernstorff, who was then Minister of State, received his dismission in consequence of the increasing influence of Struensee, who could not brook a rival in power, and had persuaded Matilda to apply for it. The King, indifferent to everything but his pleasures, easily yielded, and both the Bernstorffs quitted Denmark, to the great regret of all good and wise men.

On the 18th of February, 1772, the old Count died at Altena; and when his nephew, Count Andreas (after the ruin of Struensee and his party), visited Copenhagen in the following summer, he was earnestly solicited to accept a situation in the Government, and was shortly afterwards appointed to the post of Minister for the Foreign Department, which his uncle had filled with so much credit to himself and benefit to the nation.

He was chiefly instrumental in effecting the exchange of the Counties of Oldenburg and Delmenhorst for part of the Duchy of

to the armed neutrality of the Northern Powers. At the present hour this mischievous spirit is at work. The same blind, indiscriminate *furor* seems to animate the great majority of our political writers; and the clouds that are concentrating round our national character in every country of the Old and New Continent, forebode a storm that at no great distance of time may, by undermining the foundation of our foreign commerce, wrest the trident of the seas from the grasp of our country.

Holstein, which had long been a bone of contention between Russia and Denmark. A treaty to this effect was concluded on the 21st of May, 1773, and this matter, which was of great importance to Denmark, was thus set at rest.

On the breaking out of the American War, Bernstorff adopted and brought to perfection a wise system of neutrality, which was of essential consequence to a nation not able to contend with the great maritime Powers.

On the 28th of February, 1780, during hostilities between England and France and her allies, Denmark, Russia and Sweden formed a coalition in defence of their neutrality, which was respected at that period, and enabled the three Powers to carry on their usual trade without much interruption. This Northern coalition was, however, neither forgotten nor forgiven by Great Britain, and was one of the primary causes of her subsequent hostilities with Denmark.

To particularise the benefits that ensued to Denmark during the ministry of Count Bernstorff would be endless. Esteemed and honoured, both abroad and at home, his situation was most enviable; it was such as could not fail to attract the attention of aspiring courtiers, whose merits were completely thrown into the shade by a comparison with his personal good qualities and public virtues. A party was secretly formed, with the view of displacing him from the pre-eminent situation he held. To create disgust, and induce him to resign, every practicable obstacle was thrown in his way, and opposition raised, to thwart his plans for the public benefit. As long, however, as he could be of service to the country, he continued in office, and disregarded the shafts of envy that were levelled at him by his opponents. At length,

The antipathies created by the dethronement and exile of Queen Caroline Matilda had scarcely ceased to operate, when an unconstitutional desire to tax our colonists in North America—without admitting them to actual representation in the distant Legislature by which such burthens were to be imposed—gave rise to that unnatural and disastrous war, the sad effects of which, though painfully humiliating to our pride and formidable to our power, have as yet been slightly felt in comparison

---

perceiving that he could not stem the current of the opposition, he resigned his situation as Minister, on the 30th of November, 1780, and, like Cincinnatus, retired to the plough and his estate, without a murmur, but with the most fervent wishes for the future prosperity of the country. To his friend Munther he said, eight years afterwards, "If they dismiss me ten times, and recall me as often, I will return, if the country can be benefited by my abilities."

Rare words! the test of the intrinsic worth of a minister, of which there are few instances.

When the Prince Royal assumed the reigns of government, in 1784, Count Bernstorff was reinstated in his high office, to the great joy of the nation. In 1786 a general emancipation of the peasantry took place in Denmark, of which he had set the example on his own estate. During the following year a variety of internal regulations and improvements occurred in the financial system. In 1789, when war was declared between Sweden and Russia, and Denmark was called upon to fulfil the article of a treaty which stipulated that, in case Russia was attacked, Denmark should send an auxiliary force to her assistance, Count Bernstorff attended the Prince, who made an irruption with 12,000 men from Norway into the Swedish territories; and Gottenburg would inevitably have fallen, had not the English and Prussian Ministers interposed, and obtained a cessation of hostilities, which eventually ended in a treaty of peace.

At the commencement, and during the early part of the French Revolution, when England declared war against France, the situation of Denmark was truly critical. Here again the genius of this truly great man prevented the country from being crushed

to what may too probably be apprehended as the result of future wars more bloody and more fierce!

As soon as the leaders of the American patriots resolved to risk a war rather than admit a principle, to the baleful effects of which no probable limits could be assigned, they adopted measures to bring into their ports those naval and warlike stores which the awful contest in which they were about to engage rendered essential to their safety and success. The anti-Stadtholdian party in

---

between the mighty Powers; and although a new code of maritime laws established in the English Admiralty Court, and the laws of nations, were disregarded by the contending Powers, yet the system of neutrality, so beneficial to the Danish nation, was not departed from, and in its consequences was productive of great mercantile advantage to the country. As a token of the general satisfaction, a gold medal was presented to Count Bernstorff on the Prince Royal's birthday, the 28th of January, 1795.

The following letter, describing the circumstance, was written by a gentleman of Copenhagen at that period:

"The interest you take in the political affairs of the North of Europe induces me to inform you of what has transpired here respecting our very deserving Minister of State, Count Bernstorff, whose private character, moral principles and benignity of manners are as well known as the prudence, steadiness and honour of his conduct in public life.

"It is to him we are indebted for our present tranquillity. He was the principal cause of Denmark not joining in the present detrimental and destructive war, the fatal consequences of which make humanity bleed and blush throughout Europe.

"Though partly deprived of the benefits due to an independent nation in her lawful trade, we yet enjoy the comforts of peace, in hopes of ultimately obtaining entire satisfaction for the injuries that trade has received from the belligerent Powers.

"Acknowledging most devoutly the blessings of Heaven, we at the same time acknowledge how much we are indebted to the man whose arduous task it became to unmask perfidious insinuations and to reject haughty proposals of ruinous participation. No species of war is just but that in defence of our lives, rights

Holland, delighted at the prospect of a war between Great Britain and her colonies, were not slow in assuring the American Republicans of every kind of support in their power to afford; nor were these idle promises. They harassed and perplexed the Stadtholder by calling for the increase of the Dutch navy, and the enforcement of the doctrine, "Free ship, free goods." The Dutch Press teemed with publications intended to hurt the

---

and liberty—ruin and shame inevitably attend the offender. Such ought to be the maxims of every moral statesman, and a minister destitute of morality is a curse upon the people.

"Count Bernstorff is a blessing to us. Convinced of this, numbers of citizens have joined in proving their satisfaction and gratitude by sending him a gold medal representing a striking likeness of himself, with this inscription:

"'*Bernstorff, Minister of State in Denmark.*'

On the reverse side is a compass, inscribed:

"'*Without alteration.*'

"I need not explain the boldness of this idea; it is as explicit and true as the frailties of mortals allow.

"The medal, with the following letter, was delivered by an unknown person:

"'To the man of his King and country, the most noble Bernstorff, who proved to Europe that true State wisdom consists in justice and peace, and, supported by strenuous perseverance, is the greatest honour in all Governments. To him, discerning fellow-citizens hereby convey the enclosed proof of their gratitude.

"'The faithful subjects of these realms, in presenting the most worthy citizen with their thanks, which he deserves, preferred this memorable day, because it reminds every friend of their country of that benefit which has been effected in these latter years for the prosperity of the State and the cause of humanity.

"'*From* DANES *and* NORWEGIANS *devoted to their King and Country.*

"'*The 28th January,* 1795.'

"The subscribers, preferring a noble deed to the emptiness of public show, remain as yet unknown.

character of the British and animate the courage of the American colonists. The most wealthy merchants in Holland exported for the use of the insurgents all sorts of contraband of war. Those supplies were usually sent

> "You must observe that the 28th of January is our worthy Prince Royal's birthday, whose application to his extensive and important duties is perhaps unparalleled, and whose firmness and constant attachment to justice and honour entitle him to every distinction and encouragement. His Royal Highness, in supporting so able a minister in whatever is just, and he on the other side being a faithful friend to the Prince, the choice of the day was noble and applicable."

This testimony of the public regard was highly grateful to him. The following year another medal was struck on his own birthday, and presented to him: this was the last year of his eventful life. In May, 1797, his mental and corporeal powers were exhausted, and after a short illness, during which he was attended by Callisen and Hensler, his personal friends, and the most eminent of the faculty, and daily visited by the Prince Royal, he expired, to the great regret and sorrow of the whole nation. His funeral was honoured by the attendance of the Prince and Royal Family, and followed by persons of the first consequence in Copenhagen. The last words of Bishop Balle, in his funeral oration, were, "Happy Bernstorff! Peace to thy ashes!—a blessing to thy family; revered be thy memory!" How glorious is the death of such a man! what an example to posterity! How much more gratifying to the feelings of his surviving children is the daily sight of the simple pedestal erected by his grateful tenants, during his life-time, in commemoration of a single act of beneficence, which alone immortalised the name of Bernstorff, than the superb mausoleum that decorates the ashes of Juliana Maria at Roskild, a gloomy depository of unrelenting jealousy and ambition, and which the beholder regards with apathy and indifference!

> "A cordial *his* sustains, that cannot fail:
> By pleasure unsubdued, unbroke by pain,
> He shares in that omnipotence he trusts:
> All-bearing, all-attempting, till he falls,
> And, when he falls, writes 'vici' on his shield:
> From magnanimity, all fear above:
> From nobler recompense, above applause."

to St. Eustatius and Curaçao, and thence transported to their ulterior destination. Many of those ships and cargoes were captured by British cruisers, and condemned. Regardless of their own violation of neutral rights in plunging into a trade so likely to involve the Republic in war, they besieged the Stadtholder (William V.) with complaints and remonstrances, terming those captures that, on the broadest principle of the law of nations, were legally made and condemned, the "piratical depredations of Great Britain on their defenceless ships." They called aloud for war to avenge those imaginary wrongs, and accused William V. of having been bribed by the Court of St. James's to permit the ruin of the navy and the commerce of Holland!

Whilst the merchants of Holland were striving by every means in their power to create a war between Great Britain and the States of Holland—conscious of the overwhelming power of the foe, whose vengeance they feared even whilst they provoked it—they looked about them for the securest means of protecting their ships and commerce from its power. A year prior to the commencement of actual war, they resolved to carry on their contraband commerce under the mask of neutral flags; and the better to screen their speculations from the observation of their Government, they exported large supplies of naval stores, arms and ammunition, under the protection of neutral flags and as neutral property. About the year 1778 a meeting of the principal Baltic merchants was held at Amsterdam. That commercial leviathan,

M. Claas Taan, senior, of Zaandam,[1] acted as president. The object of the meeting was to devise means of securely carrying on their commerce under a neutral flag. On account of its local situation, the city of Embden was fixed on as the chief emporium of this vile traffic, which was founded on fraud, and could only be supported by a deliberate and organised system of forgery and false swearing. A nominal firm was for this purpose then established, under the patronage of M. Claas Taan, namely, Messrs. Gerrit and Barend Van Olst, Brouwer and Co., of Embden.

But as Denmark was a maritime State, possessing at that period thirty ships of the line, nine fifties and twenty frigates, and finding its carrying trade pro-

---

[1] The floating property of M. Taan was, at this period, on an average, equal to £1,000,000 sterling. He was sole proprietor of forty Greenland ships, besides other vessels; he possessed no fewer than thirty mills at Zaandam, the rich village on the river Y, so celebrated for its legions of windmills. It was here that Peter I. worked as a shipwright. The inhabitants were formerly proverbial for the insolence of wealth, affecting at the same time the dress and manners of boors (*i.e.*, clowns or countrymen). Mr. Hope, the banker, had about this period a foreign bill due for a very large amount, accepted by one of those village merchants. He took with him an English gentleman who was desirous of seeing the interior of their houses. They found the man of wealth clad in a coarse brown jacket, with large silver buttons, huge breeches, a vast flapped hat, and klompers (*i.e.*, wooden shoes). He was employed with a shovel, cleaning out a ditch. The proud Zaandammer, when he learnt the errand of Mr. Hope, took him leisurely into his house, and in a careless way asked him to name the coin in which he wished to receive his bill. Between gold ducats, the highest, and sesthalves, the lowest current specie, there were many kinds; and by this challenge it was clear he was prepared with a sufficient sum of each sort to pay a bill the amount of which appeared particularly large even to Mr. Hope.

digiously increased, the Danish Court seemed well disposed to protect its flag without enquiring too minutely as to the neutrality of its employment; it was, therefore, determined, as well as the Prussian, to use the Danish flag. Nominal firms were immediately established in Copenhagen and at Altena. In the former city the celebrated De Coninck,[1] the rich possessor of Drottningaard, was the principal Dutch agent. That man was employed in very large masked concerns, principally for the Dutch East India Company and the Government of Holland. His enormous fortune was acquired by the systematic commission of those crimes for which less wealthy criminals were continually being condemned to the gallows in England, and in Denmark and Holland to the severest punishment short of death, and perpetual imprisonment in irons!

Exclusive of the De Coninck's, there were several other firms of the same vile nature established in the ports of Denmark. At Altena the violation of maritime

---

[1] This man, having acquired his wealth at the risk of eternal perdition to his soul, set up at last as a man of *taste*. The fame of his plenteous table and delicious wines soon spread abroad, and *tasteful* travellers of all nations crowded to his magnificent villa to *taste* of the delicacies that abounded. The infamy of the man was forgotten in the luxuries that he dispensed. M. Jens Wolffe, who, as Danish Consul-General, must have had no small experience in such matters, though free from the taint of committing those crimes, has made tolerably free with this amateur in the arts of perjury and forgery. He has given an emblematical vignette representing De Coninck taking his wine in an extensive and magnificent library, his back turned on the books, whilst a servant appears bringing in a dish of some sort in his hand. A couple of enormously fat swine are amusing themselves in the same room, routing in the litter that seems spread on the floor!—*Vide* "Northern Tour."

neutrality was carried on to an incredible extent. The first person who set up as a dealer in false papers and false oaths was a Dutch schoolmaster named Hendrick Van Der Berg, who was employed by the brothers Messrs. Pieter and Cornelius Corver, of Zaandam. Immense commercial speculations were conducted by M. Pieter Corver—under the Danish flag, on Dutch account—in the name of Hendrick Van Der Berg. Many of those enormous Dutch mast-carrying vessels, almost as large as line-of-battle ships, were freighted with all sorts of naval stores, consigned, nominally on Danish account and risk, to the ports of Holland and France, and the new Transatlantic Republic. In this manner was a seductive, lucrative, but infamous traffic first introduced into Denmark, by which the legal and creditable paths of legitimate commerce were too generally abandoned, the name and calling of a merchant degraded, the neutrality of Denmark radically violated, and the foundation laid for those terrible scourges with which that kingdom has since been visited. At this period, the increase of commerce in the Danish ports at home and abroad was prodigiously great. The tonnage of her commercial marine apparently experienced an immense increase. Her master mariners and mates found plenty of employment, but it was of a nature that uprooted every principle of moral virtue. They were hired by such men as De Coninck to navigate vessels that belonged to subjects of belligerent Powers, particularly Holland. They earned their daily bread by daily perjuries. They were taught to laugh at the sanctity of oaths. The

15—2

example spread from the cabin to the forecastle. Mates, cooks, and the men before the mast, in case of capture by a belligerent Power, were expected to swear in corroboration of the simulated papers. From this polluted source a stream of contaminated riches flowed into Denmark, derived from the mercenary protection extended to the ships and commerce of the enemies of Great Britain. Our native merchants were, however, at this period untainted with the infamy of following those bad examples.

Count Bernstorff found the finances of Denmark in utter disorder. The expense of the Royal Court, of numerous and heavy pensions, and the interest of the National Debt made heavy drains on private property. After many great retrenchments, it was scarcely practicable to find resources to meet the current expenses. Such was the state of affairs when the first American War broke out. Count Bernstorff was well-informed as to the illegal commercial enterprises of Danish merchants. He knew of, and *tolerated*, the masked establishments set up at Copenhagen and Altena for the neutralisation of belligerent commerce. Instead of tearing up by the roots those demoralising institutions, he connived at their existence, and framed the municipal laws of Denmark to favour their operation. In doing this, the Count showed a deficiency of true political science. The ships thus covered belonged principally to Dutch merchants. It was Dutch capital that was employed. All the principal repairs were done in Dutch ports. The perjured neutralisers gained about two per cent. on the nominal transfer of the ships. An annual tribute was paid by the owner, called "protection money," equal to about four shillings per ton measurement, or two per cent. on the gross amount of all freights. For the neutralisation of cargoes, one per cent. on the amount, exclusive of a fee for each certificate. The most solemn public averments were sold in blank, with the seals of offices and the formal oath regularly attested and witnessed! Such were the leading features of that polluted traffic that was sanctioned by Count Bernstorff. That statesman was wrong, as it neither respected morality nor profit. If he had maintained the integrity of the Danish flag, the capital and industry of his countrymen would have soon created a trade really neutral, that would have been far more lucrative, permanent and untainted by crime. The Count, by winking at the criminal avarice of unprincipled merchants, became their idol. It was this secret bias that led him so strongly to advocate the rights of neutral flags, as laid down in the Treaty of Utrecht, and admitted by the Treaty of 1756 between England and France. He wished to see Denmark enriched at the expense of Great Britain, but not to wrest from the latter the sovereignty of the seas. As the flames of war extended from America to Europe, the greater was the mass of Dutch, French and Spanish commerce thrown into the hands of pseudo-neutrals. Neutral papers and neutral flags were publicly advertised for sale in the ports of Holland, France and Spain. Innumerable captures and detentions were the result. The law of nations was annihilated. The maritime rights of Great

Britain, founded on public law and essential to her safety, were trampled on and set at nought. The Danes became exasperated against England for interrupting a trade that was alike lucrative, illegal and immoral. In all the ports of Europe gigantic preparations were seen for preparing the vaunted armament that was to execute the vengeance of Europe, destroy the navy of Great Britain, and restore the liberty of the seas!

By an extraordinary combination of circumstances the most despotic Courts of Europe united against Great Britain to give liberty to the armed and revolted colonists. The Danes and the Swedes seemed to have laid aside mutual animosities; they joined in alliance with Russia. Pressed as England was at all points, even in the British Channel, by the fleets of her enemies, her naval greatness might then have received its death-wound if the coalesced Powers had been sincere and true to each other. Happily for Great Britain there existed an inveterate jealousy between Sweden and Denmark: the latter Court had the worst possible opinion of Gustavus III. Count Bernstorff foresaw that if a great naval battle took place, Catherine would so manage that her fleets, if fortune was adverse, should suffer the least, and run away with the fame—and profit, too—if victorious. He foresaw the probability of the naval power of Denmark being crushed in the contest if she once committed herself fully; thence he determined to avoid extremities. The imperious Catherine saw his drift, which was manifest by his inserting an article in the treaty with Russia stipulating that Denmark should be allowed to maintain "its former alliances." The insertion of this article neutralised Denmark, alarmed Gustavus, and filled Catherine with rage; it offended Juliana Maria, and caused equal disappointment, anger and regret in the Courts of Berlin, Versailles and Madrid.

Attempts were made to conciliate Count Bernstorff and induce him to withdraw the neutralising clause. The King of Prussia sent Prince Ferdinand of Brunswick to remonstrate on the subject. The Prince assured the Count of the permanence of his high office, if he yielded, and menaced him with instant dismission if he persisted. The Queen-Dowager, Juliana Maria, supported the arguments of Prince Ferdinand. She was anxious to see the splendour and power of the House of Hanover humbled and greatly reduced. Count Bernstorff was, however, inflexible. He retired from Denmark, accompanied by the mortifying consideration that he had offended all the great Powers; also Great Britain, by having favoured the enormous breaches of commercial neutrality which had so materially contributed to give rise to this Northern confederacy. And all the Northern Courts were displeased by his inserting an article that neutralised the naval power which Denmark was bound to supply.

The dismissal of Count Bernstorff caused a vast accession of influence to the Queen-Dowager. Guldberg, the preceptor to Prince Frederick and favourite of his mother, who was called Private Secretary to the King, was, at this period, the efficient Minister for Foreign Affairs. The influence of Count Bernstorff and the

British Cabinet being still thought too great in the Council of State, an alteration was deemed expedient, by which the deliberative power of the Boards of Commerce, Finance, and the Marine, was completely superseded. After the fall of Struensee the old mode of government was re-established. The President of the Council of State recommended all public measures to the King, who signed the mandates, which were transmitted to those Boards for execution.

After the dismissal of Count Bernstorff, an Interior Cabinet, very similar to that of Matilda and Struensee, was established. The Council of State was passed over, and the Boards were directed to execute the orders of the King, who continued in a most deplorable state of mental imbecility. The Queen-Dowager had possession of his person; and as she could obtain his signature to every document laid before him, nearly the same kind of interior government was erected as that for the establishment of which Struensee was condemned to die. By this step, Juliana obtained the most despotic power, a power that she retained till the son of the unfortunate Matilda, aided by the secret counsel of Count Bernstorff, wrested the reins of government from her hands, and drove her into a retirement whence she emerged no more.

Although deprived of office by foreign influence, Count Bernstorff never despaired of being restored. He kept up an occasional correspondence with Great Britain, and was well served by his agents at his own Court, who informed him of all that passed, and whenever opportunity served, strove to impress the

Crown Prince with the most favourable sentiments towards that statesman.

Even at this period, it is probable Juliana had not abandoned all hope of excluding the heir-apparent from the throne. He was kept as much as possible in the background. Her emissaries filled the residence with reports much to his disadvantage, representing him as stupid and intractable, and insinuating that he was affected with the same mental imbecility that had so many years incapacitated his father from governing. Christian VII. was confirmed before he was fourteen, and immediately took his place in the Council of State. The sovereignty was now vested in Juliana. The Crown Prince attained his fourteenth year, yet not a symptom was shown that indicated an intention on the part of Juliana to permit that solemn ceremony. The cause of this repugnance was evident. As soon as the Prince was confirmed she could not exclude him, except by violence, from taking his seat in the Council. She feared the influence of his presence there, well knowing that he was not the weak and talentless boy that he had been represented. It was believed that the advice of M. Guldberg prevented Juliana Maria from attempting to set aside the succession of the Crown Prince. As the period approached when his public examination must of necessity take place, and also his admission into the Council of State, a new mode of treatment was adopted. General Eichstedt, who was nominated *Governor* of the Crown Prince, on the arrest of his unhappy mother, was removed. His preceptor, M. Sporon, who was erroneously thought to be a favourite with the Crown Prince, was appointed *Secretary* of the Council, which was filled with persons in whom Juliana had the most confidence, and wherein M. Guldberg held almost unlimited sway.

In January, 1784, the Crown Prince completed his sixteenth year. In stature he was much like the King—his complexion very fair, his eyebrows very bushy for a youth of his age, his hair almost white. Though a plain likeness, he bore a strong resemblance to his unfortunate mother.

On the 28th of January, the birthday of the Prince, the Queen-Dowager augmented the pensions of several courtiers, and created eight new Knights of the Order of the Holy Ghost. Amongst them was M. Molckte, steward of the household. One of those sudden turns in politics that sometimes reconcile the most jarring interests, led to the restoration of peace between the Counts Bernstorff and Schak Ratlau. The latter nobleman had, like Count Rantzau, lent himself, in 1780, to the Queen-Dowager, and aided her in driving Count Bernstorff into retirement. Feeling himself of less consequence than he expected, or seeing a chance of bettering his fortune, he made private offers to the Crown Prince, by whom they were accepted, who displayed in his secret correspondence with Count Bernstorff a firm and sensible mind. Such was his discretion, he did not acquaint Count Ratlau of his intercourse with Bernstorff, whilst to the latter he communicated everything proposed by the former. As the eventful day approached, the Crown Prince assumed a more free and friendly demeanour towards his stepmother and her son. Without descending to any gross or culpable duplicity, he completely deceived M. Guldberg, and even his preceptor, M. Sporon. Not so with the lynx-eyed Juliana. She found means to ascertain the existence of a secret correspondence. This fact she communicated to M. Guldberg, who admonished her with much earnestness not to risk the fatal consequences that he foresaw would result from her pushing matters to extremities. He told her that he believed a crisis was at hand that would be fatal to her power, and if she acted rashly, probably to her own life and that of her son. She had wisdom enough to take in good part the counsel of a man who had shown himself in everything her firm, unshaken friend. She promised to abstain from acts of violence; and he was not so tired of being efficiently the First Minister of the Crown as to recommend a voluntary surrender of the reins of government.

Ambition being Juliana's leading passion, she could have met death with less horror than a blow that must annihilate her political power and force her into retirement. Contrary to the advice of M. Guldberg, she went to the apartment of the Crown Prince, and accusing him of holding a secret correspondence, would have proceeded to interrogation. He listened to her with the most profound attention, and when she had finished speaking, he said, with a careless air, " As you are *certain*, madam, it is so, have the kindness to inform me from whom you have derived the information? I shall then know what answer to give." She perceived there was nothing to be obtained by interrogatories, and withdrew.

Count Bernstorff was pretty well assured that M. Guldberg would not risk his life and fortune by encouraging the Queen-Dowager to defend by force her illegal power. The Count remained at his estate, but everything was guided by his wisdom. He had secured the support of some officers of high rank. The commandant of the citadel engaged, if the attempt failed, to give that fortress up to the Crown Prince, as a place of safe retreat for himself and adherents.

On the 28th of March, 1784, he being then sixteen years and two months old, the Crown Prince was confirmed in the Royal chapel of Christianborg, in the presence of the whole Court, the foreign ministers, the great officers of State, and other persons of distinction who had been invited. M. Basholm, first chaplain to the King, interrogated him as to his religious creed. The examination continued a long time, and the Crown Prince made his responses in a firm, manly, deliberate and very audible tone of voice. His demeanour was mild, dignified and collected, giving the most complete refutation to the calumnies that had been so industriously spread. Juliana was astonished and dismayed. The impression he made on the audience was such that many actually were affected even to the shedding of tears. When Count Bernstorff was assured of the firmness and capacity which the Crown Prince displayed during this trying test, he anticipated complete success when the great attempt should be made.

At length the hour arrived that was destined finally to destroy the power of Juliana and her party, and effect a change in the Danish Government almost as great as that which followed the arrest of Matilda. Having received the sacrament, the Crown Prince was admitted as a member of the Privy Council, and succeeded his uncle, Prince Frederick, as President. On the morning of the 14th of April, he took the oath prescribed. At the moment of relieving guard, when a double proportion of the garrison was under arms, he gave personal orders that no one should quit his post without permission from himself. The Council were assembled in the King's apartment; his uncle was present. The Crown Prince addressed himself to the King, his father, stating that the law now called on him to govern, to do which efficiently, he required a Council in whom both himself and the nation had confidence. He then produced a memoir that he had composed, and which, having read in a firm, deliberate tone of voice, he laid before the King and requested his signature. The poor imbecile Monarch who had during so many years been kept in strict subjection, appeared to hesitate. One of the members (Rosencrone) arose, and said, "Your Royal Highness is sensible the King cannot sign such a paper without due consideration." He had the boldness even to attempt to snatch the paper from the Prince's hand. Turning round to the Count with an air full of dignity and courage, the Crown Prince said, "It is not, sir, for you to advise the King on such an occasion, but I, who am heir-apparent to the throne, and responsible to the nation." Count Schak Ratlau was in the confidence of the Prince, and he remained silent. Guldberg was also silent, appearing thereby to acquiesce. Prince Frederick looked astonished and dismayed. The Crown Prince then laid the papers before his father, by whom they were immediately signed. The papers were at once carried by a confidential agent to the Royal Chancellory and entered in the records of the Crown. Being thus authorised to act, the Crown Prince addressed himself to the Council in a mild, yet decisive tone, and announced their dismissal.[1] He informed them that he had nominated a new Council, and appointed Count Bernstorff First Minister of the Crown. He assured the discarded members of his great regard, and qualified their grief and mortification by promising them indemnification in pensions, or some other equivalent. To his uncle he behaved with the utmost respect and deference, entreating him to honour the new Council with his presence and assist him with his advice.

From the council-room the Crown Prince went to the castle-guard and addressed the officers of the regiments of horse and foot then on duty, whom he found assembled agreeably to his orders. They immediately bound themselves by an oath to obey him. He then passed on to the Queen's magnificent apartment, to whom he communicated the important change that had taken place. Notwithstanding the blow was expected, it seemed almost to annihilate that haughty

---

[1] Rosencrone, Stehman, Molckte, Eichstedt and Guldberg.

woman. The Prince looked at her with pity, and spoke to her in the mildest terms. He told her she was at liberty if she pleased to retain the same apartments and household attendants. He gave her a choice of any of the Royal castles for her country residence; but, he also gave her to understand that she must no more interfere in affairs of State.

He left Juliana scarcely able to reply, and met the assembled new Council (Bernstorff excepted), the governor of Copenhagen, the commandant of the citadel, the commanding officers of the battalions in garrison, the colonel of the Copenhagen armed burghers, and the chief officers of police, telling them it was his orders only to which they were in future to pay obedience.

Expresses were sent every hour to Count Bernstorff to inform him how matters were going on. When the revolution was completed, the Crown Prince sent him an appointment to his former office, as Minister for Foreign Affairs, which was vacant by the dismission of Count Rosencrone, and held, *ad interim*, by Count Schak Ratlau.

These important changes were soon known in the city, and the heroic conduct of the young Crown Prince loudly applauded. The affection that the inhabitants felt towards him was soon manifested by the impatience with which they clamoured for the young Regent to appear, in whom they hoped to see revived the fine qualities of his grandfather, Frederick V. An immense multitude soon assembled near the great palace. Their shouts and huzzas penetrated every recess of that vast edifice, and smote the aching heart of Juliana, who trembled with apprehensions even for her personal safety. Dressed in a general's uniform, the modest young Prince showed himself to his people, and was hailed by plaudits that shook the whole city. Fearless and alone, attended only by a single domestic, he walked through the midst of the multitude and the principal streets of Copenhagen. He thus perambulated the town without the interference of the military, the crowd keeping at a respectful distance. The windows and balconies were crowded with handsome and well-dressed females, who waved their hands and handkerchiefs, bowing as he passed. These courtesies he returned, and thus escorted by a people in whose affections he already reigned, the Crown Prince re-entered the portals of Christianborg. This was the most brilliant day of his life. This Prince has lived to experience deep and heavy misfortunes. He may have adopted injurious measures, but the purity of his intentions, the integrity of his heart, were never questioned; nor, when his metropolis was wrapped in flames and his dominions partitioned, did he ever lose the respect and confidence of his people. There is no test equal to that of adversity. When a nation preserves its attachment to a Prince overwhelmed by misfortunes, it may safely be concluded he merited by his virtues the regard that is bestowed.

To return from this digression: the high steward of the palace, and M. Jacobi, reader to the King, were dismissed. Four chamberlains were appointed, to whom was entrusted the care of the King's person, and to provide him amusements. M. Schack was appointed Grand Master of the Ceremonies, an office not including the right of access to the King. Upon his retirement from that office, it was bestowed on M. de Numsen, director of the customs at Elsineur, son to the lady who had the care of the Crown Prince in his infancy. This gentleman was highly esteemed for his talents and acquirements. He had travelled much, and resided in several Courts, was possessed of a fine taste, great politeness, and a thorough knowledge of the world. He was, besides, a munificent patron of learning and the fine arts. M. Sporon, the Prince's preceptor, was dismissed, being too much devoted to Juliana to expect any gratitude from the Crown Prince. His dismissal followed so soon at the heels of his appointment that he had scarcely received the congratulations of his friends on account of the acquisition before he stood in need of their condolence on its loss.

Within a few days after these great events, Count Rosencrone retired to his estates in Jutland. He was indemnified by a pension equal to about six hundred pounds sterling per annum. He carried with him into retirement the reputation of an honest, well-meaning man. The mildness of his deportment caused his dismissal to be regretted, not only by those who had the honour of his acquaintance, but by all who had occasion to transact business with him as Minister for Foreign Affairs. His family were then recently ennobled, and he was first employed by the Court in the diplomatic line.

M. Stehman was appointed to a valuable post at Hardersleben. This gentleman owed his fortune principally to his zeal and industry. He was a laborious calculator rather than a splendid orator. Count Schimmelman, son to the Minister of that name so celebrated in the annals of Denmark, succeeded M. Stehman as Minister of Finance.

Instead of oppressing M. Guldberg, who had so principal a hand in the misfortunes of his unhappy mother, the Crown Prince allowed him to remain high steward of the household of Prince Frederick, with pensions to the amount of a thousand pounds sterling per annum. This gentleman possessed talent more than equal to Struensee's, with a judgment incomparably superior. He was temperate, inquisitive and industrious. He had but little taste for light amusements, and was seldom seen at balls or galas. He was devoted to domestic duties—a strong indication of a virtuous mind. He was twice married; his wives were sisters, daughters of a miller residing near Fredensborg. These pages show the favour he enjoyed from Juliana and her son, Prince Frederick. That he lent himself too implicitly to the views of his Royal patron may be admitted. It was, perhaps, his only road to power. He had, at least, the merit of enjoying his good fortune with exemplary moderation, and exhibiting a fidelity to those by whom he was advanced that is highly honourable to his character.

General Eichstedt, after his dismissal from Court and from his colonelship of horse-guards, retired to his estates, honoured with the high post of Lord Chamberlain of Denmark.

Infinitely to the honour of the Crown Prince, he set an example to all the ministers and servants of the Crown in the respectful delicacy with which he treated his dejected, disconsolate step-mother and his uncle. He strove by the kindest deportment to soften the stroke that wrested a sceptre from her hands. His mildness and humility affected her proud spirit more than any other mode of conduct could have done. She saw he pitied and forgave her, and it almost broke her heart. She soon withdrew from the metropolis, fixing her residence at Fredensborg. No hope remained of her ever regaining the power she had lost. Sullenly resigned, she strove to appear not to value what had passed away, equal to the tranquillity and retirement it procured her. She resolved to devote her time to prepare for another and a better world, and her wealth to charitable purposes. It must in candour be admitted, if the motives that animated her conduct in effecting the fall of Matilda were base, the use that she made of the power thus obtained offered no small atonement.

Above all, the mildness and fortitude that distinguished the Crown Prince on this trying occasion entitled him to admiration and esteem. There was a pensiveness imprinted on his features that showed he had not been nursed in the lap of fortune. He sought to obtain his legal inheritance, but he avoided everything that looked like exultation or triumph. Firm and temperate at the moment of peril, his demeanour was marked by modesty and discretion. When his enemies were overthrown, humanity prevented him from exposing to loss and degradation those whom he dismissed from their offices. The ministers whom he had removed were generally respected as men of probity and talent. In the day of prosperity they had conducted themselves with moderation. The fine arts, sciences, commerce, manufactures and agriculture were encouraged. Their greatest fault lay in the part which some of them had acted in the sad and terrible events of 1772. This was the real cause why the Crown Prince dismissed them. There was scarcely an individual amongst them whom he did not in some way or other indemnify, displaying at this early age a degree of wisdom and clemency that gave the fairest promise of his becoming a just and magnanimous Sovereign.

The new ministers appointed by the Crown Prince at the revolution of 1784 were: Count Bernstorff, Minister of Foreign Affairs and President of the German Chancellory; the Baron Rosencrantz, President of the College of Admiralty; the Baron Schak Ratlau, Chancellor of the University of Copenhagen; General Von Huth, Commander-in-Chief of the Artillery and President of the College of War; and M. de Stamp, President of the Danish Chancellory.

During the absence of Christian VII. on his travels in England and France, Baron de Rosencrantz had the direction of the War Department. He was a man of superior intellect and liberal endowments. His manners were polished and graceful, his knowledge of the world extensive. He possessed everything requisite to shine in a regal Court.

Baron Schak Ratlau was valued for his talents and acquirements in literature and the fine arts. He enjoyed the esteem and confidence of Denmark by his noble and generous conduct at the commencement of Struensee's administration. At the time of this great change, General Von Huth had arrived at the venerable age of seventy-five years, yet he appeared to possess the activity of a man of forty, and all his mental faculties were still verdant. He owed his elevation principally to his merit. He was born in Hesse Cassel. After serving in several wars, he entered the Danish service as a lieutenant-colonel, under the administration of Count St. Germaine. He was plain and unassuming in his manners, and, exclusive of his professional fame, he enjoyed an unsullied reputation for morality and unbending integrity.

The minister who presided over the Danish Chancellory was also possessed of qualities that, equally with his compeers, had acquired confidence and esteem. The four first of the new ministers were Knights of the Elephant, corresponding in rank with that of the Garter in Great Britain; De Stamp was invested with that of Dannebrog. From this period the Crown Prince dedicated his time to the acquirement of wisdom and experience, whereby to qualify himself to reign. Not content with presiding in the Council, he paid daily visits to his ministers, and most frequently to Count Bernstorff. He also attended the courts of justice, as well to observe the conduct of the judges as to gain a practical knowledge of the Danish jurisprudence.

According to the authority of that intelligent writer,

Mr. Coxe (vol. v., p. 177), the only foreigner who was supposed to have had any prior knowledge of these transactions was Mr. Elliot, who then resided as British Envoy at Copenhagen, having repaired thither from Berlin. The King of Great Britain, uncle to the Crown Prince, was the first Sovereign to whom the Prince Royal communicated the success of his daring enterprise. Alas! how little did that virtuous Sovereign or his young nephew imagine what dreadful visitations, in the course of a few years, the fleets and armies of Britain would pour on Denmark! Had it been foretold, it would have been regarded as some frightful vision springing from a distempered brain. From this period, the reign of Frederick VI. may be considered as commencing, the interesting events of which will be related in the proper place.

THE SWEDISH OLIGARCHY

The following short chapter is introduced merely to remind the reader of some of the leading events that occurred in Sweden after the death of Charles XII., and the better to elucidate the state of that kingdom when Gustavus III. overthrew the oligarchy in 1772.

CHAPTER X

THE Swedes have ever been celebrated for their valour and love of freedom. No nation on earth merits a higher character for every manly virtue. Under victorious princes, they gained abundance of glory, but it was at the expense of their independence. Gustavus Adolphus, considered merely as a warrior, justly merited the title of "The Great"; but his deep inroads on the constitutional rights of the people prevented his having any valid pretensions to that nobler appellation, "The Good." It is a well-known trait of the character of Charles XII. that when the Archbishop of Upsala was about to place the diadem upon his head, the demi-barbarian, rudely seizing the splendid ornament, placed it himself on his head.

The death of that indifferent monarch, but great soldier, was regarded as a blessing by a great part of the nation. And if the Order of Nobility had not found means to erect an oligarchy upon the ruins of his despotism, the peaceable establishment of a free Government might have indemnified Sweden for all the calamities which had originated in his vast and irrational ambition.

The sister of Charles XII., the Princess Ulrica Eleonora, for the sake of securing a crown that might have been contested, renounced in her own name and in that of her descendants and successors all claim to absolute power, and formally recognised the right of election to be in the nation in Diet assembled. Her husband, Frederick I., signed the Charter agreed to by his consort; he adopted the Lutheran religion, and was elected and crowned King of Sweden.

The Charter of 1720 was the work of the faction called the "Caps," who plumed themselves as patriots because they had stripped the Crown of undue prerogatives; and they would have merited the appellation if, instead of founding a grasping and devouring oligarchy, they had limited their own odious privileges and extended the liberty of the three inferior Orders.

The power of the King, by the letter of the Charter of 1720, was reduced to a mere cipher. The monarch had no longer the power to declare war or make peace, levy taxes, raise recruits, appoint officers of State, or dispose of the property of the Crown. The King had two votes in the Senate, and, if the voices were equal, the casting vote in such cases lay with the King.

The Senate and Nobility possessed all the power and patronage of Government. The three inferior Orders, namely, the clergy, burghers and peasants were oppressed, degraded and mocked by a nominal share in the legislative power, but void of real authority or influence.

The following are the principal articles contained in the Charter extorted by the Senate and Nobility from the King and Queen of Sweden in 1720 and 1723, viz.:

"The supreme power ought to reside for ever in the Assembly of States, composed of the representatives of the four Orders of citizens, the nobility, clergy, burgesses, and the immediate peasants of the Crown.

"The States, whether convoked or not, shall assemble every third year to review the conduct of the Senate, colleges and other departments in the execution of the laws entrusted to them, and to adopt such measures as may be necessary for the welfare and glory of the realm.

"The Crown of Sweden shall not be held by any Prince under the age of twenty-one years; and the States shall have the right of appointing tutors for the education of the Royal Family.

"The legislative power shall be wholly in the States, whose consent shall be necessary to give validity to the decrees passed by the King and Senate in the intervals between the meetings of the Diets.

"The States reserve to themselves the right of making war, but, in case of invasion or domestic commotions, the King, in concert with the Senate, may take measures for repelling force by force, without waiting for the meeting of the States, which shall, however, be convoked without delay.

"The King may coin money, but the standard shall be regulated by the States.

"The King shall not upon any occasion leave the kingdom without the consent of the States.

"In case of a vacancy in the Senate, three candidates, natives of Sweden, shall be nominated by the States, of whom His Majesty shall accept one.

"During the illness or absence of the King, the Senate shall sign all public Acts.

"All the superior military officers, from field-marshals to colonels inclusively, shall be appointed by the King.

"The States, assembled in Diet, shall give redress to all persons prejudiced by the regulations or decisions of the States.

"The ancient privileges of the Senate shall be for ever inviolable, but no new privilege relating to any separate Order can be valid without the consent of the whole."

To these, in 1723, were added the following:

"The King, in concert with the Senate, may convoke the States before the expiration of the three years.

"Upon the death, absence or illness of the King, the Senate in a body may convoke the States, which they may also do when the welfare of the country or the liberty of the States is in danger.

"If, in the above cases, neither the King nor the Senate shall convoke the States within the time prescribed, the States shall declare everything done in the interval, both at home and abroad, null; of which they shall order notice to be given by the Governor of Stockholm, and the governors of the different provinces, that the States may assemble of their own accord at the proper time and place.

"When the throne is vacant, the States, whether convoked or not, shall assemble at Stockholm thirty days after the death of the King, and shall proceed to a new election.

"The individuals who compose the States shall bind themselves by an oath not to propose, agree to, or execute anything that has a tendency to change the form of government; and whatever shall be decreed by the States to the prejudice of the liberty and independence of the nation, shall be null and invalid.

"The Senate and the King shall be responsible for their conduct in the intervals between the meetings of the Diet.

"There shall be a secret committee for affairs not proper to be fully discussed; and this shall be composed of the three first Orders, to the exclusion of the peasants; all matters referred from the whole body shall be settled here, and the members shall be absolutely prohibited from conferring with foreign ministers.

"The States shall make the laws, but they shall be signed by the King and executed in his name. In default of the King, the Senate shall sign, and cause them to be executed.

"Each Order shall have a vote in the regulation of affairs relating to the nation in general, and the plurality of the four votes shall decide the question; but where the just privileges of any single Order are concerned, the matter must be decided by a unanimous vote of all the Orders."

The defects of such a system of government are so palpable, they need no elucidation. For the exercise of the power wrested from the Crown, two fierce and powerful factions contested; that which Russia supported was called the "Caps"; that devoted to the furtherance of French politics was known by the appellation of the "Hats." The Caps, to amuse the nation, professed their determination to cultivate the friendship of Russia, and promote internal and external peace, agriculture and manufactures. The Hats sought for partisans by extolling the value of a French alliance, stimulating the nation to aspire to the reconquest of the provinces that formerly belonged to Sweden. These two factions, with varied success, carried on their machinations for half a century! alternately or simultaneously in the pay of France, Russia, England or Denmark.

The martial spirit of the Swedes led them to forgive Charles XII., not only his losses in the field of battle, but his despotic principles. It could not be denied that his fierce and ungovernable ambition had covered Sweden with mourning, but it was sorrow unalloyed by dishonour. National pride was gratified in contemplating the exploits of the conqueror, whilst his fame poured a blaze of imperishable glory over his impoverished and exhausted country. His faults were all forgotten, and if they wept, it was rather on account of his fall than of the sufferings he had entailed on his bleeding country. Such being the feelings of the great bulk of the population, as it might have been foreseen, the pacific measures of the Caps were publicly condemned as being servile and disgraceful. And with diminished resources, and an impoverished exchequer, the prevailing faction rashly ventured on a war with Russia. The loss of an army of brave men, Count de Lewenhaupt, and part of the Swedish territories in Finland and Lapland, furnished lasting cause of regret in Sweden for having suffered itself to be led astray by factious chiefs, who, under the plausible pretext of paramount regard to the public good, had no better object in view than the augmentation of their own power and revenues. During this war the King had, perhaps, a secret interest in thwarting, as far as he could, the measures of the Senate by which his power was shackled and his splendour eclipsed. In revenge, the Court of Versailles instigated the States, or rather the oligarchy, to add new trammels to those already fastened on the power of the monarch, by exercising the control of the Senate over the personal property of the King. On the 25th of March, 1751, at the advanced age of seventy-one years, died Frederick I., who was succeeded by Adolphus Frederick. This Prince had been married some few years to the Princess Louisa of Prussia, sister of Frederick the Great, a woman of rare endowments and uncommon cultivation. She was the early patron of several of those great men who afterwards extended the sphere of human knowledge and shed an imperishable lustre on their country. Sir Charles Linné, K.P.S., Bergmann and Menanderhjelm were among the number of her scientific friends.

This great woman—who really merited the appellation of "the Minerva of the North"—was peculiarly the object of Senatorial vengeance. By the thirteenth article of the Ordinance of 1723, it was enacted that the States of Sweden were empowered to inspect the jewels of the Crown as well as those of the Royal Treasury; and merely to wound the feelings of the illustrious foreigner—who was alike eminent for beauty, dignity and fine accomplishments —the Senate demanded to inspect her jewels, pretending, as an excuse, that their *high mightinesses* had heard that the Queen had sent them to Berlin! Count Tessin, the Swedish Ambassador at Berlin, had delivered the jewels in question to the Queen as her private property. They required the production of jewels that were become the private property of the Queen, with the view to compare them with the inventory. The Queen said to the senator who had demanded them, "I shall not admit of any inspection, nor, after such an indignity, will I retain them. As soon as they can be separated from my own gems, the whole that I received as a present shall be returned." The dignified severity of her looks, the firmness of her tone and manner, made the audacious noble not only look, but *feel* humbled. The States, goaded by the

Senate to do whatever was required of them, complained to the King, not only of Her Majesty the Queen having shown contempt towards the Senate, but also towards the nation and great officers of the Crown. "It should be remembered that the Queen came to Sweden as the King's consort, and to increase the authority of the Crown." After stating several causes of complaint alike puerile and malignant, they concluded their rude and impertinent address by observing that "the States of Sweden did not wish for any alterations in the sentiments of the King towards the Queen, but that the Queen should feel more respect for the nation."

The King, who was calculated to have excelled in the practice of domestic virtues, had not sufficient firmness to repel this insolence as he ought. Fearful of giving rise to internal commotions, the mild and benevolent man strove by humility and submission to soothe the anger of the oligarchs. He descended to make an elaborate apology for the Queen, imputing all that was offensive to her ignorance of the Swedish language, urging, with marked deference as to style and expression, that the jewels having remained ten years in her possession without any inspection having been called for, she considered the measure as implying distrust of her honour, and the more insulting, as the diamonds, having been given to her as a present, were in fact her private property.

The States, however, led by the oligarchy, persisted. The moderation displayed by the King only encouraged the audacity of the predominant faction, and notwithstanding all the protestations of Adolphus Frederick, the insulting and humiliating measure was carried into execution.

One of the *remonstrances* presented from the Diet of 1756 contained the following singular expressions, viz.: "The States beseech Your Majesty to remain master of the Court, and King of Sweden, and *humbly pray* that all further correspondence on this subject may cease."

The King wishing to be allowed to appoint the tutors to whom was to be entrusted the education of his children, had selected a second governor for the Crown Prince—a privilege that the States would not permit him to exercise; the place was declared to be unnecessary, the second governor was dismissed, and this resolution was accompanied by an insulting letter to the King. To show the plenitude of their power and rudeness, they transmitted a peremptory order, couched in the shape of a humble request, to dismiss the governor, and appointed Count Scheffer in his place. Urged by his Queen, whose proud heart was half-broken by these bitter humiliations, the King mustered resolution enough to protest against the right of the States to this prerogative over his children; but so overwhelming was the power of the ruling faction, that his wishes and his rights, as a parent or Sovereign, were equally disregarded. Count Scheffer took possession of the King's eldest son, soon after which several other officers were appointed to be immediately about his person. This was unquestionably done to inspire the young Prince, even in his days of childhood, with sentiments of awe and reverence toward the Order of Nobles and the Senate. As to the inferior Orders, they were merely passive machines, moved and removed at the pleasure of their superiors.

Nor did the humiliations to which the monarch was subjected by the venal and rapacious nobles end here. To give legality to resolutions subversive of the Royal authority, and made without the consent, or even the knowledge of the King, the Senate caused a fac-simile of the sign-manual to be engraved, which was affixed to such documents as they wished to promulgate unknown to the King! The nation, instead of finding its liberty restored by the Charter of 1720, saw itself the prey of an unprincipled aristocracy, that trampled on the just prerogatives of the Crown and the rights of the people; that levied taxes, which they caused to be collected and disposed of as they saw good, from the burthen of which their estates were exempted. Indifferent to the horrors of war or the blessings of peace, they put up for sale to the highest bidder, in the political market of Europe, the resources, courage and influence of a brave and high-spirited nation.

Several opportunities occurred that might, if improved, have led to the sure and sudden overthrow of the abhorrent faction that ruled with despotic sway in Sweden. But such was the King's fear of exciting a civil war, and thereby exposing Sweden to utter subjugation, that he submitted to the degrading yoke of a venal aristocracy, that was alike fatal to the prerogatives of his crown and the liberties and honour of the people. Instead of waiting for an opportunity of breaking asunder the fetters imposed by the oligarchy, he preferred incessant but unavailing efforts to render them less intolerable and galling.

At the instigation of his spirited and accomplished Queen, the King secretly, if not openly, encouraged Counts Brahe and Horne, and other noblemen and burghers attached to the faction called the Hats, to endeavour to organise a force, military and insurgent, competent to seize on the capital and overthrow the Old Hats. It appeared by the evidence published that the domestics of the King, as low as valets and footmen, were employed to excite, by their discourses, the populace of Stockholm to take up arms against the Hats. It was through this channel the conspiracy was detected. The inferior agents were first arrested. The chiefs might have escaped, as there was ample time, and they were admonished by the sorrowing Queen to lose no time in avoiding the destruction that impended. By a fatal confidence in the King, Counts Horne and Brahe remained, and were arrested. It is recorded that they were tortured in the cruellest manner to force them to accuse the King and Queen, which they indignantly refused. The King had the mortification to be forced to ratify their condemnation, and sign their death-warrant. The Countess Brahe, a high-born and beautiful woman, far advanced in pregnancy, prostrating herself at the feet of Count Fersen, a leader of the Hats, in vain implored the callous statesman for her husband's life. He perished with his friends on the scaffold. Of their adherents, some were imprisoned and others exiled; and thus terminated the effort made to put down the despotic sway of a venal nest of rapacious peers.

Instead of her husband, if the Queen Louisa Ulrica had swayed the sceptre of Sweden, soon would that great woman have overthrown the fell tyranny of a detestable faction, who were strong only because her gentle-hearted husband was, comparatively speaking, weak. Her elevated soul was wrung with unutterable anguish when she heard of the sufferings endured by her faithful friends, without the power to rescue or even to relieve them. Disdaining to show homage where her bosom was filled with intense scorn and just abhorrence, she omitted no opportunity of displaying, as far as a due regard to her own dignity warranted, the contempt and aversion she cherished towards the cruel and unfeeling oligarchy, beneath whose hands the best and bravest of her friends had perished.

If Louisa Ulrica had possessed a mind like that of Catherine II., ambition and a thirst of vengeance might have led her to have given Adolphus Frederick a premature passport to eternity, and have caused herself to be declared, during the minority of her son, administratrix of Sweden. If she deplored the too great forbearance that marked her husband's policy, she honoured the goodness of his heart, knowing it was not any deficiency of personal courage by which his conduct was regulated, but a conscientious regard to his coronation oath, and an unconquerable dread of giving rise to a civil war. The Queen never ceased to lament, whenever their memory occurred to her, the sad fate of her brave and unfortunate friends; but, if ever she entertained, she soon dismissed all thoughts of vengeance from her bosom. She was really virtuous—unaffectedly religious. Repressing as far as she could the workings of indignation and ambition, she applied her great and capacious mind to the cultivation of literature, the fine arts and sciences. She could not be prevented from superintending the education of her children. She engaged the King in numerous journeys through the different provinces of Sweden; and seeking out genius in obscurity, transplanted it to a more genial soil, where its fine qualities might freely expand. And many of those deservedly great names that have conferred more real lustre on the Swedish nation than all the heroes of the Gustavian line, owed all their eminence, next to Nature, to her fostering hand.

Acting upon a system of economy that was untainted by meanness, with an income inferior to many private gentlemen of England, she expended it so judiciously that she left behind her many costly monuments that embellished Sweden, reflecting equal honour on her taste and judgment. The Palace of Drottningholm, distant about seven English miles from Stockholm, was her favourite residence. That magnificent structure—which is equal in extent and magnificence to any Royal palace in Great Britain—was enriched by innumerable additions, internal and external, derived from her own industry, wealth and taste.

On a plan of her own designing, for the purpose of enjoying greater retirement, she built a tasteful little palace in the park at Drottningholm, calling it "China Lustslot," *i.e.*, the Chinese Rural Palace. Its architectural merit consisted in its resemblance to the country palaces of the Emperor of China. It consisted of a centre, and, on either side, of two smaller pavilions, or *corps du logis*. Here her virtuous husband amused himself in mechanical pursuits, such as carving, turnery, and the less elegant toils of a whitesmith; and here the Queen devoted her leisure hours to the noblest of human pursuits, that of wisdom and science. Surrounded by the greatest names known in the annals of Swedish science and literature, and by domestic blessings, in this, and other enchanting spots, this illustrious woman strove to banish from her mind the bitter indignities that she had endured as nominal Queen of Sweden.

After the judicial murder of her friends, the wrongs and insults to which she was exposed were multiplied. Through the feelings of the Queen, the reigning factions strove to wound the King. She was accused of betraying State secrets, and carrying on a traitorous correspondence with the Court of Berlin. Like the harpies of the poets, the oligarchs obtruded their baleful influence into the inmost recesses of the palace. They interfered with the King's table, that was always distinguished by a liberal economy, and even debarred the King and Queen of appointing their domestic chaplains, who, in the Lutheran Church of Sweden and Denmark, may be almost regarded as *confessors*. After various *changes of ministry*, the Hats and Caps were alternately above or below the political horizon, but always selfish, corrupt and despotic, and alike inimical to the just prerogatives of the Crown and the liberties of the people. To stem or escape the overwhelming flood of legislative and oligarchical corruption and despotism, the Queen, aided by the Crown Prince, prevailed on Adolphus Frederick to make one bold and decisive effort to shake off the degrading yoke that humbled the Crown and debased the people. The commencement of war between Russia and the Porte, and the death of Count Lowenhjelm, the inveterate opposer of French politics, favoured the views of the Hats, and encouraged the cautious King to hazard the proposal of abdicating his throne. Pursuant to the opinion of his secret advisers, the King, to the surprise and vexation of the Senate, refused to sign a public document they had presented, and demanded the convocation of an extraordinary Diet, as affording the only remedy for the disorders complained of by his subjects. After refusing to sign this Act, the King, on the 12th of December, 1768, expressed his intention of abdicating in the following terms, viz.:

"If, contrary to all reasonable expectation, the Senate should reject this proposal, I shall be forced to relinquish the burthen of a government rendered intolerable by the wretchedness of the people, who are taxed beyond their power of compliance. When my faithful counsellors shall have assembled the States, the reasons which have induced me to abdicate shall be communicated to them. In the meantime, I peremptorily forbid the use of my name to any Act of the Senate. (Signed) "ADOLF FREDERICK."

An answer to this letter, though demanded in forty-eight hours, was not returned at the end of five days, a decisive proof how greatly the senators were perplexed. Finding no reply was likely to be given, the King went personally to the Senate. Pretending to want time for deliberation concerning his demand of convoking an extraordinary Diet, and with respect to His Majesty's abdication, those conscientious men expressed their hope that he would desist from a measure incompatible with his oath and the prosperity of the nation. In reply, the King told the usurpers (for such they were) that their answer was only to be considered as a refusal, and thenceforward he should interfere no farther with the measures of government.

It was with great difficulty, and only by the entreaties of his Queen[1] and eldest son, that Adolphus

---

[1] The following letters, written by Queen Louisa Ulrica to her son, afterwards Gustavus III., are highly honourable to her character, and well worthy a place in this brief memoir, viz.:

LETTRE I.

"J'ai été touchée vivement, mon cher fils, de la sensibilité que vous avez témoignée à mon départ. Je ne vous cache point que votre amitié m'est chère, et qu'il y a peu de mères qui puissent aimer plus tendrement leurs enfans que je ne fais; mais, à DIEU ne plaise que je vous aimasse d'une amitié aveugle! ce seroit vous trahir, et non pas vous aimer. Je suis attentive à toutes vos actions, et je n'ai point à me reprocher de lâche complaisance pour vos défauts; je me flatte même, que ce sera, un jour, un des liens qui vous attachera plus intimement à moi.

"Continuez, mon cher fils, à être exact à remplir tous vos devoirs: je mets au-dessus de tout le culte et la vénération que vous devez à l'Etre Suprême. Souvenez-vous que les vertus morales sont en danger si elles ne sont soutenues par celles chretiennes, et que les âmes élevées ont pour Dieu des sentiments qui partent du cœur,

Frederick could be wrought up to the adoption of that apparently resolute conduct; almost immediately after which the Crown Prince went in great state to the Royal Chancellory to demand, in his father's name, the fac-simile of the Royal signature that is already mentioned. His demand being refused, Gustavus went to the other State departments, declaring at each place that his father had abdicated, and delivering to each of the members a printed statement of His Majesty's reasons for having recourse to that extreme measure.

---

et qui leur donnent cette noble assurance dans toutes les actions de leur vie. Que la vôtre, mon cher fils, soit longue et que Dieu vous fasse la grâce de vous mettre au rang de ces princes qui servent de modèle aux siècles à venir, ce sont, mon cher fils, mes vœux: ils sont sincères, et vous assurent de la tendresse infinie avec laquelle je serai à jamais

"Votre tendre mère,
"Lou. Ulrique."

Letter I.—Translation.

"It was not without great emotion that I saw you, my dear Gustave, so sensibly affected with my departure, for I freely own to you that your affection is extremely dear to me, and that there are few mothers who love their children with more tenderness than myself; but God forbid that my love for you should ever make me blind to your faults!—this were to betray, instead of loving you. I am attentive to all your actions, without having any reason to reproach myself with a weak indulgence for your defects; and I flatter myself that this will one day be a means of attaching you yet more closely to me.

"Continue, my dear Gustave, to be exact in fulfilling your several duties, the principal of which is the veneration and worship due to the Supreme Being. Remember that moral virtue is in great danger when it is no longer supported by Christianity, and that all great minds have a sincere love for, and confidence in their Creator,

The Senate, mortified and humbled, sent a deputation to the King, whom, to all appearance, they found inflexible—a line of conduct in which he persevered till, by a second deputation, the Senate consenting to call the States together, induced him to resume the reins of government, which, by-the-bye, he neither had, nor seriously intended to resign.

The extraordinary Diet met on the 28th of April, and the Senate not daring to negotiate the treaty without the participation of the States, all the measures of Russia and England were disarranged.

---

which gives them that noble assurance so visible in every action of their lives. That your life may be of long duration, and that God may be graciously pleased to place you in the rank of those princes who become a model to future ages!—these are my constant prayers; they are sincere, and, therefore, assure you of the tender affection with which I shall ever be,
" Your kind mother,
" Lou. Ulrique."

Lettre II.

" Je vous avois promis, mon cher fils, une plus longue lettre par le courier, et je me fais un plaisir de vous tenir parole. Je n'entrerai pas en detail des beautés des provinces, de leur situation, de leur commerce, et de leurs manufactures; le sujet sur lequel je veux vous entretenir est infiniment plus intéressant; c'est des habitants, de leur zèle, et de l'amour infini qu'ils témoignent au roi. A quoi serviroient ces vains titres et ces grandeurs s'ils n'étoient accompagnés de l'affection du peuple. Le vrai bonheur, mon cher fils, est de pouvoir faire celui des autres; heureux celui qui en a le pouvoir! mais quelque peu que l'on puisse en avoir, il doit toujours avoir cet objet. Les princes qui s'éloignent de ces maximes sont des tirans que la Providence a fait naître comme des instrumens de sa vengeance et dont les noms ont l'horreur du genre humain.

" Dieu vous a donné, mon cher fils, des talens et une âme sensible; gardez vous toujours que ce cœur ne devienne la dupe

Thus the intrigues and the gold of France again began to acquire the ascendency. The King returning to the Senate, assured that body of his approbation of their conduct, asserted the purity of his own views, and declared the welfare of the nation to be his only aim.

The conduct of the Hats on this occasion proved

---

de l'esprit; c'est un écueil qui a souvent terni les plus belles vies; que la votre aie la piété pour guide! c'est le plus sûr remède contre tous les égaremens.

"Continuez, mon cher fils, à vous faire une étude de la vertu. Vous voulez savoir quel en sera le succès? Il sera proportionné à vos efforts. Pourquoi balancer? On n'est point sage par hazard. Les biens, les honneurs, les dignités peuvent aller au devant de vous; mais la vertu ne nous previendra jamais; elle ne s'obtient que par le travail et par un travail continu; mais ce travail doit-il vous rébuter dès qu'il vous procure la possession de tous les biens? N'espérez donc jamais pouvoir allier la volupté avec la gloire, la mollesse avec la récompense de la vertu.

"C'est peut-être trop de morale pour une lettre. Je vais finir celle-ci en vous communiquant mon contentement sur les vôtres. Votre sincérité répare en partie la faute que vous avez commise. Celui qui se résigne est à moitié corrigé; faites en sorte, mon cher fils, que vous n'ayez plus de pareilles confidences à me faire. Donnez-moi, par votre conduite, des preuves convaincantes de votre amitié. Soyez assuré de la mienne, qui ne finira qu'avec la vie, étant à jamais

"Votre tendre et bonne mère,
"L. U."

LETTER II.—Translation.

" I promised you, my dear Gustave, a long letter by the courier, and I have a pleasure in keeping my word. I shall not be particular in describing the beauties of these provinces, their situation, commerce and manufactures. I will rather tell you of the inhabitants, their zeal and affection for the King, which is a subject infinitely more interesting. Of what use were all these vain titles and grandeur, if not accompanied by the people's love? They would

how great was their reliance, in the ensuing Diet, upon the support of France. Various expedients were adopted with a view to support that party, and a considerable subscription was raised in favour of the French faction by the principal merchants of Sweden.

By these energetic measures, and the quantity of

---

be troublesome burdens and crowns of thorns. True felicity, my dear Gustave, consists in the power of making others happy: fortunate is the man who is endowed with this power! but be our share of it ever so small, this ought always to be its principal object. Those Princes who depart from these maxims are tyrants whom Providence created to be the instruments of its vengeance, and whose names are the horror of mankind.

"God hath given you talents, and a heart not without sensibility; be careful lest it become a dupe to your understanding; it is a rock on which many a sensible man hath split. Choose piety for your pilot, and you need not fear that you will err in your course.

"Continue, my dear Gustave, to make virtue your chief study. Would you know your success beforehand? It will be proportioned to your efforts. Why should we balance a moment? We shall never grow good by chance. Wealth, honours, dignities, may come of their own accord; but virtue must be eagerly pursued. She is not to be obtained without continued labour: but ought this labour to affright us, when we know that it will procure us all that is desirable? You must never hope to unite sensuality with glory, nor indolence with the reward of virtue.

"This is, perhaps, too much morality for a letter. I shall finish this in telling you with how much satisfaction I received yours; your sincerity is some reparation of the fault you have committed. He who acknowledges his guilt is not far from amendment. Behave, my dear Gustave, so as not to have any more such secrets to entrust me with. Let your future conduct convince me of your affection. You may be assured that mine for you will never cease but with my life, being ever your tender and affectionate mother,

"L. U."

money distributed by the French minister, the Hats obtained important electioneering advantages over the Caps. In spite of all the efforts of Russia, England and Denmark, General Count Ferson was elected Marshal of the Diet, and of the secret committee, all the individuals composing which were devoted to his will. It was fortunate for the Caps that the Hats were split into two parties: of these, the Court or Royal party, like the *ultra Royalists* of France in 1815, were for rendering the Crown absolute; the other party, called the "Old Hats," had no other view than to supplant their antagonists and gain possession of the *loaves and fishes* of Sweden, without doing anything in favour either of the Crown or the people.

The first act of the secret committee was the dismission of the senators who had been appointed under the influence of Russia and England; but still, all that could be obtained of this Diet by the French Court, which had lavished such large sums to obtain its appointment and favour, was a declaration dictated by that anti-Britannic spirit which appears so powerfully to animate Sweden and most of the Continental nations of Europe at the present hour. Its tenour was as follows, viz., "That the English only aimed at the empire of the sea and the extension of their commerce, which they were desirous of acquiring at the expense of other nations; that Sweden, therefore, could not consider England as her friend, and though it was the interest of Sweden to be upon good terms with the neighbouring Powers, she could not enter into any alliance with them; that Sweden reckoned France and the Porte as her natural allies, and also Spain and Austria as the friends of France."

The plan, between one Diet and another, of giving to the King and the Senate the power of forming alliances and declaring war, was successfully resisted by Colonel (afterwards General) Baron Pechlin, a man of great ability and integrity, at the head of the party called the "Old Hats." If it had succeeded, all the military resources of Sweden would have passed into the hands of the French minister, who would have immediately plunged Sweden into a war with Russia.

The plan which France had formed to overturn the Swedish Government, and kindle a Northern war in Europe, thus completely failed. The expensive expedient of employing the States to effect this purpose was found to be useless, and no other and more effectual means could be devised. The daring and enterprising spirit that marked the character of the Swedes, and rendered a revolution, if attempted by a bold and sudden stroke, by no means improbable, was counteracted by the mild and pacific character of the King, of whom it was said, that he could never be brought into any measure by which the safety or interest of his family were likely to be involved in danger. The love of tranquillity seemed to increase with his years; his wise and virtuous Queen, shocked at the blood that had been shed during her husband's reign by each of the gladiatorial factions, refrained from urging him to any further efforts. She rested her hopes on the abilities and courage of her sons, particularly the Crown

Prince. At the express request of the Duke de Choiseul, he had been invited to Paris, a circumstance that revived the hopes of the Court party, who confidently expected that it would lead to some effectual step for the establishment of the Royal authority, and the overthrow of the two factions who alternately ruled the dominions of Sweden. Such was the state of that agitated kingdom when the death of the King, on the 13th of February, 1771, suddenly changed the face of affairs.

The character of this monarch is so fully developed in the preceding pages that there is nothing to add, except the observation that, as he was never suffered to reign, there are no grounds whereon to rest his public character. During the whole of his nominal sovereignty, Sweden was governed by conflicting factions, who waged war and negotiated peace, not as the safety or interest of Sweden required, but as those Powers commanded whose gold had paid for their venal suffrages. Yet, during the reigns of Frederick I. and Adolphus Frederick, these very abuses gave a strong impulse to the factious nobles to cultivate their intellectual power, in hope, by their talents and eloquence, to obtain a share in the division of the power, profit and patronage that had been wrested from the Crown at the death of Charles XII. During this half-century, Sweden produced many great orators and distinguished statesmen, but they were bound in the fetters of party. Seldom were they permitted, if they even were inclined, to render any important service to their plundered and insulted country. For the space of half a century, under a nominal monarchy, Sweden was in fact an oligarchy. The Senate and the Order of Nobles during that period exercised all the essentials of monarchy; hence it would be a work of supererogation to give the characters of kings who never exercised the sovereign power. In the succeeding reign, the tables were turned upon the oligarchs. The whole kingdom groaned under their tyranny and abhorred their venality. The blood that had been reciprocally shed by those fierce, venal, conflicting factions, and the general detestation in which both parties were held, kept back the people from ranging themselves round the banners of either. Under the withering influence of their intriguing chiefs it was in vain to hope for anything beyond a change of masters. Thence, the Prince who succeeded his father on the throne, like Frederick III. of Denmark, had little more to do than to follow the impulse of popular indignation, which, operating in the same pernicious way as in Denmark, rendered the people more ardent in their wishes to see the foul and accursed oligarchy broken up, and driven far from the throne of Sweden, than to make terms with the monarch advantageous to her freedom, and equally fatal to the vile factions which had so long and so successfully preyed on the vitals of their country.

Louisa Ulrica, now Queen-Dowager of Sweden, sustained a heavy affliction in the death of her mild and benevolent husband. The early promise of excellence displayed in the wonderful capacity of her eldest son was blasted as he approached to manhood by the deep dissimulation of his mind and the propensities to which he was addicted. Her second son, Charles (who yet fills the throne of Sweden), gave himself implicitly up to the views of Gustavus. Her third son, who died at Montpelier, showed her more deference than either Gustavus or Charles; his capacity was, however, less brilliant. Her daughter, Sophia Albertina, was possessed of a great share of personal virtue, a capacity as vast and varied as her splendid brother, and unsullied by his vices. The period had now arrived when this illustrious woman hoped to see avenged the wrongs and indignities she had for nearly thirty years sustained from the oligarchy that usurped all the prerogatives of the Crown; but the vices with which she knew Gustavus to be deeply fraught forbade the hope of ever seeing him deserve the title of a patriot King. She never doubted that his mind was adequate to any enterprise, but with real sorrow she anticipated that he would rear monarchical despotism on the ruin of the two conflicting factions. Her mild and benevolent views aimed at the adoption of a constitutional form of government, that should leave the people nothing to wish for by any future change. Absorbed in secret grief, she took no steps whatever of a political nature; and the absence of Gustavus, her eldest son, and of Frederick, the youngest (Duke of Ostra-Gothland), who were then in Paris, afforded the reigning faction, as they weakly supposed, the most favourable opportunity of confirming the durability of their usurped authority, and riveting indissolubly their vile shackles on the King and people.

Perhaps the profound dissimulation which, beyond any other quality, marked the character of Gustavus, was owing to the necessity his father and mother had been under of speaking on affairs of State with the utmost reserve, and having one set of opinions for the Senate and ministers of the Crown and another for their confidential friends. Be that as it may, in native talents and acquirements, in presence of mind and undaunted courage, Gustavus equalled the most accomplished men in Sweden; but, in *hypocrisy* he had no equal; he towered above them all, as the flight of the imperial eagle stretches into regions beyond the reach of birds of humbler wing. His associates were young, gay, dissipated courtiers, alike free from private morals or public principles—his ready tools and obsequious instruments.

GUSTAVUS III.

CHAPTER XI

Sophia Magdalena, consort to Gustavus III.—Auspicious commencement of his reign—His secrecy and self-command—Profound dissimulation—The Diet of 1771—Further proofs of deep hypocrisy—Outwits the Senate—Overthrows the oligarchy in 1772—His gross impiety on that occasion—Anecdote of Count Ugglas—Gustavus lives apart from his Queen—The Duchess of Sodermanland—A Royal expedient—Increased splendour of the Court—Gustavus encourages trade and manufactures—Becomes a monopolist of brandy distilleries—General discontent—Insurrections—Failure of his commercial speculations.

THIS extraordinary monarch was twenty-five years of age at the death of his father, Adolphus Fredcrick. Gustavus III. was born on the 24th of January, 1746. He was married in his twentieth year to Sophia Magdalena, Crown Princess of Denmark. His lovely young bride was sister to Christian VII., and daughter of Frederick V., by Louisa, daughter of George II. and Queen Caroline. The handsome and accomplished young couple were married in the beginning of November, 1766 — the two disastrous matches, namely.

that of Christian with Caroline Matilda, and Gustavus with Sophia Magdalena, taking place at the same time.

Seldom had a Prince so fair an opportunity of serving his native land and of becoming the idol of a grateful people. And never was there a monarch more liberally gifted by Nature or embellished by education. The path to imperishable glory lay wide before him. Everything conspired to court his steps. But, alas! dissolute company and perverted habits had deeply polluted his mind long ere the sceptre passed into his hand.

Although to remove far away from his ill-fated consort—whom he hated because he had injured—might, as was alleged by Gustavus himself to one of the senators, have had its influence in determining him to go on his travels, the grand object was to procure aid from the French Court whereby to enable him to overturn the oligarchy. With these negotiations he was far advanced at the beginning of 1771.

Gustavus was much too sagacious, however immoral, to believe that such polluted beings as those who were his minions could be safely depended upon. When, therefore, the news of his father's death arrived, he carefully shut up his real views in the recesses of his own mind, and appeared to his profligate companions perfectly contented with the nominal authority that devolved upon him. And when one of those sycophants hinted at the pleasure he should feel in seeing the oligarchy laid low and the power of the Crown exalted, Gustavus, assuming an imperious frown, sternly forbade such discourse in future, telling the parasite that he looked on the senators as his best friends and safest counsellors, and, without a blush, accusing his illustrious mother of being the turbulent instigator of all the misfortunes and dissensions that had occurred during his father's reign.

At this period the Court of Versailles was at its meridian splendour; its voluptuousness and corruption were at its height, and ripe for the punishment that awaited its deep iniquity.

Calculated to shine in any station and to excel in every pursuit, it is no wonder that Gustavus succeeded in obtaining more favourable conditions than any other negotiator could have effected. He obtained 6,000,000 livres—one-fourth of which was to be paid immediately, and the remainder in three successive yearly payments. The final arrangement of this affair kept Gustavus some months in Paris. The fact is, he wanted to secure this money to aid the blow he meditated against the oligarchy. The ambassador at Paris was a member of the Senate. Gustavus had, therefore, a delicate and a difficult task to perform; but arduous indeed must have been that labour, the difficulties of which he could not have surmounted.

It is dubious if Gustavus even entrusted his brother Frederick with his views. It is already shown in how decisive a tone he curbed the loquacity of one of his courtiers. Nor was it in trifles only that the young King sought to blind and mislead his powerful and wily antagonists. He received their counterfeit pretensions of loyalty as sterling, and he repaid them with their own base coin—nay, he even went beyond them in expressions of attachment and devotion. In reply to their notification of his accession to the throne, he transmitted to the mistrustful oligarchs the most eloquent and fervent protestations of his entire satisfaction with the existing order of things. He assured that Senate, whose speedy humiliation he contemplated, and under whose tyranny he writhed, of his entire devotion to *their* counsels, and that with his heart's blood would he defend "*the purity of their doctrines, and the existence of their political power!*" He expressed his abhorrence of all violence, and in the least equivocal terms that language could supply; and upon his word of honour, as a King and a gentleman, he declared his firm determination faithfully to fulfil whatever the existing law prescribed, and to act conformably to the form of regency of the year 1720, to which he had already sworn! To leave the less reason to doubt the sincerity of his intentions, Gustavus declared he should consider and treat as traitors to their country, and personal enemies to himself, those who, secretly or openly, or in any manner, should seek to establish an *arbitrary government* in Sweden. This masterpiece of Royal eloquence and dissimulation he concluded with the solemn invocation, attesting his sincerity, "May God so help me!"

Whilst vast and important designs filled his mind, Gustavus apparently gave himself up to his licentious companions and polluted pursuits. He attended the select parties of the beautiful and meretricious females of the Gallic Court. With those he did not long remain a favourite, for it could not be concealed that this Prince did not pay homage at the shrine of Venus. During his abode in Paris, Gustavus employed himself in obtaining, whether from the Treasury of France or the Porte, the largest possible subsidy, as well as in endeavours to secure the firm support of France in the revolution he contemplated. Matters being at last satisfactorily arranged, Gustavus quitted Paris on his return to assume the vacant throne of Sweden. As he passed through Berlin, he spent a few days with the King, his maternal uncle. Without assuming any appearance of secrecy or mystery, he found means to see his uncle once alone, and that unknown to his attendants.

Gustavus was received in Stockholm with acclamations of joy; when he met 'the Senate, his manner was respectful and conciliating. He repeated verbally the professions he had transmitted from Paris. He paid a visit of condolence to the Queen-Dowager, his mother, but seemed desirous of avoiding any particular conference. His young and neglected spouse he scarcely deigned to notice, and that interesting Princess, loaded with the trappings of Royalty, was one of the least happy women in Sweden. It was in vain Louisa Ulrica sought interviews with her son. He was seldom to be seen except in company with Armfeldt, or some other of his vile associates, whose presence was intolerable to this high-minded woman. Amidst all his affected gaiety and dissipation, his mother saw the drift of his actions; and if entreaties, tears, and the most solemn admonitions could have reformed his habits and turned his thoughts, he would have been the saviour of his country by giving it liberty. Wearied by her remonstrances, the haughty Prince forbade her visits, which treatment, as the politic Prince perhaps foresaw, tended to confirm the oligarchs in the belief that their criminal plot had succeeded, and that Gustavus, being entangled in the evil courses to which he was first allured by their secret agents, was no longer to be dreaded. Probably the rude treatment his mother experienced was inflicted from a wish to produce this very impression.

Master of himself, and the sole keeper of his secrets, Gustavus shunned all private conferences with the chiefs of the Court faction.[1] He appeared to prefer the company of the reigning oligarchs. Meantime, he omitted no opportunity of acquiring the affection of the populace. Three days in the week he set apart to give audiences to the people. He listened with well-dissembled earnestness to their details. He not only redressed those grievances that lay within his reach, but he relieved the wants of some, whilst to all he was courteous and condescending in the extreme, and thus he became the idol of the multitude.

In May, 1771, a Diet was assembled at Stockholm, in which, contrary to expectation, the Caps were found to have secured the ascendency. Neither surprised nor dismayed by this unexpected circumstance, the young King, on the 25th of June, at the opening of

---

[1] Sir John Carr, in his "Northern Summer," page 153, very gravely tells his readers that Gustavus planned the Revolution of 1772 "in the recesses of the rocks at Haga!" Surely someone imposed on his credulity!

the Diet, made a speech that was so modelled that, whilst it covered his own views, it pleased the contending factions. In the course of his harangue, Gustavus said: "Born and educated amongst you, from my earliest infancy I have been taught to love my country. It is my greatest happiness that I am a Swede, my greatest glory to be a citizen of a free country. To behold it happy is the first object of my wishes. To govern it, in a state of freedom and independence, is the last object of my ambition." He concluded a speech transcendently eloquent and most gracefully pronounced, with the following well-chosen phrases: "Do not, I conjure you, consider these as empty professions, falsified, perhaps, by the secret emotions of my heart; but receive them as the faithful expression of what that heart feels, which is too honest not to be sincere, and too haughty ever to prove false to its engagements."

This artful speech, which abounded in general maxims of the most noble kind, appeared to give complete satisfaction to both parties. A grand deputation was appointed the next day to return him the thanks of the Diet, and it was ordered to be printed.

Although the King kept aloof in the way described, the Court party made every possible effort to obtain some concessions; but they found the Caps too vigilant to be deceived and too strong to be subdued. One great object with them was to procure a relaxation of some of the points introduced by the Charter of 1720 into the coronation oath, that restricted the power of the Crown within such very

SOFIA MAGDALENA
SISTER OF CHRISTIAN VII, AND
WIFE OF GUSTAVUS III

After the painting by Karl Gustaf Pilo, in the National Gallery at Stockholm

he ____ ____ a speech that was so modelled that, whilst it ____ his own views, it pleased the contending factions. In the course of his harangue, ____ said: "____ and educated amongst you, ____ my ____ ____ I have been taught to love my country. It is my greatest happiness that I am ____, ____ ____ glory to be a citizen of a free ____. To behold it happy is the first object of ____ ____. To govern it, in a state of freedom and independence, is the last object of my ambition."
It ____ a speech transcendently eloquent and ____ ____fully pronounced, with the following well-____ ____ ____ ____ ____re you, consider ____ ____ ____ ____ by the ____ ____ of my heart; ____ receive them as the ____ ____ ____ ____ feels, which is too ____ ____ to be ____, and too haughty ever to prove false in its ____."
This, ____ ____ ____ ____ ____ ____ ____ maxims ____ ____ ____ ____ ____ to give complete satisfaction to both parties. A grand deputation was appointed the next day to return him the thanks of the Diet, and it was ordered to be printed.

Although the King had acted in the way described, the Court party made every possible effort to obtain some concessions, but they found the Caps too ____ to be deceived and too strong to be subdued. One great object with them was to procure a ____ of some of the points introduced by the Charter of 1720 into the coronation oath, that restricted the power of the Crown within such very

the Diet, made a speech that was so modelled that, whilst it covered his own views, it pleased the contending factions. In the course of his harangue, Gustavus said: "Born and educated amongst you, from my earliest infancy I have been taught to love my country. It is my greatest happiness that I am a Swede, my greatest glory to be a citizen of a free country. To behold it happy is the first object of my wishes. To govern it, in a state of freedom and independence, is no less object of my ambition." He concluded a speech eminently eloquent and most gracefully pronounced, with the following well-chosen phrases: .... assure you, consider these no empty professions falsified, perhaps, by the secret sentiments of my heart; but receive them as the faithful expression of what that heart feels, which is too honest not to be sincere, and too haughty ever to prove false to its engagements."

.... complete satisfaction to both parties. .... was appointed the next day to convey the thanks of the Diet, and it was ordered to be printed.

Although the King kept aloof in the way described, the Court party made every possible effort to obtain some concessions; but they found the Caps too vigilant to be deceived and too strong to be subdued. One great object with them was to procure a relaxation of some of the points introduced by the Charter of 1720 into the coronation oath, that restricted the power of the Crown within such very

SOFIA MAGDALEVA
SISTER OF CHRISTIAV VII, AND
WIFE OF GUSTAVUS III

*After the painting by Karl Gustaf Pilo, in the
National Gallery at Stockholm*

narrow limits. The discussions which resulted prevented the coronation from taking place that year. Such was the coolness of the King's conduct, that he appeared to feel little, if any, interest in these matters, apparently regarding them as mere party questions.

The coronation of Gustavus III. was performed on the 22nd of May, 1772, with an uncommon degree of pomp and magnificence; and he took the oath prescribed without faltering, although fully determined not to observe it! When the different Orders of State came to take the oaths of fidelity and to pay him homage, Gustavus then said, "Assured of your affections, and sincerely resolved to merit that blessing, and to establish my throne on your love and happiness, the public engagements into which you are about to enter would, in my opinion, be superfluous, if it were not, by the ancient laws and customs of Sweden, required at your hands. Unhappy is the king who stands in need of the bond of oaths to secure himself on the throne, and who, not assured of the hearts of his subjects, is constrained to reign only by the force of laws, when the love of his subjects is denied him."

Notwithstanding these fine speeches, the Caps were still suspicious of Gustavus, whose secret vices they well knew, but the vastness of whose genius they were yet, by one terrible lesson, to learn. It was a conflict between professed deceivers, and the King won the prize. At the very instant that he expressed to the different Orders of the State his determination to maintain the existing state of things, *he had secretly written and finished the new constitution* that was to abrogate the existing oligarchy, and establish, under the mask of a free government, an hereditary despotism in Sweden.

With his youthful Queen, the King no longer kept up even the appearance of affection or regard; his mother he saw but seldom; his brothers he sent away from Stockholm—Prince Charles to Scania, and Frederick to East Gothland: his motives for this are only to be conjectured. He might have been animated by a wish, at such a crisis, not to have the whole family cooped up within the metropolis; he might have been fearful even of *their* fidelity, for it is clear, from the profound depths of his own hypocrisy, he could have no belief that any such things as honesty and sincerity existed in the human breast; again, the desire to derive support from their military talents, and influence on the minds of the soldiery, might stimulate him to send them into those provinces at this critical period.[1]

In accomplishing the Revolution of 1772, Gustavus displayed qualities that amazed and confounded the hated and degraded oligarchs. The most insulting of

---

[1] The limits assigned to this memoir exclude a detailed relation of the Revolution of 1772. The reader is, therefore, referred to "A History of the late Revolution in Sweden," by Francis Sheridan, Esq.; to the "Travels in Poland, Russia and Sweden," by William Coxe, A.M., &c.; and more particularly to the account contained in a work published in London about 1790, by Harlowe, St. James's Street, entitled, "Characters and Anecdotes of the Court of Sweden," vol. i., p. 195, &c.

all his acts was his requiring the fallen nobles, surrounded by hostile bayonets and loaded cannon, to join him in singing psalms to praise God for the revolution that had been accomplished, and by which their own political ruin was effected. It combined the most perfect cruelty with the worst species of impiety, and dishonoured the profligate King infinitely more than it disgraced those whom it was intended to insult and mortify.

From the moment that this devouring oligarchy was destroyed, a new race of men appeared at the Court of Sweden. The bold and haughty senators, each of whom thought himself on a level with his Sovereign, degraded and dispersed, humbled and subdued, sullenly retired, overwhelmed with grief, shame and dismay, carrying with them to their estates the scorn and reproaches of their country, and in their place appeared a set of voluptuous and depraved parasites, such as might be expected to abound in an Asiatic Court, and such as Sweden never knew till Gustavus displayed them in his train and invested them with high commands. Except that many of them were of humble origin, they might not inaptly be compared to the *ultra Royalists* of the present day in France. With them the King was the source of all honour and of power; he was the representative of God on earth; and, like God, in their corrupted creed, he had a right to dispose at pleasure of his creatures! At the head of these base minions were Armfeldt and other dissolute nobles, whose vices were at once a stain to manhood and a scourge to their country.

The celebrated Count Ugglas—the secret and unconstitutional adviser of Gustavus IV., Adolphus—owed the foundation of his future greatness to this Revolution; for just as it was completed, the triumphant King, flushed with victory over a venal, detested aristocracy, walked into his Chancellory in the Royal Palace. Delighted with the occurrence, this Ugglas, then a young man and a writer in the Chancellory, forgetful how vast was the distance between his situation and his Sovereign, went up to him with his head erect, and every feature dilated with joy, and seizing him by the hand, and giving him a hearty slap on the shoulder, exclaimed, "Thou art worthy to be our King! Gustavus for ever!" More pleased than offended with a familiarity that denoted the sincerity of his good wishes, Gustavus took Ugglas under his peculiar protection, and laid the foundations of his future greatness. Under Gustavus IV., Adolphus, M. Ugglas was created a Count, and enriched with the spoils of the kingdom. He was the secret adviser of that unfortunate Prince, and, in conjunction with the execrable Armfeldt, highly instrumental in promoting those despotical measures that led to his dethronement and banishment.

As the King did not cohabit with his Queen, to prevent the Gustavian race from becoming extinct, he deemed it advisable that his brother Charles should marry. The Princess of Lubeck Eutin (now Queen of Sweden) was fixed on as his bride. She was then young, beautiful, accomplished, of a sweet disposition, and warmly beloved by her Court and attendants. The

Duke, her husband, who was completely a libertine, still persevered in his amatory pursuits, and the hopes of those seemed likely to be disappointed who waited in anxiety for an heir to the throne.[1]

Some time after this Royal marriage, which was celebrated by the Court with distinguished splendour, it was officially announced that the young and beautiful Duchess was

"As ladies wish to be who love their lords."

The nation felt deeply interested in the event; and so near was the Duchess supposed to be to her time that the cannon on the batteries that were intended to communicate the happy event of her safe delivery to the metropolis were kept ready charged — when, most unexpectedly and suddenly, these pleasing expectations all vanished, and, instead of an heir to the Crown, it was announced that the young Duchess had mistaken her situation, and had been troubled with a "false conception."

Probably the Duchess was never pregnant, but that a *near relation* to her husband was, and it was out of

---

[1] "The Swedes universally lament that he (Gustavus III.) has no children by his Queen; and it is on this account that his next brother, Prince Charles, is now married. The King is said not to be of an amorous complexion, or attached to women."—Wraxall's "Tour, &c.," p. 127.

"It has been asserted, and I believe with truth, that his (Gustavus III.) sensibility towards the female sex was far from being lively; he seldom cohabited with his Queen. Strange to tell, gifted with acute feelings, and a warm and brilliant imagination, this accomplished Prince, descended from a race of beautiful females, displayed an example of almost monkish continence."—Sir John Carr's "Northern Summer," p. 130.

compassion for her that the young and generous Princess encountered the risk of assuming the appearance of pregnancy, in order to adopt as hers the infant with which her amiable relative was teeming.

There are circumstances connected with this delicate subject that it might not be advisable to publish, though essential to historical truth. The Queen-Mother, Louisa Ulrica, certainly doubted the probability of her sons ever becoming fathers. And this strange belief in a mother is said to have been the cause why the Queen-Dowager questioned the reality of the pregnancy of the young Duchess. She certainly suspected that Gustavus and the Duke himself were privy to the intended fraud—and who will believe that the Duke was innocent? Several times the Dowager-Queen hinted her suspicions to Gustavus, who would not hear a word on the subject. Determined not to be trifled with, it is said that she threatened to make public her suspicions if the reality of the appearance of pregnancy were persevered in.

The Friherre Benzelstjerna is said to have been the nobleman whom Louisa Ulrica sent to the Duchess to announce that, if she did not lay aside the assumed appearance, her mother-in-law was determined to institute a public enquiry. This was a blow that could not be parried. The Duchess made a frank avowal that she was *not* pregnant, and said, laughing as she spoke, "Well, never mind! if it is not so at present, it may happen in a short time!"

It is truly difficult to believe that, unknown to her husband, the Duchess could carry false appearances so far as to have her pregnancy officially announced to the nation, and solemn prayers offered up in the churches for her safe delivery. And it is no less so to suppose that the Duke would dare to attempt such a fraud without the sanction of the King, his brother. The author of a work, entitled, "Characters and Anecdotes of the Court of Sweden" (vol. i., p. 7), alluding to this singular occurrence, observed that this *disappointment* of her hopes, "*put the King as well as the Duke very much out of humour.*" It is believed both were privy to this attempt to substitute an heir to the throne. This failure gave rise to an expedient still more extraordinary, adopted two years afterwards, to which Gustavus IV., Adolphus, is said to be indebted for his existence.

Whilst these events were passing, a marked change was observed in the conduct of the King, who assumed a degree of state quite at variance with his professions of economy. He lavished the wealth of the kingdom in feasts and tournaments, and swelled his household establishments to an extent far beyond what Sweden had ever before witnessed. Louisa Ulrica almost ceased to rejoice at the humiliation of the oligarchs, since, instead of those high-born and powerful lords, she saw the Court filled with a race of servile and unprincipled parasites and flatterers, who, fattening on the prevailing profusion, applied all their influence to strengthen and increase that love of pageantry and magnificence which was already too conspicuous. She beheld with sorrow and regret that, in less than two years, not only the admiration, but even the esteem of the liberal and cultivated part of his subjects, was rapidly on the wane. She foresaw that this boundless waste must lead to acts of rapacity and injustice, which, accumulating from year to year, might ultimately produce some catastrophe fatal to his life and power. When an opportunity of remonstrating with Gustavus presented itself, she never failed to embrace it. Impatient of wholesome counsel, and forgetful of the obligations he was under to his illustrious mother for those accomplishments which dazzled mankind, Gustavus treated her advice with contempt, and haughtily forbade its repetition.

In the affectionate Albertina, her only daughter, who had arrived at the full maturity of beauty, virtuous in principle, and no less accomplished than the ungrateful Gustavus, and in the society of a few select and loyal nobles of the old Court, the Queen-Mother endeavoured to console herself for his want of filial affection. Prince Frederick was, however, kind and attentive; but the depraved habits of her two eldest sons had totally alienated their affections. Whilst Louisa Ulrica mourned over the ruin she could not help anticipating from their vicious courses, she took every precaution to conceal her sorrows from the world, and, on all occasions, strove to palliate their conduct.

Notwithstanding the passion of Gustavus for the possession of unlimited power, the display of his fine taste, and a degree of magnificence in his Court that was incompatible with the impoverished state of the finances, the first six years of his reign were, speaking comparatively, usefully employed. He applied with great industry his extraordinary talents to the improvement of the commerce, husbandry and finances of Sweden. That he did not perfectly understand the principles by which trade is created and improved was evident by the failure of all the plans he adopted; he was, however, *sincere* in these endeavours to benefit his country; his motives, therefore, must not be too narrowly scrutinised. He established manufactories at Stockholm and Gothenburg to relieve the wants of the destitute poor by finding them employment, which he furnished with raw materials. In Stockholm alone, in 1773, twelve thousand poor persons were thus employed. If kings engage in trade they will be sure to lose their capital. It turned out so with Gustavus; those *forced* establishments ultimately failing, after having occasioned an enormous waste of treasure. Gustavus gave the first great impulse to the better cultivation of Finland. He encouraged the importation of corn, and prohibited dealers from keeping it in store, whereby to enhance its price, adopting the most decisive measures to counteract those monopolisers whose ever-grasping avarice, backed by enormous wealth, sought to increase overflowing coffers, although the poor and destitute perished by its effects in the streets or by the highway side.

The expenses of the Court were swollen to an unprecedented sum, the love of the King for grandeur impelling him to assume a degree of splendour that might have better suited the vast and powerful Empire ruled by Catherine II.

A dignitary of the Church of Sweden once said to Gustavus, "There are two things with which a wise

King of Sweden would not meddle, namely, *religion* and *brandy!*" The first, Gustavus was wise enough to leave to the priesthood, but the second offered a temptation not to be resisted. In 1772, the King had declared he was firmly bent on the suppression of all monopolies; at the same time he prohibited private stills. Previous to this period, every Swedish farmer was at liberty to distil from corn or other substances. For the sake of revenue, Gustavus prohibited this right, which rendered him unpopular, and gave rise to many petty insurrections, to suppress which he was forced to have recourse to his standing army. During three years he persevered in these unpopular measures. The prohibition was, however, recalled in 1775: the privilege of distilling brandy was wholly monopolised by the Crown, which was granted to a limited extent to individuals, on the payment of a certain sum, for a fixed period of years. The want of a sufficient number of contractors or farmers of this Royal monopoly, forced the King to abandon his plan. His next determination was to become, himself, the only distiller in Sweden! He set about this enterprise with his usual ardour. Gustavus flattered himself he had discovered a new *Potosi* in his poor and barren kingdom. He interdicted the importation of foreign brandies, bought up (probably at his own price) the materials used by private distillers, and enacted very heavy penalties in case of this Royal monopoly being infringed.

Complaints, murmurs, execrations and menaces were heard in the metropolis and in every province of his kingdom. The Fourth Estate (peasants) sent deputations to the King, remonstrating in bold and energetic terms against the assumption of this monopoly, and demanding the restoration of their old, indisputable right of distilling brandy for their own consumption. Disregarding these remonstrances, the King still persevered, when serious commotions broke out in various parts of Sweden. Even in the metropolis it was found necessary to station guards at the Royal brandy factories, to prevent their being destroyed by the indignant populace. He was so stubborn, or rapacious, that rather than relinquish a revenue thus gained, he hazarded his crown and life.

Many of his regulations relative to commerce were judicious; these were adopted at the suggestion of persons who best understood its principles: wherever the King preferred his own theories, however plausible they might appear, abstractedly considered, they invariably failed when put to a practical test.

CHAPTER XII

Vast projects of Peter the Great—Their progressive realisation—Gustavus attempts to counteract Russia—Catherine II. and Gustavus—Their opposite views and preparations—Great national undertakings began or completed by Gustavus at Carlscrona and Sveaborg—Visits his provinces—Reforms local abuses and punishes several unjust judges—His great and varied talents and acquirements—Effeminacy of his Court—Honours paid by Gustavus to the memory of Sir Charles Linné—Suffers his invaluable collection to be sold—Embellishes Stockholm—Practises the utmost profusion—Recommends frugality to his subjects—Sumptuary laws—Corrupts the national manners—Lavishes his treasures on idle pageantry.

WHEN Peter I., on the sylvan shores of the deep, broad, majestic Neva, laid the foundations of the future capital of European Russia, estimating in his capacious mind the growth of power with civilisation, he probably considered that his successors would extend the northwest frontier till it should embrace the whole of the territories then appertaining to Sweden and Denmark.[1]

---

[1] In "A Sketch on the Military and Political Power of Russia," the author (who by acclamation is pronounced to be Lieutenant-General Sir Robert Wilson), speaking of Peter I., observes:

"In the years between 1701 and 1711 the Czar Peter was

Gustavus III. was often heard to assert that, if he were Czar of Russia, in defiance of all Europe combined, in seven years he would realise that project and give law to all the world! The provinces wrested from Sweden by the disastrous wars that were ended by the Treaties of Abo and Nystadt gave Russia the command of the Baltic, and of an invaluable source of commercial prosperity. Gustavus knew the vast ambition of Catherine II.; he envied her magnificence and dreaded her power. If she usurped the throne of her husband (Peter III.), she inherited the spirit of Peter I., treading in the path which that noble savage had marked out. When Catherine heard of the Revolution of 1772 being accomplished, she was at once astonished and

---

contending, with various success, against the Swedes, Turks and Poles for an advance of his European frontier.

"In the year 1713, having conquered Riga and Livonia, he built the city of St. Petersburg, transporting 30,000 from Archangel to be the inhabitants, and inviting foreigners, particularly the English, to settle there.

"In the year 1714 he developed his naval projects, which have been suspended, but never abandoned by his successors.

"In the year 1721 he declared himself Emperor of All the Russias; and on his death, in 1729, the world added and preserved to his memory the posthumous title of 'The Great.'

"From the year 1729 to 1762, although Russia, under six Sovereigns, some of whose reigns were short and tragical, proceeded in the attainment of internal strength, solidity and trade; although, in the reign of Elizabeth, she had connected herself with England and acquired a military character, still she had not taken her station as a great European Power.

"When Catherine II. mounted the throne, only 22,000,000 of people paid her homage.

"During her reign of thirty-three years, according to the best

grieved. The nobles and courtiers who were in her pay had not prepared her mind for such a result. But when informed of the extreme magnificence of Gustavus, and that in point of ceremony he equalled the Court of Versailles, and in splendour emulated, if not eclipsed, every other throne in Europe, she was secretly pleased, not doubting but his love of pageantry would soon disgust his subjects, and probably enable the nobility to renew those fetters that were so suddenly snapped asunder. Compared with the pecuniary resources of Catherine, Gustavus III. was an indigent Prince. The Prince Potemkin, and perhaps several other of her favourites and first-rate nobles, possessed a revenue far exceeding the entire income allotted for the support of the whole of the Royal Family of Sweden. It was, therefore, with real pleasure that Catherine heard of the magnificence that prevailed at the Court of Gustavus; and on more

---

authorities of the time, the number was augmented to nearly 36,000,000, by acquisition and natural increase of population."

"Alexander commenced his reign in the year 1800, with over 36,000,000 of people:

"The acquisitions of his predecessors had been enormous, but they had not yet completed the line of frontier.

"The guns of the Swedes could be heard in St. Petersburg. Denmark and Sweden had considerable navies.

"Aland covered the Swedish coasts from insult or sudden invasion, when the Gulf of Bothnia might be frozen; and Sveaborg commanded the navigation of the mouth of the Gulf of Finland.

"When Alexander came to the throne, 36,000,000 of people acknowledged his authority; but at this day (1817), by increase and acquisition, there cannot be less, at the lowest calculation, than 42,000,000—and not of Asiatic houseless hordes wandering in deserts, but chiefly of Europeans."—Pp. 116, 117, 121 to 128.

than one occasion she derided his pigmy efforts, calling him by coarse and insulting epithets, of which the least offensive were "The little King" and "The amateur player of Stockholm."

Amongst crowned heads, occurrences trivial as these have sometimes had powerful influence on the destinies of nations. The sarcasms of Catherine, perhaps with additions and embellishments, were reported to Gustavus, who suffered them to make too deep an impression on his mind. From this period a strong feeling of personal enmity was blended with the hostility of Gustavus to the politics of the Empress Catherine II.

The King exerted himself with inconceivable activity to place his army and navy on a formidable footing, for he aspired to the maritime sovereignty of the Baltic. When Gustavus had any great object in view, he was seldom very nice regarding the means of attainment. His uncle, Frederick of Prussia, accused him of intending to burn the Danish Royal navy by incendiaries, hired for that purpose: perhaps he also intended to treat the Russians in the same way. Gustavus, secretly determined to make a sudden irruption into the Russian territories the first favourable opportunity, made as great exertions to build a formidable navy as if all Sweden were an island, whose safety, like that of Great Britain, depended upon her fleet. The works begun by Gustavus at Carlscrona[1]

---

[1] Carlscrona, the capital of the province of Bleking, and the residence of the governor, is situated upon the shore of the Baltic Sea, and built upon a large insulated rock. The road to

were of stupendous magnitude, the expense far exceeding the value of any possible benefit that could rationally be expected. They were calculated to strike every spectator with amazement, and to immortalise the name of the Royal founder, rather than prove of utility commensurate with the prodigious disbursement they occasioned. It is difficult to convey an adequate idea of the immense labour expended on the docks at

---

it is over two other islands, which are joined to the mainland by three large bridges, and contain two suburbs of considerable size, but dirty and ill-built, being inhabited only by the lower sort of people. The city takes its name from its founder, Charles XI.

"I was conducted to the port by an officer, who had been in our Service under Mr. Dedel. This port is very large and convenient, being almost surrounded with docks, and having a long bridge, on the two sides of which vessels not in use are kept at moorings. I reckoned here twenty-eight vessels of the line and frigates, amongst which were one of one hundred guns, one of ninety-six, one of eighty-four, two of seventy-four, and several of sixty and fifty. The whole fleet, including five vessels now equipping, consists of thirty-seven vessels of the line and nine frigates. The five vessels thus fitting out, and four others which were in the water, but unrigged, were built in the course of four years. There were several upon the stocks, either wholly, or almost in skeleton; and I was shown one of these vessels, which was constructed in six weeks, all the parts having been prepared beforehand. The plan of reviving and increasing the naval force was concerted about four years ago; a part of the year 1782 was spent in preparing and collecting the materials, and in 1783 they began to build. It is intended to build four vessels annually till the fleet shall be restored to a respectable situation; and, to defray the expenses of this plan, the King has suspended the execution of half the works at the new dock. These works are, indeed, stupendous, and exceeded all the highly-wrought expectations which I had conceived from the accounts given of them. Twenty-nine years have been already spent in forming them, and they yet want much of completion. At the entrance is a basin hollowed in the rock, of about fifty feet in depth,

Carlscrona. If the London or Liverpool docks had been excavated out of rocks of granite, the enterprise would not have been as difficult for England to perform as those at Carlscrona were for Sweden. The Swedish engineers, Polheim and Thunberg, although their talents have been much underrated by careless or superficial British tourists, were men of vast genius and profound science, and the first projectors of these

and surrounded by quays of freestone, at which four men-of-war may at the same time receive or discharge their stores. From this basin, canals of communication are formed, that, by means of large locks, afford a passage for each vessel into its own dock, of which there are twenty for ships of the line, and ten for frigates.

"One of these separate docks, with its canal and lock, is entirely finished. The bottom is composed of freestone, joined and cemented with pozzuolana, a sort of cement, brought for that purpose from Italy, and laid in a bed, which has been hollowed in the rock, exactly of the shape of a ship's keel. Along the whole length of this dock they have contrived galleries of stone, by means of which they erect the beams or scaffoldings, when the vessel is rendered entirely dry, in order to be repaired. The walls which support the roofs and separate the docks from each other are formed of the same freestone and cement, and are at least of the thickness of twenty feet up to the height of the vessel's upper deck. There platforms are constructed for the reception of the guns of each vessel, which are delivered and received through large arched openings communicating with the platform and with the inside of the dock.

"The roof is of timber, plated on the outside with iron, and so contrived as to bear all the levers used in loading and unloading the vessel. When the dock is to be rendered perfectly dry, the water is suffered to run through a vent in the bottom, which they open by a machine prepared for that purpose; it is then received in a basin hollowed immediately under the dock, and from thence is forced, by means of a windmill, into the other basin before-mentioned.

"These covered lodges, when the plan is perfected, will form

works. The nation was, in a manner, impoverished by the expense. The King, however, persevered, and at the time of making war on Russia he had created a navy too powerful for Sweden to be long able to maintain, yet totally inadequate to the attainment of

---

a large semi-circle; but the second is yet unfinished, and, from the immense expense of the undertaking, it seems doubtful whether the whole number will ever be completed. At present they are chiefly employed upon the improvement of the ancient dock, which will, probably, be not less useful than the new one. Indeed, it is by no means certain that vessels can be preserved by this method longer than by those now in use; and, even if this is admitted, it will still remain to be enquired how far the millions expended in forming the docks, sluices, basins and canals are likely to be repaid by the savings proposed.

"This new dock was begun in the late reign, upon a plan suggested by one Thunberg, now a very old man, who has the direction of the works constructing upon the Gothe Alf. The ancient dock, which is a sort of canal of 350 feet in length and 30 in depth, was hollowed in the rock, and entirely completed between the years 1715 and 1724. It was planned by Polheim, and is situated between the port and the new dock, communicating, on the one side, with the dockyard and port, and, on the other, with the sea, by means of two canals of such size as to admit the passage of first-rate men-of-war. Both canals are enclosed by very large flood-gates, and before that which opens towards the sea they have placed a movable dam of very ingenious construction, in order to protect the sluice from the violence of the waves. When a vessel has entered the dock in order to be caulked, they shut the gates, place the dam before them, and an immense pump is put in motion, either by men or horses, which in twelve hours renders the dock entirely dry.

"The port of Carlscrona, which is very deep and easy of entrance, is capable of containing a hundred ships of the line. It is defended by two strong forts, whose fires cross each other, and are undoubtedly able to sink any fleet that should attempt to force a passage. They are both built upon rocks in the sea; the one called Kongsholm (King's Island), the other Drotnings-kiar, or Queen's Rock."—*Vide* "Journey through Sweden," v. 148, &c

the sovereignty of the Baltic—a shallow sea, unsafe for large ships and shut up by ice several months every year. The genius of Gustavus gave birth to the largest navy Sweden ever possessed, which was soon after destroyed, by his inexperience and presumption, in the Bay of Wiborg.

This magnificent and enterprising Prince undertook another work, equal in magnitude and expense, but of a far higher order in point of national importance, in completing the fortress and the naval docks built upon, or rather excavated in, the granite islands that cover the entrance to a large bay near Helsingfors, in the Gulf of Finland. His object in this was of a twofold nature, *i.e.*, to protect Sweden from invasion on the side of Russia by land or sea, and to facilitate an invasion of that country by the Swedish fleet or army.

When Sweden was compelled to cede a considerable portion of Finland to Russia, it became necessary to construct new fortresses to protect the country that remained. The Swedish generals and engineers represented a cluster of island rocks that stretch across the entrance from the Gulf of Finland to the shore near Helsingfors as the spot most eligible for the site of a new fortress and the formation of a secure haven for the Swedish navy. General Ehrensward had the chief direction of this enterprise, and the works were commenced in 1748. The plan of the intended fortress was highly approved; it was named Sveaborg, *i.e.*, the Safeguard of Sweden. From this period down to the year 1775, upwards of 5,000,000 dollars were expended, and still the works were incomplete.[1]

When Gustavus III. visited Sveaborg, being struck with the advantages of its local situation, he determined to improve upon the original plan, so far as to be considered as the second founder. Secretly bent on war, under the specious mask of defensive prepara-

---

[1] The following description of Sveaborg is extracted from the "Travels of Mr. Coxe in Sweden," vol. iv, p. 13, &c.:

"But one of the most curious and important fortresses in the Swedish dominions is Sveaborg, situated near Helsingfors.

"Seven islands, lying within the circumference of four miles, compose this fortress, namely: Långärn, the nearest to Helsingfors, 600 feet in length and 500 in breadth; Wästra Swartö, south-east of Långärn, 1,400 feet in length and 800 in breadth; Little Ostra Swartö, 800 feet square; Stora Ostra Swartö, 3,000 feet in length and 1,600 in breadth; Wargön, lying in the centre, 2,400 feet in length and 2,000 in breadth—it is the principal island, and contains the governor's house; sixth, Gustafsvärd, south-east of Wargön, 1,600 feet in length and 1,200 in breadth; seventh, Skantz Landet,* south of Gustafsvärd, an island as big as both Wargön and Stora Osträ Swartö, but of which only 600 feet are to be fortified.

"The works are really stupendous, and worthy of the ancient Romans. The walls are chiefly of hewn granite, covered with earth, from 6 to 10 feet thick, and in a few places not less than 48 feet high. The batteries, which begin upon a level with the water, and rise in tiers one above another in all directions, commanding the only channel through which large vessels can sail to Helsingfors, render the passage of an enemy's fleet extremely dangerous, if not impracticable.

"In Wargön is a dry dock, capable of containing eleven or

* The orthography of Mr. Coxe, in Swedish proper names, is, in general, erroneous. The names of the islands on which the celebrated fortress Sveaborg was constructed were copied from a map of Helsingfors, laid down by N. G. Wirming, and engraved by H. Akerland and E. Personne, 1808. In this map there is no mention of such an island as Skantz Landet; probably Mr. Coxe meant Bockholmen. According to the scale laid down in the above-named map, it is probable that Mr. Coxe is wrong in the dimensions given to those islands.

tions, he resolved there to accumulate such vast military magazines as should, at any favourable moment, admit of a sudden and formidable invasion of Russia; carrying his anticipations so far as the capture of St. Petersburg, the destruction of the Russian marine, and transporting to Stockholm, as a trophy of victory, the magnificent equestrian statue of Peter the Great that Catherine II. had commanded Falconet to prepare for the decoration of her residence! Such were

---

twelve frigates, hollowed in the solid rock, 800 feet long, 200 broad and 14 deep.* It is divided into three equal parts by two brick walls, which run lengthways; each part will contain four frigates, and may be closed with sluice-gates, so that each vessel lies separately from the other. The whole is covered with a wooden pent-house roof, in order to preserve the frigates from the rain: this basin contained eleven frigates. At one extremity of this dock is a basin 200 feet square, closed at each end with sluice-gates, which serves for the entrance and exit of the frigates, and likewise for repairing and building ships. At the other end another basin was finished, of the same dimensions, for a man-of-war, which may likewise serve for the passage of the frigates, whenever the other is employed in repairing or building of ships. The magazines for the stores and artillery are built on the edge of the water, which is of sufficient depth to admit each vessel close to the quay, to be equipped without trouble. There is an excellent port for seventy sail of the line, and a small harbour, no less secure, for ten frigates.

"The garrison, in October, 1784, consisted of 350 soldiers and 600 marines; but when the whole fortifications are completed, will require 12,000 men. For the purpose of building and fitting out ships at Sveaborg, the Swedes procure oak from Gothland, part of the flax from Finland, and hemp and masts from Riga. Such, in October, 1784, was the state of Sveaborg, a fortress which, even in its present unfinished state, will be capable of harassing the Russians in case of war, and which, should it be completed, may justly be called the Gibraltar of the North."

* This depth is certainly too shallow, although Swedish frigates are smaller and draw less water than British.

the flattering visions in which the ambitious Gustavus indulged. Nor was Catherine a passive spectator of his conduct. That great woman penetrated his real views, and filled not only his metropolis, but his Court, with her secret agents. She chiefly depended upon the indigent nobility and officers of Finland. The result showed, at the critical moment of peril, how well she was obeyed by those mercenary and restless chiefs. That venal and rapacious oligarchy —whose criminal conduct reduced Sweden to a state that afforded Gustavus III. an opportunity of establishing, if he had pleased, despotism by law—had greatly neglected the Swedish army and navy. They were loudly and generally accused by the nation of having appropriated to their own use, and distributed amongst their partisans, the revenue of Sweden. Gustavus took care to convince his people of the dilapidated state in which he found the army, navy and fortresses; and he zealously strove to supply everything that was wanting to effect their restoration. He distributed clothing, tents and new muskets to each regiment; the fortresses were all put into a state of defence and furnished with artillery. A new manual exercise was introduced, in which the troops were manœuvred by Gustavus in person. He suppressed the sale of military offices and commissions, increased the pay of the officers, and introduced such regulations as secured them, at the age of fifty, the means of retiring on full pay for the rest of their lives.

Gustavus made frequent journeys through different provinces, that he might, from personal observation, judge of the real state of trade, manufactures, agriculture and the interior police. In one of these tours through Nerike, the most beautiful and picturesque province of Sweden, the King acquired great popularity by the dismissal of the governor, on a charge of malversation. The seneschal and the treasurer of Dalecarlia were also dismissed; but the example which produced the most powerful impression was the sentence pronounced by Gustavus upon the principal court of justice held at Jönköping, the capital of Ostra-Gothland. The accused were obliged to appear in person at Stockholm. The cause was pleaded publicly before the King, who said, in his opening speech, "I have delivered you from an oppression that rendered all justice venal. I have made laws for securing the rights of the poorest of my subjects, and those laws have been violated. I owe an example of justice to posterity." Four members of the high tribunal of Jönköping, having been found guilty, were dismissed from their offices, and several others were suspended from the exercise of their judicial functions.

These acts are really an honour to Gustavus, as was also his relieving the farmers (who were then, as at present, generally very indigent) from the oppressive burthen of supplying post and courier horses gratis for the use of the King and Royal Family. He took an exact census of the people; and used his utmost efforts to increase the population of Sweden, by encouraging strangers, particularly mechanics and artists in metal, to settle in his kingdom, and by striving to induce those

Swedes to return who had already emigrated to foreign lands.

So accomplished a gentleman was Gustavus, that there was scarcely a professor of literature, or any of the liberal or elegant arts, but he was able to excel each in his own peculiar study. He was spoken of as a prodigy of talent, a Mæcenas in liberality, which, joined to the magnificence of his Court, attracted crowds of painters, poets, musicians, theatrical dressers, dancers, &c. Those who possessed very superior merit were retained, and all who greatly excelled were munificently rewarded. In the distribution of his patronage he betrayed the selfishness of his motives. He spared no expense to gratify his love of pageantry; the superb spectacles with which he treated the inhabitants of Stockholm served to ingratiate him with the most elegant of the fair sex, as well as the vulgar populace. It also attracted public attention from the silent but rapid progress he was making towards the establishment of a monarchical despotism. Nor was he ignorant that, from his own superior taste and matchless elegance, he should be looked upon as the great presiding genius that gave the first design, and the last finish, to everything that was superlatively excellent. Whilst the treasures wrung from an indigent nation were thus profusely lavished on the votaries of the fine arts, few indeed were the geometricians, astronomers, chemists, mineralogists, or engineers whom he liberally encouraged. His Court was filled with soft and effeminate courtiers, generally devoid of principle, whom he had selected and advanced, in many instances, from obscure stations. Gustavus was himself an elegant and witty dramatic writer. He would have made, perhaps, the best actor in Sweden, and incomparably the first of managers. He introduced and patronised the Swedish opera. The scenery was equal, if not superior, to any in Europe. It was designed and executed under his personal inspection; for he was competent to instruct the first masters. The dresses displayed equal taste and splendour: Gustavus drew designs for the costumes. Before his classic eye, all anomalies vanished: the actors and actresses became kings and queens. The dramatic amateurs of France and Italy were forced to own that the elegance and grandeur of their drama was equalled, if not outdone, in a Northern metropolis, where it was least to have been expected. If any stranger had seen the King engaged with theatrical dancers, singers and dressers, he would have thought the King was so absorbed by those pursuits he could have neither time nor inclination for higher objects. After instructing the performers, Gustavus would return to his palace, perhaps to meet an archbishop, and confer concerning a new version of the Bible; to receive an engineer, relative to the works at Carlscrona, Sveaborg, or Trollhätta; to discourse with and encourage manufacturers of the coarsest and the finest wares; who generally went away pleased and astonished at a man that seemed to understand the secrets of their trade equally well with themselves, and able to elucidate the most abstruse points of every subject that was connected with their various occupations. He studied the prejudices of the peasantry of every province; and when anyone felt himself deeply injured by the judges or officers of the Crown, if the individual repaired to Court, the King would patiently listen to his complaint; and if Gustavus saw he was likely to gain great applause, he seldom hesitated to dismiss a judge or an officer for whom he cared but little, or against whom he might entertain a private pique.

Gustavus' would often assist in person at the Academy of Sciences, on which occasions he threw into his manners so great a degree of deference and gravity that he appeared like a tyro receiving instruction from sage masters rather than a Sovereign; by this artful demeanour he ruled, as he pleased, the Academy, of which he became the idol. To procure greater *éclat*, he often sent questions, under a fictitious signature, that led to some new discovery in science, or improvement in agriculture.

The pedestrian bronze statue of Gustavus Vasa, the great founder of the Gustavian line, and the colossal equestrian statue of Gustavus Adolphus[1] are

---

[1] "Larcheveque did not live to finish this superb statue; it was completed by his great pupil, Sir John Tobias Sergell, K.P.S. This great favourite of the Swedes is represented in complete armour, excepting the head, which is encircled with laurel; his right hand holds a truncheon, pointing downwards; the King is gracefully seated on the horse (a likeness of his favourite charger), and the animal has great spirit. The following are the dimensions: height, from the bottom of the pedestal to the top of the hero's head, 40 feet; from the bottom of the horse's feet to the top of the hero's head, 18 feet; height of the hero, if standing, 14 feet; length of the horse, from the head to the crupper, 10 feet. The pedestal, which is of marble laid on blocks of grey polished granite, is ornamented

monuments worthy of the heroes to whose glory they were consecrated, and of the magnificent Prince in whose reign they were erected. They are equally as fine as the statues of Charles I. and James II. in London. The King himself furnished the design for the medal struck in memory of Sir Charles Linné: on one side was the bust of that great naturalist; on the obverse, a figure of Cybele, in a mournful attitude, surrounded by attributes of the mineral, vegetable and animal kingdoms: the inscriptions, "*Deam luctus angit amissi*"; and on the exergue, "*Post Obitum*, A.D. January, 1778. *Rege Jubente*." Gustavus attended the next meeting of the Academy of Sciences, in which the eloquent and graceful King delivered an impressive oration in commemoration of the illustrious dead. In a speech from the throne, addressed to the Diet of 1778, he lamented the irreparable loss that Sweden had recently sustained; yet this same monarch suffered the Linnæan collection to be purchased by a private foreigner and taken to England! Gustavus could have prevented the sale of that invaluable and national treasure if he had pleased; and the irreparable loss sustained by Sweden is alone imputable to his neglect, if not to his parsimony and indifference as to matters of scientific pursuit.

As soon as he began to reign, Gustavus commenced

---

with medallions of his favourite generals."—*Vide* Mr. Coxe, vol. iv., p. 73. In a note to p. 70 is a quotation from the "Voyage de deux François," wherein mention is made of a statue of Gustavus's minister, Oxenstjern, of nine feet high, placed under the equestrian hero. *It has never been cast!* This glaring blunder has been since copied by Sir John Carr, who, having seen this noble work of art, ought to have avoided a mistake so obvious.

embellishing his metropolis; and if he had lived to complete the edifices planned by himself and his favourite architect Desprez, he might have rendered Stockholm equal to St. Petersburg in magnificence, and far superior as to the classical chastity and elegance of the architectural decorations; but his unfortunate subjects, whose property, seized by rapacious tax-gatherers, paid for all these embellishments, would have been drained of their last dollar, and the labouring peasant, alike destitute of employment and food, have been left to perish of famine. Thus boundless was the love of magnificence in a callous, unfeeling Prince, who preferred such costly gratifications to the prosperity of his people.

Fifty thousand dollars were expended on a tournament held in 1776, at the Royal palace at Ekolsund.[1]

---

[1] Ekolsund, or Ekholmsund as it is sometimes spelt, is situated about forty-three miles north of Stockholm, on an arm of the great lake called Mälaren. It was for many centuries one of the Crown estates, and a Royal residence. The palace, occasionally inhabited by Gustavus, was never finished. Its situation is most delightful; and its boundaries, in lakes, forests and cultivated lands, included nearly, or quite, forty square miles. Being more than commonly pressed for money, Gustavus sold this fine estate to Sir Alexander S——, from whom it has descended to his heir-at-law, the present owner of that name, resident in North Britain.

To the antiquarian this is hallowed ground, a greater number of rude sepulchral monuments, called Runic stones, mostly of a date more remote than the eleventh century, being seen here, and at Lislena, than perhaps at any other spot in Sweden. Two of those tombstones, of an unusually large size and elaborately wrought, are set up, one on either side of the avenue leading from the main road to the palace. They are supposed to be extremely ancient, and are remarkably well wrought.

It was as magnificent as regal wealth and exquisite taste could render it. In the character of a foreign knight, Gustavus affirmed "That love is more lively and more permanent in the hearts of those that latest become subjected to its influence." It is almost super-

---

Sir Alexander S——, to whom Gustavus III. alienated this fine estate, was a very singular character, whose life was marked by striking vicissitudes. He was by birth a North Briton, and was an elderly man at the time of the Revolution of 1772. He acquired an ample fortune by commerce in Stockholm; but sudden and heavy losses falling upon him, he was ruined in everything, except his character. As that was untainted, a few wealthy merchants subscribed a sum that enabled him to begin the world anew. He was so prosperous that he became richer than ever. As his years and wealth increased, he became so extremely penurious as to begrudge himself the commonest necessaries of life. He was even in the habit of pilfering sugar and biscuits from the public coffee-houses he frequented; and, perhaps, at his death, his greatest trouble was that he could not take his adored riches with him to another world.

M. P. Hambré, Esq., a gentleman well known in Stockholm, was, in 1808, owner of the hotel in Paul's Gatan (street) that formerly belonged to the States-General of Holland, and was inhabited by their minister at the Court of Stockholm. This gentleman married a relation of Sir Alexander S——'s, and had the management of the estates of Ekolsund, by whom some of the preceding particulars were communicated to the author. M. Hambré was distinguished by talents, learning and patriotism. The feudal system, to which he was an enemy, prevails at the present day (1817) in Sweden, almost in the same degree that it did a century since in the Highlands of Scotland. M. Hambré released the numerous peasantry who lived on the lands of Ekolsund from personal services, and, letting the lands on the same kind of leases as in England, left the cultivator master of his time and resources.

The method of cultivating large estates in Sweden is by letting portions of land to labouring farmers, giving them a certain quantity of seed-corn, and live and dead stock, the owner or occupier taking in return, on a limited number of days in the

fluous to say that the King was victorious: for what courtier would dare to snatch the prize from his Royal master's hand? But had they been ever so well inclined, it is exceedingly probable he would still have been the victor. The celebrated Major Muncke—whose name has already been mentioned in pages

---

year, the labour of the farmer and all his family, horses, carts, &c.—a mode that was objectionable in many ways, but principally because that the vassal was forced at all times to attend to his master's concerns, to the frequent injury, and even ruin, of his own. Another method was to hire *stòtt drangarne, i.e.,* victualled servants. Those are usually placed in a house by themselves, have a stated quantity of provisions given them, and a female drudge to cook their food. A third method is to employ *torparers, i.e.,* villagers, to whom a small piece of land, a cow and a fixed quantity of corn, &c., is given, exclusive of a small daily pay. The wages were low, but, with all its defects, this mode secures the poor a decent subsistence, and is, therefore, worthy of consideration at a moment when so large a proportion of the labourers in Great Britain and Ireland are suffering the extreme of want in the midst of surrounding plenty.

Some time subsequently the owner of this vast estate let the whole of it to a Scotch gentleman named Dundas, who came with his wife and family to settle in this beautiful but secluded spot. Mr. Dundas was ennobled by Gustavus IV., Adolphus,[*] in the spring of 1808, soon after which, unhappily for his future peace, he removed his family from Ekolsund and returned to Scotland.

The system introduced by M. Hambré at Ekolsund proved injurious to Mr. Dundas, who was looked on with envy, both as a monopoliser of land and a foreigner; and the peasants, being released from annual servitude, went where they pleased to look for work, and he had very great difficulty in procuring a sufficient number of labourers, particularly in seed-time, and to get in his hay and corn harvests.

[*] To this unfortunate Prince the merit is due of having endeavoured to improve the condition of the peasants; and in all enclosures of common pasture heaths, he compelled the enclosers to allot a certain portion, *for ever,* to each cottage, which the wealthier proprietors were bound to enable the possessor to cultivate.

36 and 39 of this volume — won the prize in the carousal.

Whilst Gustavus thus indulged his taste for excessive splendour, he endeavoured to suppress, by sumptuary laws, that spirit of luxury which, infecting

---

Mr. Dundas communicated to the author many interesting particulars respecting the vicinity of Ekolsund. The Mälaren (the Archipelago of Sweden) extends from the Island of Aland to Arboga, and is studded with innumerable islands, mostly covered with evergreens, continually presenting objects really picturesque. Mr. Dundas's opinion was that the water had formerly flowed much higher than at present. He said that in rocks that are now clad with trees, and some distance from the Mählar, there have been found vast and massive iron staples and rings inserted, that appeared as if meant to serve as moorings to vessels. He also mentioned several cylindrical holes, excavated by the ancient inhabitants in the granite rocks, for which no specific use could be conjectured, except for grinding corn, before mills were invented.

The following anecdotes were related to the author, relative to Gustavus III. and Ekolsund:

"As the King was giving directions to a favourite gardener, His Majesty complained of the flowers being plucked and the grass plots tumbled, saying, 'You should keep the lackeys and kitchen girls out of this garden, as they, I suppose, are the offenders.' 'Pardon me, gracious King,' said the gardener, 'those are not the guilty persons, as I am able to keep *them* away myself.' Suspecting the truth, with a smile of good-nature beaming on his expressive features, Gustavus said, 'Well, if you think so, pray tell me whom do you suspect?' 'Your own gay courtiers, my King. It is the gallant knights and fair ladies who are so fond of this retired spot; and as long as Your Majesty's Court remains here, the roses will be plucked and the grass too much pressed.'"

At the time of this festival, the Queen, the Duchess and a number of the nobility were in the drawing-room, standing near the windows, when a huge elk, his lofty antlers borne high above the water, was seen swimming across the lake. The Queen asked what it was, and someone said it was an elk that had been hunted;

the trading classes, called, as he thought, for the pruning knife. Instead of setting the example of economy and retrenchment where the vice itself had originated, he taught the theory of economy, and persevered in the practice of all his former profusion! He introduced a national dress for each of the four Orders of the State.[1] The Court ladies in the new costume were laughed at and lampooned; the Countess Höpken, one of the most beautiful and elegant women in Sweden, compared them, decked in red ribbons and red trimmings, to *boiled lobsters!*[2] This affair furnished Gustavus with employment for two or three years, which he might have accomplished in as many months, if he had begun by introducing retrenchment and economy into his own Court.

At this period the citizens of Stockholm, as they took their breakfasts, frequently lamented the extravagant habits of their King, and foreboded bankruptcy and insurrection as the ultimate result. About noon, a Royal page arrived with tickets, inviting the grumbling husbands, and their wives and daughters, to be present at some new and superb spectacle. In an instant the females, all in ecstasy, lauded the fine spirit of their gallant and accomplished King! They must, to be sure, appear like somebody on such an occasion.

---

when the young Duchess, with a playful smile, said, "Oh, no! Your Majesty, it is no elk; it is Admiral ——, bathing!" It may not, perhaps, be necessary to add that the admiral alluded to was generally considered as a notorious *cornuto*.

1 It was partially in use in 1808.
2 *Vide* "Characters and Anecdotes of the Court of Sweden."

Thus was extravagance and dissipation introduced into the bosom of private families, to the total exclusion of that frugality so strongly recommended. Gustavus knew the character of every person of any note in Stockholm; he studied that of their wives and daughters, and artfully paid particular attention to those females whose husbands and fathers were most averse to his erratic career, by which means, if he caused domestic dissension, he partially neutralised public discontent, having a great majority of the ladies always on his side! Such was the influence of his graceful demeanour, insinuating address, and almost magic eloquence, that it is not at all singular he should in a manner fascinate every person whose goodwill he was desirous of attaining.

His ardent mind and fertile genius acted as a perpetual impetus to things that were new, grand, and out of the common track; thence resulted a constant succession of magnificent *fêtes*, spectacles, ballets, tournaments and national operas of the most splendid and imposing kind, the latter not unfrequently of his own composition.

It was really a calamity to mankind that this wonderful man was born the next heir to a throne. Had his station been less elevated, and his education equally good, and if he had cultivated his genius with equal assiduity, he might have formed a human prodigy, in genius, acquirements and morals, equal to the Admirable Crichton!

But in the character and fate of this monarch the well-known maxims are strongly exemplified, that an exalted station is not significant of happiness, nor always calculated to win the esteem of surrounding attendants; whilst, if the same individual had been born in a lower rank, all would have been successful about him and pleasant within him.

LIST OF ILLUSTRATIONS

MEMOIRS OF
THE COURTS OF SWEDEN AND DENMARK

VOLUME I

	PAGE
CAROLINA-MATILDA . . . . *Fronts.*	
LOUISA OF ENGLAND	32
COUNT STRUENSÉE	80
FREDERICKSBORG PALACE	152
CHRISTIAN VII	208
SOFIA MAGDALENA	280

www.ingramcontent.com/pod-product-compliance
Lightning Source LLC
Chambersburg PA
CBHW020312240426
43673CB00039B/778